THE BLOODAXE BOOK OF
20TH CENTURY POETRY

ALSO FROM BLOODAXE BOOKS

Poetry & Posterity

EDNA LONGLEY

Edna Longley's latest collection of critical essays marks a move back from Irish culture and politics to poetry itself as the critic's central concern. She considers how poets are read and received at different times and in different contexts, and from Irish, English and American viewpoints. But her interest in the reception of poetry is still very much influenced by debates about literature and politics in a Northern Ireland context, and in the book's final essay she relates poetry to the "peace process".

Poetry & Posterity presents detailed readings of several important figures included in *The Bloodaxe Book of 20th Century Poetry*, including Edward Thomas, Auden, MacNeice, Kavanagh, Larkin, Hughes and Heaney, as well as an incisive account of other 20th century anthologies.

Edna Longley's other two critical books from Bloodaxe also include relevant essays: in *Poetry in the Wars*, her classic work on Ireland, poetry and war, she discusses the poetry of Edward Thomas, MacNeice, Douglas, Larkin, Mahon, Heaney and Muldoon, while in *The Living Stream: Literature & Revisionism in Ireland* she explores the work of many writers, including Yeats, MacNeice, Heaney, Durcan and Muldoon.

Strong Words
modern poets on modern poetry
edited by W.N. HERBERT & MATTHEW HOLLIS

Poetry has never been so rigorous and diverse, nor has its audience been so numerous and engaged. *Strong words?* Not if the poets are right. As Ezra Pound wrote: 'You would think anyone wanting to know about poetry would go to someone who *knew* something about it.' That's exactly what Bloodaxe has done with this judicious and comprehensive selection of British, Irish and American manifestos by some of modern poetry's finest practitioners, including Pound, Yeats, Eliot, Auden, Frost, Lowell and Stevens, as well as over 30 specially commissioned statements from leading contemporary writers, amounting to a new overview of the poetry being written at the start of the 21st century.

As well as representing many of the most important poets of the last hundred years, *Strong Words* also charts many different stances and movements, from Modernism to Postmodernism, from Futurism to the future theories of poetry. This landmark book champions the continuing dialogue of these voices, past and present, exploring the strongest form that words can take: *the poem.*

THE Bloodaxe Book OF
20TH CENTURY POETRY
FROM BRITAIN AND IRELAND

edited by
EDNA LONGLEY

BLOODAXE BOOKS

ISBN: 1 85224 514 X

First published 2000 by
Bloodaxe Books Ltd,
Highgreen,
Tarset,
Northumberland NE48 1RP.

Reprinted 2001

www.bloodaxebooks.com
For further information about Bloodaxe titles
please visit our website or write to
the above address for a catalogue.

Bloodaxe Books Ltd acknowledges
the financial assistance of Northern Arts.

The publication of this book forms
part of an education project supported
by the National Lottery
through the Arts Council of England.

MILLENNIUM FESTIVAL

Official Supporter

Cover printing by J. Thomson Colour Printers Ltd, Glasgow.

Printed in Great Britain by
Cromwell Press Ltd, Trowbridge, Wiltshire.

CONTENTS

PREFACE

Every anthology draws artificial circles around its contents. One circle is the category of the "century". Of course, this is a useful way to indicate that no poem or poet exists in a vacuum. Poets tune into their contemporaries and into contemporary history. That collective work, now entering the 21st century, is what a living tradition means. Yet tradition also stretches further back. It involves what the American poet Donald Hall calls 'conversation' with 'the dead great ones'. 20th century poetry is full of conversations with dead poets from Homer onwards. Again, just as various poetic movements quarrelled and overlapped during the century itself, so poets around 1900 were defining themselves against their immediate predecessors. All this traffic with the past underlines the point that modern poetry is not (as is sometimes claimed) an entirely new species. Certainly it has responded to new circumstances and ideas – but poetry has always done so. And, during the 20th century, poets renewed all the genres whereby poetry tries to make sense of human experience: love poetry, the poetry of family and friendship, the poetry of unhappiness, elegy, epic, pastoral, satire, praise-poems, religious poems, war poems. It was usually critics rather than poets who doubted poetry's scope and stamina during a century which certainly tested them. Yet the testing – as I think this anthology of British and Irish poetry illustrates – was not to destruction.

The 20th century was a remarkable century for poetry in the English language. W.B. Yeats thought so as early as 1936 when he said in 'Modern Poetry: A Broadcast': 'The period from the death of Tennyson until the present moment has, it seems, more good lyric poets than any similar period since the 17th century'. To agree with that statement you need not agree with Yeats's own taste as represented by *The Oxford Book of Modern Verse* (1936). What counts is his stress on the lyric poem. Yeats dates modern poetry from the 1890s when he and other poets, under the influence of French symbolism, 'wished to express life at its intense moments, those moments that are brief because of their intensity':

> In the Victorian era the most famous poetry was often a passage in a poem of some length, perhaps of great length, a poem full of thoughts that might have been expressed in prose. A short lyric seemed an accident, an interruption amid more serious work...The aim of my friends, my own aim, if it sometimes made us prefer the acorn to the oak, the small to the great, freed us from many things we thought an impurity.

The lyric is hard to define except as 'a short poem'. But Yeats's word 'intensity' associates the 20th century lyric with a special drive

toward verbal and formal concentration. Here, indeed, poets such
as Yeats and T.S. Eliot saw the 17th century lyric (Donne, Herbert,
Marvell) as a challenging model. They were also stimulated by other
highly compressed poetry: the classical Greek lyric, the Japanese
haiku.

This anthology is essentially an anthology of 20th century lyrics.
I do not mean that every poem speaks in a first-person voice or that
there are no poems with, for instance, a narrative element. The
common factor is concentration: language 'at its intense moments'.
Except for T.S. Eliot's *The Waste Land* and Basil Bunting's *Brigg-
flatts*, I have not included extracts from long poems. Yet these
extracts are not exceptional in another sense. They show how the
acorn has affected the oak, the lyric the epic. Lyric poems (son-
nets, for example) have long been combined into sequences. But
The Waste Land and Yeats's 'Nineteen Hundred and Nineteen', if
by different formal means, intensified the practice of interweaving
poems to create complex perspectives. Among other effects, this
helped the modern lyric to move between the private and public
spheres. Sequence-building (crowned by the care with which a poet
like Yeats or Philip Larkin or Paul Muldoon organises a whole
collection) continues to assert the lyric's scope. A recent example
is Simon Armitage's 'The Whole of the Sky'.

The idea that modern poetry is a new species – or poetry a
doomed species – is bound up with the idea that modernity is a
new condition. That idea centres on the cultural changes produced
by technology. Although poetry had been mixed up with city life
since before Catullus's Rome, the modern city presented problems
of scale. How could the poetic imagination, with its roots in oral
culture and close-knit community, cope with mass-production or
mass-culture? Edward Thomas wrote of the multiplying suburbs:
'these streets are the strangest thing in the world...Poets have not
shown how we are to regard them.' In fact, poetry has proved its
resourcefulness by developing its urban imagination. The urban
landscapes in this anthology include T.S. Eliot's 'Unreal City', Louis
MacNeice's oppressive 'Birmingham', Philip Larkin's deceptively
blank 'Coventry', Ciaran Carson's labyrinthine 'Belfast'. Up to a
point, all these poets give the city a nightmarish aura which sug-
gests that reservations linger. On the one hand, there has been a
shift from Eliot's mix of fascination and distaste to W.H. Auden's
matter-of-fact opening: 'I sit in one of the dives / On Fifty-Second
Street'. Modern urban idioms are now in every poet's lexicon. On
the other hand, poetry has also resisted the modern city (Yeats did
so) for the reasons implied by Thomas. It often takes time for

words and images to sink to a level where they can be imaginatively absorbed.

Words and images are primary in poetry. So if poetry shows a time-lag where it meets the urban vortex of change, this is because it works differently from prose. It is never enough to describe or comment. Poetry's meanings are embodied, and complicated, by form. In the 1930s some poets were – rightly – laughed at because they put pylons into poems that had not assimilated the pylon's contexts. W.H. Auden speaks for the deeper opening-up to contemporary life which he and other poets effected during that decade, when he says that poetry moves between the 'Aristocratic' and 'Democratic' principles. The Aristocratic principle as regards subject-matter is: 'No subject-matter shall be treated by poets which poetry cannot digest. It defends poetry against didacticism and journalism.' The Democratic principle is: 'No subject-matter shall be excluded by poets which poetry is capable of digesting. It defends poetry against limited or stale conceptions of what is "poetic".'

"Urban" and "rural" poetry should not be seen as opposites – not only because subject-matter is, in fact, rarely straightforward in poetry. Many poets draw on both country and city, and "pastoral" has always been a way of talking about contemporary society. Modern pastoral is very rich; and may be so precisely because social change has thrown into relief, as well as into jeopardy, older relations between humanity and its environment. This explains why poets' imagined worlds often depend on places where modernity has arrived slowly. Here poets from regional England (Thomas Hardy, D.H. Lawrence) are as representative as poets from remote parts of Scotland or Ireland (Edwin Muir, Patrick Kavanagh). For these poets, as more recently for Seamus Heaney, the split between traditional world-pictures and modernity was a fact of autobiography that became a source of art. Country poetry (poetry that turns a particular locality into a microcosm) reflects on older communal meanings in a way that questions modern living. Nature poetry (poetry occupied with the natural world) reflects on our earthly habitat. Both kinds of pastoral have ecological implications. Indeed, the ecological perspective now apparent in Edward Thomas's work shows how poetry's longer-term vision pays off. In the year 2000 the belief that poetry must explicitly notice the city seems archaic as well as literal-minded. Birds, animals, insects, landscapes, trees and flowers play many parts in modern poetry. Even where there is no ecological point, this interdependence makes the point. Jo Shapcott imagines her 'life as' a bat, a frog, an iguana. For Ted Hughes, a poem itself takes shape as a fox's movements. Hugh

MacDiarmid begins a poem: 'It is with the poet as with a guinea worm...'

Modernity in its guise as modern war has profoundly reshaped poetry. My choices for this anthology suggest that war poetry was a central 20th century genre – one that touched and changed other genres. Not every anthologist of modern poetry would agree. War poetry, so often ghettoised in its own anthologies, tends to be defined by content alone. This seems an Anglo-American quirk. Countries with experience of invasion know, as war poetry knows, that war transforms everything including the structures that represent it. It heightens poetry by heightening history. Charles Sorley in 1914, Keith Douglas in 1939, recognised that the language and rhythms of most poetry had become obsolete. Both also wished that the experience of war would revolutionise English society. The trenches and Douglas's poems of the Desert War, not to mention Ireland, at least changed the horizons of the English lyric. So did the Home Front poetry of both world wars. Here pastoral poetry and love poetry are invaded by forces that question their premises. This applies to such poems as Ivor Gurney's 'The Mangel-Bury', Henry Reed's 'Lessons of the War', Alun Lewis's 'Goodbye', Stevie Smith's 'I Remember'. War heightens not only historical awareness but everyday existence. It illuminates not only death but life. Modern war also did as much as Charles Darwin or Karl Marx to make poetry question Christianity and other established systems.

War can be confined neither by space nor by time. Robert Garioch and Edwin Morgan have written retrospective war poems in which war measures other things. More generally, as Paul Fussell shows in *The Great War and Modern Memory*, collective memory is still coming to terms with 1914–18, let alone later catastrophes. The structure as well as content of memory is at stake – particularly so in a medium whose own structures deeply depend on remembering and being remembered. It seems no accident that Edward Thomas wrote 'Old Man', a poem about the perplexities of memory, in December 1914. Poetry, which once took the shock of modern war fast, is still taking it slowly. Above all, perhaps, the Great War transformed elegy. Elegy became a means of political protest. It became elegy for wider cultural loss and for the death of God. War made consolation more difficult in private as well as public elegy. This introduced the further question, voiced by Wilfred Owen in the Great War and Theodor Adorno after the Holocaust: should poetry be silenced by suffering that exposes its inadequacy or presumption? Hence the tendency of war poetry to cross-examine its own procedures. By speaking from the angle of a gunner looking

through his 'dial of glass', Douglas's 'How to Kill' implicates poetry
in the guilt of violence. The legacy of war poetry, or its continuation
by other means, includes Thom Gunn's elegies for AIDS victims as
much as Philip Larkin's 'MCMXIV'. It appears comprehensively in
poetry from Northern Ireland after 1969. Civil war dissolves clear
boundaries between public and private zones, and hence between
poetic genres. This explains why so-called "Troubles" poetry takes
its bearings from many 20th century poetic responses to war, in-
cluding Yeats's engagement with earlier Irish conflicts. Finally, war
marked 20th century poetry even by default, as when the Great
War impelled Robert Graves to concentrate on love poetry.

Nevertheless, some critics see war poetry as conservative because
of its generally traditional verse-forms. Wilfred Owen's protest
poems attack lingering Romantic idioms, but their own medium is
stanza or couplet, however new he made them sound. It may be,
indeed, that traditional forms are more efficient at getting a mes-
sage across. Auden says: 'The poet who writes "free" verse is like
Robinson Crusoe on his desert island: he must do all his cooking,
laundry and darning for himself.' The poets of the Great War
prompted poets of the 1930s to employ traditional forms for their
own kinds of protest and warning. Thus in Auden's 'Epitaph on a
Tyrant' or 'September 1, 1939' (a poem also influenced by Yeats's
public voice) rhyme and stanza sharpen the anti-Fascist point.
Later, James Fenton was equipped by Auden to write his poems
of Vietnam, Cambodia and post-Holocaust Germany.

All this is not to deny the huge impact of *The Waste Land*. T.S.
Eliot's sequence, edited by Ezra Pound, showed that poetry need
not be written in regular stanzas or regular lines; nor need it be
constructed as a consecutive meditation, argument or plot. Yet
The Waste Land has been canonised by academic criticism in a
way that may overrate its formal influence. When critics invoke
Eliot as the sponsor of poetic "modernism", they are usually sug-
gesting that modernity has made it impossible to write in traditional
forms and from a stable central vantage-point. This is because
modern philosophy has shown perception to be relative, and made
ideas of coherence impossible to sustain. Thus poets can only work
with cultural 'fragments' and fragmented forms. Today, "post-
modernist" poets are praised for highlighting the instability of
language itself. Some of this thinking seems anti-poetic and anti-
creative (besides being disproved by 20th century poetry in practice).
Further, "modernism", as a critical concept applied to poetry, derives
from Eliot's and Pound's American perspectives on English and
European literature. These perspectives are crucial to what might

best be called the "modern movement" in poetry. But the countries of the British Isles also moulded that movement in ways that reflected their own cultural conditions. And all the mutual stimulus provoked variation rather than imitation. Hence the range of modern poetry in English. For instance, a long aesthetic argument between Yeats and Pound came to stake out the field of formal possibility. Yeats's concentrated stanzas are at the opposite pole from Pound's capacious, allusive and discontinuous *Cantos*.

American modernism takes deepest root where it stirs personal or cultural vibrations. In Ireland, James Joyce has proved a more immediate counter-model to Yeats partly because his approach to the English language is allied with a subversion of authoritarian systems, including the Catholic Church and the British state. The self-consciousness about language in contemporary Northern Irish poetry has similar contexts. Poems criticise languages of power, decipher cultural codes, and imply that words and images are part of the political problem. This awareness that the English language can be spoken with different inflections from different angles is accentuated by the presence of the Irish language and Ulster Scots dialect. Yet if poets such as Paul Muldoon or Ciaran Carson or Medbh McGuckian show that we cannot take language for granted, they also use it richly. Similarly, to have fun with traditional forms (like Muldoon with the sonnet) does not rule out remaking them.

Scotland, where Gaelic and Scots also shadow English-language poetry, where poets also combat authoritarian systems, has been more noted than Ireland, England or Wales for experimental poetry. Local factors and some modernist linguistic impulses met in Hugh MacDiarmid's "Synthetic Scots". (MacDiarmid and Pound share a spirit of presbyterian iconoclasm which they apply to "English" poetry.) Later, Edwin Morgan and Ian Hamilton Finlay created "concrete poems" that sought to fuse verbal and visual art. Yet in neither case did this mark an absolute break with traditional forms. Their love of experiment again signals subversion, together with a utopian desire for new kinds of form, new kinds of order. Free verse, too, has many mansions. Besides the liberties taken by T.S. Eliot, it covers rhythms that seem born from moment to moment but do not disrupt sequential logic in other ways. D.H. Lawrence's psalm-like incantations are the supreme example.

In fact, Lawrence was greatly influenced by Walt Whitman. I draw another artificial circle when I exclude American poets apart from Eliot and Sylvia Plath. Certainly, personal factors caused these poets to become intimately involved with poetry in England (as Thom Gunn became involved with poetry in America). Their combined influence on British and Irish poetry is incalculable. Yet a feature of Plath's artistic relation to Ted Hughes was that both poets were excited by precursors from all quarters (Yeats, Dylan Thomas, Marianne Moore). My circle is artificial not because poetic nationality must be anxiously measured, but because the 20th century witnessed such various poetic traffic to and fro across the Atlantic. That included Yeats's strong presence in American poetry.

Conversely, one American visitor who helped (and still helps) to recharge the formal batteries of the English lyric was Robert Frost. Frost's emphasis on speech rhythms directly inspired Edward Thomas. He showed Thomas how to write a free blank verse as well as how to bounce 'sentence-sounds' off the walls of a stanza. Like Yeats, Graves and Hugh MacDiarmid, Frost gave the lyric a more dramatic structure. This includes dialectic – the drama of argument – and 'the quarrel with ourselves', as Yeats terms it. Many 20th century lyrics render modern relativity and doubt, as they do inner quarrels, by a dramatic counterpoint. This can occur between tones of voice, between stanza-form and syntax, between one poem and another. Traditional form does not stop a poem from being ambiguous or open-ended. For Louis MacNeice, all poems contain 'in varying degrees...an internal conflict, cross-talk, backwash, come-back or pay-off'. Some poets, including MacNeice in his later work, further changed the lyric tune by making syntax the primary agent of rhythm. But differences of artistic emphasis are dialectical too. While Keith Douglas was stressing 'significant speech', Dylan Thomas was reinventing the singing line. One way in which this anthology suggests the vitality of traditional forms, the variety of 20th century poetry, is by including a scatter of short poems – not small poems, but poems that epitomise lyric concentration. Another is by showing that the sonnet, also an epitome, is still going strong. Don Paterson writes in the introduction to his selection of *101 Sonnets* (1999): 'Unity of meaning is an ideal that is impossible to represent in any sustained, linear, complex utterance – but it's what, crazily, our human poetry tries to do. So a sonnet is a paradox, a little squared circle, a mandala that invites our meditation.'

Paterson defines a poem as 'no more or less than a little machine for remembering itself'. Form connects a poem's origin in feeling or perception with its destination in memory. It marks poetry's own origin as an art of memory. The formal principle is also a pleasure principle. It 'invites' us, as Paterson says, even to experience what we might want to forget (like Owen's 'warnings'). There are a number of poems about poetry in this anthology. The lyric poem relishes or scrutinises its own patterns, not in an introverted way

but as part of relishing and scrutinising life. This is one message of
Yeats's 'Byzantium', Sylvia Plath's 'Metaphors', Simon Armitage's
'Zoom!'. Some poets particularly make us recognise that language
and rhythm are bodily functions, physical sensations, which carry
over into movements of mind. Hughes does so in 'The Thought-
Fox', Heaney in 'Personal Helicon' – poems about the sources of
poetry. Partly thanks to modern psychology, modern poetry has
explored the relation between mind and body, between the con-
scious and unconscious self, between the self and the world, with
new complexity. Of course, the forms that dramatise states of mind
can be as disturbing in their effect as those that dramatise states of
war. Plath's vivid images and seductive rhythms often imply dis-
tance or alienation from what they evoke.

Some critics argue that poetry can no longer claim to cover the
whole human personality or the whole of life: there are no "uni-
versals". But perhaps, as with other aspects of the modern poetic
enterprise, greater awareness of the difficulties has intensified the
effort. The drama of lyric poetry begins where the merely personal
ends. And this is where readers become interested. Bonds with
lovers, parents, children or a community are fairly ubiquitous even
if cultural modes differ. The 20th century made its own difference
by adding more poems (not all by women) in the voice of female
desire, in the voice of mother, daughter or wife. The numerous
poems about parents also hint at poetry's mysterious autobiograph-
ical roots. Artistic self-definition is entangled with family bonds in
Seamus Heaney's 'The Harvest Bow', Selima Hill's 'The Fowlers
of the Marshes', Ian Duhig's 'Nothing Pie'. And poetry continues
to be entangled with eroticism. The modern Muse has not abdicated
but become more varied in complexion. Stevie Smith's Muse is a
'strong' female 'Angel'. Fleur Adcock's 'Excavations' and Medbh
McGuckian's 'Mr McGregor's Garden' treat male muses in a manner
alien to Graves's 'White Goddess'.

Changing definitions of femininity and masculinity are one cultural
story that might be read from 20th century poetry in these islands.
But perhaps we should be cautious. As regards poetry, the con-
temporary stress on culture may put the cart before the horse – as
did a stress on class in the 1930s. Intense lyrics tell unpredictable
stories, and identity in poetry appears no less problematic than
subject-matter. 20th century British and Irish poetry at once crosses
supposed cultural boundaries and illuminates the fine print of cul-
tural difference. Roderick Watson says in his introduction to *The
Poetry of Scotland: Gaelic, Scots and English 1380-1980*: 'the "Scottish
poetic tradition" is a much more complex, interactive, rich, many-

stranded and fulfilling thing than any simple opposition between
"Highland" and "Lowland"; "fantasy" and "realism"; "English",
"Scots or "Gaelic" can sustain'.

Watson's 'interactive' scenario extends to modern "British Isles"
poetry. (I do not include Gaelic or Welsh poetry here, since other
kinds of anthology do the job better.) As compared with national
anthologies, this book may disclose different dynamics as regards
both poetic and cultural tradition. Mutual national awareness,
including painful awareness, has certainly been a shaping factor. It
is not just that the "Celtic" countries have been unable to ignore
England or English poetry. Poets interested in the condition of
England, Ireland, Scotland or Wales share approaches as between
nationalities, differ in their approach as within nationalities. The
range of poetry from Northern Ireland illustrates all the complica-
tions. The range of poems in Scots is not confined to a political
stake in Scottishness. And Englishness – a more popular concern
than often supposed – is filtered through diverse sensibilities and
images. We can track its metamorphoses in Edward Thomas, Auden,
Larkin, Geoffrey Hill, the contrasting Yorkshires of Hughes and
Armitage. Some poems (including war poems) criticise ideas of
exclusive nationality. Others draw attention to national interactions
by reflecting on mobility. Carol Rumens imagines Northern Ireland
from a consciously English angle. Fleur Adcock's 'Foreigner' feels
alien in England. Yet Adcock's genealogical fancy 'Swings and Round-
abouts' suggests the danger as well as pull of "roots". Perhaps genea-
logy, topography and nationality are versions of a deeper cultural
theme that seems to matter greatly in all poetic quarters: belonging,
community, home. The dialectic between country and city feeds
into this – especially where local microcosms act as wider communal
models – as does the interest in (not only indigenous) myth and
folklore. Such dwelling on home may be further proof that modern
poetry has reason for its time-lags and backward looks.

As for artistic interaction: influences move promiscuously around
these islands, from one cluster of energy to another (which is how
poetry seems to happen). But this, like the varied ways in which
poets receive American or continental influences, also reveals cul-
tural difference. For instance, while both Philip Larkin and Derek
Mahon learned from Yeats's forms, Mahon as an Irish poet had to
cope with other Yeatsian legacies. Yet, as already indicated, cul-
ture itself affects poetic structures. To take one example: much
modern poetry confirms Matthew Arnold's intuition that poetry
would, in some sense, replace religion. It is not just that poets
such as R.S. Thomas and Geoffrey Hill have gone on writing fine

religious poetry. From 1900 to the millennium, poetry is full of displaced or redirected religion. Christianity shapes the vision and forms even of poets who disown it, like Thomas Hardy. Yeats was drawn to poetry as compensation for the loss of God. Conversely, *The Waste Land* can be read as a search for God. Besides the continuing link between poetry and Anglicanism, many effects of presbyterianism on Scottish poetry, of Catholicism on Irish poetry, are clearly marked (not that any of the countries is religiously homogeneous). On the one hand, as regards belief, the modern poet says with William Empson's contemplator of the 'Supreme God in the ethnological section': 'Let us stand here and admit we have no road'. On the other hand, this becomes the imaginative basis for finding new roads, new myths. Poets often represent their own brand of spirituality as superior to orthodox religion. Calvinistic religion gets a particularly bad press for its life-denying and art-denying attitudes. This is a common story from, among others, Dylan Thomas in Wales, MacDiarmid in Scotland, Lawrence in England, Mahon in Northern Ireland. However, to negate poetry can be to inspire it. Fundamentalist fervour has also been recast in positive ways – as in Lawrence's whole poetic mission or when Mahon's poem 'Nostalgias' sings along with a 'lost tribe...singing "Abide with Me"'. A post-religious sense of loss gives modern poetry its persistent metaphysical dimension. From another angle, the interchanges between poetry and religion illustrate the point that poetry comprises an intricate cultural map of the 20th century in these islands.

My brief introductions to each poet offer, as this anthology does more generally, some perspectives on 20th century poetry from Britain and Ireland. There are other views, other maps, and no anthology can include everything. Obviously the poems themselves also speak for themselves.

EDNA LONGLEY

THOMAS HARDY

(1840–1928)

Thomas Hardy anticipates every crossroads of modern poetry in the British Isles. He stands between folk-traditions and literature; region and metropolis; Christianity and the post-Darwinian crisis of faith; Victorian and modern consciousness; prose-fiction and poetry; 'things [that] go onward the same' and modern war. Aside from a period in London as an apprentice architect, he spent all his life in Dorset. From the late 1890s, partly owing to attacks on the 'obscenity' of his novel *Jude the Obscure* (1896), Hardy devoted himself to poetry. His first collection was *Wessex Poems and Other Verses* (1898), and he published eight more collections of lyrics. Hardy's late start as a poet held back his reputation. But Edward Thomas was an advocate; W.H. Auden was inspired by his 'metrical variety'; and Philip Larkin, for whom Hardy's 'dominant emotion' is 'sadness', thought him the best poet of the century.

The ambiguous title of his second collection, *Poems of the Past and the Present* (1901) suggests more than that Hardy published poems written years earlier or based on old drafts. This very habit belongs to his intense meditation on obsolescence and mortality: the monstrous fact that the present becomes past. He could 'bury an emotion in my heart or brain for forty years' before turning it into a poem. If his poetry does not alter, this is because alteration is structural. Its language veers between local idiom, ambitious abstraction, ballad-simplicity and elaborate syntax. Its rhythms reminded Thomas of 'old people dancing an old dance'. Its scenes are 'haunted' (a favourite word) by vistas of loss. Hardy's 'Wessex' microcosm turns his personal hauntings into a communal narrative. When he was accused of letting a 'pessimistic' philosophy govern his vision, he replied that his poems were 'dramatic or impersonative', he had no fixed ideas, and that he based his hope on 'loving-kindness, operating through scientific knowledge'. Hardy can be more a Victorian moralist than a fully 'dramatic' poet, just as his forms can be less various than they appear. Yet his love poems to his dead wife Emma, with their delicately searching rhythms, consummate his dedication to a Muse of mourning.

The Darkling Thrush

I leant upon a coppice gate
    When Frost was spectre-gray,
And Winter's dregs made desolate
    The weakening eye of day.
The tangled bine-stems scored the sky
    Like strings of broken lyres,
And all mankind that haunted nigh
    Had sought their household fires.

The land's sharp features seemed to be
  The Century's corpse outleant,
His crypt the cloudy canopy,
  The wind his death-lament.
The ancient pulse of germ and birth
  Was shrunken hard and dry,
And every spirit upon earth
  Seemed fervourless as I.

At once a voice arose among
  The bleak twigs overhead
In a full-hearted evensong
  Of joy illimited;
An aged thrush, frail, gaunt, and small,
  In blast-beruffled plume,
Had chosen thus to fling his soul
  Upon the growing gloom.

So little cause for carolings
  Of such ecstatic sound
Was written on terrestrial things
  Afar or nigh around,
That I could think there trembled through
  His happy good-night air
Some blessed Hope, whereof he knew
  And I was unaware.

[31 December 1900]

The Self-Unseeing

Here is the ancient floor,
Footworn and hollowed and thin,
Here was the former door
Where the dead feet walked in.

She sat here in her chair,
Smiling into the fire;
He who played stood there,
Bowing it higher and higher.

Childlike, I danced in a dream;
Blessings emblazoned that day;
Everything glowed with a gleam;
Yet we were looking away!

The Convergence of the Twain
(Lines on the loss of the 'Titanic')

I
In a solitude of the sea
Deep from human vanity,
And the Pride of Life that planned her, stilly couches she.

II
Steel chambers, late the pyres
Of her salamandrine fires,
Cold currents thrid, and turn to rhythmic tidal lyres.

III
Over the mirrors meant
To glass the opulent
The sea-worm crawls – grotesque, slimed, dumb, indifferent.

IV
Jewels in joy designed
To ravish the sensuous mind
Lie lightless, all their sparkles bleared and black and blind.

V
Dim moon-eyed fishes near
Gaze at the gilded gear
And query: 'What does this vaingloriousness down here?'...

VI
Well: while was fashioning
This creature of cleaving wing,
The Immanent Will that stirs and urges everything

VII

Prepared a sinister mate
For her – so gaily great –
A Shape of Ice, for the time far and dissociate.

VIII

And as the smart ship grew
In stature, grace, and hue,
In shadowy silent distance grew the Iceberg too.

IX

Alien they seemed to be:
No mortal eye could see
The intimate welding of their later history,

X

Or sign that they were bent
By paths coincident
On being anon twin halves of one august event,

XI

Till the Spinner of the Years
Said 'Now!' And each one hears,
And consummation comes, and jars two hemispheres.

The Walk

You did not walk with me
Of late to the hill-top tree
        By the gated ways,
        As in earlier days;
        You were weak and lame,
        So you never came,
And I went alone, and I did not mind,
Not thinking of you as left behind.

I walked up there to-day
Just in the former way;
  Surveyed around
  The familiar ground
  By myself again:
  What difference, then?
Only that underlying sense
Of the look of a room on returning thence.

After a Journey

Hereto I come to view a voiceless ghost;
  Whither, O whither will its whim now draw me?
Up the cliff, down, till I'm lonely, lost,
  And the unseen waters' ejaculations awe me.
Where you will next be there's no knowing,
  Facing round about me everywhere,
    With your nut-coloured hair,
And gray eyes, and rose-flush coming and going.

Yes: I have re-entered your olden haunts at last;
  Through the years, through the dead scenes I have tracked you;
What have you now found to say of our past –
  Scanned across the dark space wherein I have lacked you?
Summer gave us sweets, but autumn wrought division?
  Things were not lastly as firstly well
    With us twain, you tell?
But all's closed now, despite Time's derision.

I see what you are doing: you are leading me on
  To the spots we knew when we haunted here together,
The waterfall, above which the mist-bow shone
  At the then fair hour in the then fair weather,
And the cave just under, with a voice still so hollow
  That it seems to call out to me from forty years ago,
    When you were all aglow,
And not the thin ghost that I now fraily follow!

Ignorant of what there is flitting here to see,
    The waked birds preen and the seals flop lazily;
Soon you will have, Dear, to vanish from me,
    For the stars close their shutters and the dawn whitens hazily.
Trust me, I mind not, though Life lours,
    The bringing me here; nay, bring me here again!
        I am just the same as when
Our days were a joy, and our paths through flowers.

[Pentargan Bay]

The Oxen

Christmas Eve, and twelve of the clock.
    'Now they are all on their knees,'
An elder said as we sat in a flock
    By the embers in hearthside ease.

We pictured the meek mild creatures where
    They dwelt in their strawy pen,
Nor did it occur to one of us there
    To doubt they were kneeling then.

So fair a fancy few would weave
    In these years! Yet, I feel,
If someone said on Christmas Eve,
    'Come; see the oxen kneel

'In the lonely barton by yonder coomb
    Our childhood used to know,'
I should go with him in the gloom,
    Hoping it might be so.

During Wind and Rain

They sing their dearest songs –
He, she, all of them – yea,
Treble and tenor and bass,
    And one to play;
With the candles mooning each face....
    Ah, no; the years O!
How the sick leaves reel down in throngs!

They clear the creeping moss –
Elders and juniors – aye,
Making the pathways neat
    And the garden gay;
And they build a shady seat....
    Ah, no; the years, the years;
See, the white storm-birds wing across!

They are blithely breakfasting all –
Men and maidens – yea,
Under the summer tree,
    With a glimpse of the bay,
While pet fowl come to the knee....
    Ah, no; the years O!
And the rotten rose is ript from the wall.

They change to a high new house,
He, she, all of them – aye,
Clocks and carpets and chairs
    On the lawn all day,
And brightest things that are theirs....
    Ah, no; the years, the years;
Down their carved names the rain-drop ploughs.

In Time of 'The Breaking of Nations'

I

Only a man harrowing clods
    In a slow silent walk
With an old horse that stumbles and nods
    Half asleep as they stalk.

II

Only thin smoke without flame
    From the heaps of couch-grass;
Yet this will go onward the same
    Though Dynasties pass.

III

Yonder a maid and her wight
    Come whispering by:
War's annals will cloud into night
    Ere their story die.

[1915]

The Fallow Deer at the Lonely House

One without looks in to-night
        Through the curtain-chink
From the sheet of glistening white;
One without looks in to-night
        As we sit and think
        By the fender-brink.

We do not discern those eyes
        Watching in the snow;
Lit by lamps of rosy dyes
We do not discern those eyes
        Wondering, aglow,
        Fourfooted, tiptoe.

Shortening Days at the Homestead

The first fire since the summer is lit, and is smoking into the room:
  The sun-rays thread it through, like woof-lines in a loom.
  Sparrows spurt from the hedge, whom misgivings appal
That winter did not leave last year for ever, after all.
  Like shock-headed urchins, spiny-haired,
  Stand pollard willows, their twigs just bared.

Who is this coming with pondering pace,
Black and ruddy, with white embossed,
His eyes being black, and ruddy his face,
And the marge of his hair like morning frost?
  It's the cider-maker,
  And appletree-shaker,
And behind him on wheels, in readiness,
His mill, and tubs, and vat, and press.

Christmas: 1924

'Peace upon earth!' was said. We sing it,
And pay a million priests to bring it.
After two thousand years of mass
We've got as far as poison-gas.

W.B. YEATS

(1865–1939)

William Butler Yeats grew up in Dublin, Co. Sligo and London. His class, the southern Irish Protestant gentry, had already lost power and position in Ireland. Yeats's early poetry blends mysticism, folklore and Irish mythology into yearning cadences. These interests were, in part, a substitute for Christian faith, of which he felt 'robbed' by Darwinism. Frustrated love for the Irish nationalist activist Maud Gonne was also close to his poetry's origins. (She married the 1916 leader, John MacBride.) During the 1890s Yeats became central to two literary movements: the Irish Revival and the fallout of French symbolism, including the doctrine of 'art for art's sake'. The mix was productive but explosive. 'The Fascination of What's Difficult' (1910) shows how Irish conflicts tested Yeats's faith in the 'holy blood' of art. Yet they also stiffened his poetry's rhetoric, roughed up its rhythms and made its symbols (such as the swan) more vital. This failed sonnet gains from what 'ails' it.

J.M. Synge's drama was another influence on Yeats's transition from his 'Celtic Twilight' style to the 'difficult' poetry of *Responsibilities* (1914) and later collections. The need to defend Synge's *Playboy of the Western World* (1907) against nationalist attacks influenced him too. Fears for Irish literature partly explain why 'Easter 1916' is an ambiguous response to the Easter Rising. More completely pessimistic is 'Nineteen Hundred and Nineteen', whose contexts include the Anglo-Irish war (a Black and Tan soldier killed the 'murdered' mother), the Great War and the Russian Revolution. Yeats called this sequence 'a lamentation over lost peace and lost hope'. Its doubts about western civilisation parallel those of T.S. Eliot's *Waste Land*. Despite becoming a senator of the Irish Free State (1922-28) and winning the Nobel Prize (1923), Yeats continued to feel that his values were threatened by modernity and by change in Ireland. However, 'Byzantium', at one level, celebrates the resilience of the creative spirit: 'Those images that yet / Fresh images beget'.

Strong contrasts are in keeping with the philosophical system that Yeats sets out in *A Vision* (1925). Here he patterns history as a series of antithetical 'gyres' or spirals. In 'The Second Coming', Europe's 'blood-dimmed tide' heralds an ominous new gyre. *A Vision* may be Yeats's way of claiming that poetry covers all human life. It also implies that creativity as well as destruction depends on conflict. These ideas both reflected and reinforced the dramatic character of Yeats's lyric: the manner in which one perspective, tone, image, word or poem answers another. And, by seeking 'a powerful and passionate syntax', Yeats gave a dramatic force to traditional stanzas. Rhythmical crosscurrents carry the turbulence of his engagement with mortality, sexuality and history. Actual historical figures, such as the 1916 leaders executed by the British, have roles in Yeats's lyric drama. The apocalyptic ending of 'Nineteen Hundred and Nineteen' refers to Dame Alice Kyteler, who was tried for witchcraft in 14th century Kilkenny, and her alleged demonic partner.

The Fascination of What's Difficult

The fascination of what's difficult
Has dried the sap out of my veins, and rent
Spontaneous joy and natural content
Out of my heart. There's something ails our colt
That must, as if it had not holy blood
Nor on Olympus leaped from cloud to cloud,
Shiver under the lash, strain, sweat and jolt
As though it dragged road metal. My curse on plays
That have to be set up in fifty ways,
On the day's war with every knave and dolt,
Theatre business, management of men.
I swear before the dawn comes round again
I'll find the stable and pull out the bolt.

The Cold Heaven

Suddenly I saw the cold and rook-delighting heaven
That seemed as though ice burned and was but the more ice,
And thereupon imagination and heart were driven
So wild that every casual thought of that and this
Vanished, and left but memories, that should be out of season
With the hot blood of youth, of love crossed long ago;
And I took all the blame out of all sense and reason,
Until I cried and trembled and rocked to and fro,
Riddled with light. Ah! when the ghost begins to quicken,
Confusion of the death-bed over, is it sent
Out naked on the roads, as the books say, and stricken
By the injustice of the skies for punishment?

The Wild Swans at Coole

The trees are in their autumn beauty,
The woodland paths are dry,
Under the October twilight the water
Mirrors a still sky;
Upon the brimming water among the stones
Are nine-and-fifty swans.

The nineteenth autumn has come upon me
Since I first made my count;
I saw, before I had well finished,
All suddenly mount
And scatter wheeling in great broken rings
Upon their clamorous wings.

I have looked upon those brilliant creatures,
And now my heart is sore.
All's changed since I, hearing at twilight,
The first time on this shore,
The bell-beat of their wings above my head,
Trod with a lighter tread.

Unwearied still, lover by lover,
They paddle in the cold
Companionable streams or climb the air;
Their hearts have not grown old;
Passion or conquest, wander where they will,
Attend upon them still.

But now they drift on the still water,
Mysterious, beautiful;
Among what rushes will they build,
By what lake's edge or pool
Delight men's eyes when I awake some day
To find they have flown away?

Memory

One had a lovely face,
And two or three had charm,
But charm and face were in vain
Because the mountain grass
Cannot but keep the form
Where the mountain hare has lain.

Easter 1916

I have met them at close of day
Coming with vivid faces
From counter or desk among grey
Eighteenth-century houses.
I have passed with a nod of the head
Or polite meaningless words,
Or have lingered awhile and said
Polite meaningless words,
And thought before I had done
Of a mocking tale or a gibe
To please a companion
Around the fire at the club,
Being certain that they and I
But lived where motley is worn:
All changed, changed utterly:
A terrible beauty is born.

That woman's days were spent
In ignorant good-will,
Her nights in argument
Until her voice grew shrill.
What voice more sweet than hers
When, young and beautiful,
She rode to harriers?
This man had kept a school
And rode our wingèd horse;
This other his helper and friend

Was coming into his force;
He might have won fame in the end,
So sensitive his nature seemed,
So daring and sweet his thought.
This other man I had dreamed
A drunken, vainglorious lout.
He had done most bitter wrong
To some who are near my heart,
Yet I number him in the song;
He, too, has resigned his part
In the casual comedy;
He, too, has been changed in his turn,
Transformed utterly:
A terrible beauty is born.

Hearts with one purpose alone
Through summer and winter seem
Enchanted to a stone
To trouble the living stream.
The horse that comes from the road,
The rider, the birds that range
From cloud to tumbling cloud,
Minute by minute they change;
A shadow of cloud on the stream
Changes minute by minute;
A horse-hoof slides on the brim,
And a horse plashes within it;
The long-legged moor-hens dive,
And hens to moor-cocks call;
Minute by minute they live:
The stone's in the midst of all.

Too long a sacrifice
Can make a stone of the heart.
O when may it suffice?
That is Heaven's part, our part
To murmur name upon name,
As a mother names her child
When sleep at last has come
On limbs that had run wild.
What is it but nightfall?
No, no, not night but death;
Was it needless death after all?

For England may keep faith
For all that is done and said.
We know their dream; enough
To know they dreamed and are dead;
And what if excess of love
Bewildered them till they died?
I write it out in a verse –
MacDonagh and MacBride
And Connolly and Pearse
Now and in time to be,
Wherever green is worn,
Are changed, changed utterly:
A terrible beauty is born.

[25 September 1916]

The Second Coming

Turning and turning in the widening gyre
The falcon cannot hear the falconer;
Things fall apart; the centre cannot hold;
Mere anarchy is loosed upon the world,
The blood-dimmed tide is loosed, and everywhere
The ceremony of innocence is drowned;
The best lack all conviction, while the worst
Are full of passionate intensity.

Surely some revelation is at hand;
Surely the Second Coming is at hand.
The Second Coming! Hardly are those words out
When a vast image out of *Spiritus Mundi*
Troubles my sight: somewhere in sands of the desert
A shape with lion body and the head of a man,
A gaze blank and pitiless as the sun,
Is moving its slow thighs, while all about it
Reel shadows of the indignant desert birds.
The darkness drops again; but now I know
That twenty centuries of stony sleep
Were vexed to nightmare by a rocking cradle,
And what rough beast, its hour come round at last,
Slouches towards Bethlehem to be born?

Nineteen Hundred and Nineteen

I

Many ingenious lovely things are gone
That seemed sheer miracle to the multitude,
Protected from the circle of the moon
That pitches common things about. There stood
Amid the ornamental bronze and stone
An ancient image made of olive wood –
And gone are Phidias' famous ivories
And all the golden grasshoppers and bees.

We too had many pretty toys when young;
A law indifferent to blame or praise,
To bribe or threat; habits that made old wrong
Melt down, as it were wax in the sun's rays;
Public opinion ripening for so long
We thought it would outlive all future days.
O what fine thought we had because we thought
That the worst rogues and rascals had died out.

All teeth were drawn, all ancient tricks unlearned,
And a great army but a showy thing;
What matter that no cannon had been turned
Into a ploughshare? Parliament and king
Thought that unless a little powder burned
The trumpeters might burst with trumpeting
And yet it lack all glory; and perchance
The guardsmen's drowsy chargers would not prance.

Now days are dragon–ridden, the nightmare
Rides upon sleep: a drunken soldiery
Can leave the mother, murdered at her door,
To crawl in her own blood, and go scot-free;
The night can sweat with terror as before
We pieced our thoughts into philosophy,
And planned to bring the world under a rule,
Who are but weasels fighting in a hole.

He who can read the signs nor sink unmanned
Into the half-deceit of some intoxicant
From shallow wits; who knows no work can stand,
Whether health, wealth or peace of mind were spent
On master-work of intellect or hand,
No honour leave its mighty monument,
Has but one comfort left: all triumph would
But break upon his ghostly solitude.

But is there any comfort to be found?
Man is in love and loves what vanishes,
What more is there to say? That country round
None dared admit, if such a thought were his,
Incendiary or bigot could be found
To burn that stump on the Acropolis,
Or break in bits the famous ivories
Or traffic in the grasshoppers or bees.

II

When Loie Fuller's Chinese dancers enwound
A shining web, a floating ribbon of cloth,
It seemed that a dragon of air
Had fallen among dancers, had whirled them round
Or hurried them off on its own furious path;
So the Platonic Year
Whirls out new right and wrong,
Whirls in the old instead;
All men are dancers and their tread
Goes to the barbarous clangour of a gong.

III

Some moralist or mythological poet
Compares the solitary soul to a swan;
I am satisfied with that,
Satisfied if a troubled mirror show it,
Before that brief gleam of its life be gone,
An image of its state;
The wings half spread for flight,
The breast thrust out in pride
Whether to play, or to ride
Those winds that clamour of approaching night.

A man in his own secret meditation
Is lost amid the labyrinth that he has made
In art or politics;
Some Platonist affirms that in the station
Where we should cast off body and trade
The ancient habit sticks,
And that if our works could
But vanish with our breath
That were a lucky death,
For triumph can but mar our solitude.

The swan has leaped into the desolate heaven:
That image can bring wildness, bring a rage
To end all things, to end
What my laborious life imagined, even
The half-imagined, the half-written page;
O but we dreamed to mend
Whatever mischief seemed
To afflict mankind, but now
That winds of winter blow
Learn that we were crack-pated when we dreamed.

IV

We, who seven years ago
Talked of honour and of truth,
Shriek with pleasure if we show
The weasel's twist, the weasel's tooth.

V

Come let us mock at the great
That had such burdens on the mind
And toiled so hard and late
To leave some monument behind,
Nor thought of the levelling wind.

Come let us mock at the wise;
With all those calendars whereon
They fixed old aching eyes,
They never saw how seasons run,
And now but gape at the sun.

Come let us mock at the good
That fancied goodness might be gay,
And sick of solitude
Might proclaim a holiday:
Wind shrieked – and where are they?

Mock mockers after that
That would not lift a hand maybe
To help good, wise or great
To bar that foul storm out, for we
Traffic in mockery.

VI

Violence upon the roads: violence of horses;
Some few have handsome riders, are garlanded
On delicate sensitive ear or tossing mane,
But wearied running round and round in their courses
All break and vanish, and evil gathers head:
Herodias' daughters have returned again,
A sudden blast of dusty wind and after
Thunder of feet, tumult of images,
Their purpose in the labyrinth of the wind;
And should some crazy hand dare touch a daughter
All turn with amorous cries, or angry cries,
According to the wind, for all are blind.
But now wind drops, dust settles; thereupon
There lurches past, his great eyes without thought
Under the shadow of stupid straw-pale locks,
That insolent fiend Robert Artisson
To whom the love-torn Lady Kyteler brought
Bronzed peacock feathers, red combs of her cocks.

Leda and the Swan

A sudden blow: the great wings beating still
Above the staggering girl, her thighs caressed
By the dark webs, her nape caught in his bill,
He holds her helpless breast upon his breast.

How can those terrified vague fingers push
The feathered glory from her loosening thighs?
And how can body, laid in that white rush,
But feel the strange heart beating where it lies?

A shudder in the loins engenders there
The broken wall, the burning roof and tower
And Agamemnon dead.
                            Being so caught up,
So mastered by the brute blood of the air,
Did she put on his knowledge with his power
Before the indifferent beak could let her drop?

Byzantium

The unpurged images of day recede;
The Emperor's drunken soldiery are abed;
Night resonance recedes, night-walkers' song
After great cathedral gong;
A starlit or a moonlit dome disdains
All that man is,
All mere complexities,
The fury and the mire of human veins.

Before me floats an image, man or shade,
Shade more than man, more image than a shade;
For Hades' bobbin bound in mummy-cloth
May unwind the winding path;
A mouth that has no moisture and no breath
Breathless mouths may summon;
I hail the superhuman;
I call it death-in-life and life-in-death.

Miracle, bird or golden handiwork,
More miracle than bird or handiwork,
Planted on the star-lit golden bough,
Can like the cocks of Hades crow,
Or, by the moon embittered, scorn aloud
In glory of changeless metal
Common bird or petal
And all complexities of mire or blood.

At midnight on the Emperor's pavement flit
Flames that no faggot feeds, nor steel has lit,
Nor storm disturbs, flames begotten of flame,
Where blood-begotten spirits come
And all complexities of fury leave,
Dying into a dance,
An agony of trance,
An agony of flame that cannot singe a sleeve.

Astraddle on the dolphin's mire and blood,
Spirit after spirit! The smithies break the flood,
The golden smithies of the Emperor!
Marbles of the dancing floor
Break bitter furies of complexity,
Those images that yet
Fresh images beget,
That dolphin-torn, that gong-tormented sea.

Politics

> *In our time the destiny of man presents
> its meanings in political terms.*
> THOMAS MANN

How can I, that girl standing there,
My attention fix
On Roman or on Russian
Or on Spanish politics?
Yet here's a travelled man that knows
What he talks about,
And there's a politician
That has both read and thought,
And maybe what they say is true
Of war and war's alarms,
But O that I were young again
And held her in my arms.

EDWARD THOMAS

(1878–1917)

Edward Thomas called himself 'mainly Welsh'. He grew up in London, but developed a passion for Nature. Hating the economic forces that had destroyed agricultural communities and expanded cities, Thomas absorbed, as his poetry shows, the literary and folk traditions of the English countryside. After studying history at Oxford, he lived in rural southern England, particularly Steep in Hampshire. He supported his family by writing reviews, country books, biography and criticism. Overwork caused (sometimes suicidal) depression and creative despair. This self-styled 'hurried & harried prose man' could not find a 'form that suits me'. Yet books such as *The South Country* (1909) and *In Pursuit of Spring* (1914) fertilised the poetry which – prompted by Robert Frost – Thomas began to write in December 1914. An influential poetry-reviewer, Thomas had praised Frost's *North of Boston* as 'revolutionary'. And its 'absolute fidelity to the postures which the voice assumes in the most expressive intimate speech' clarified his own artistic direction. 'The sun used to shine' celebrates the poets' friendship. It also suggests Thomas's darker inspiration – the Great War. Although overage, he enlisted in the Artists' Rifles (July 1915). He was killed at Arras (April 1917) before his first collection, *Poems*, appeared.

Thomas's poetry dramatises the inner journey of one who 'ceaselessly, unreasonably grieves'. It may also be the first ecological poetry in that it subordinates the human eye and human presence to natural systems. Similarly, Thomas rejected imperialism and defined English nationality in terms of locality or "home". His thinking about England was conditioned by social change, war and his ecological sense of habitats and history. 'The Combe' opens up a long perspective on the present. 'As the team's head brass', which registers change in the very fabric of its blank verse, revises Hardy's 'In Time of "The Breaking of Nations"'. Thomas's language, images and forms renew traditional properties of English poetry. His variations on the quatrain, for instance, are extraordinarily subtle. Yet he also fears ruptures of the links between humanity and earth, present and past, 'word' and 'thing', that his poetry is still able to effect. 'Rain' (in which 'Myriads of broken reeds' alludes to dead soldiers) builds up a complex and chilling symbol of dissolution.

Old Man

Old Man, or Lad's-love, – in the name there's nothing
To one that knows not Lad's-love, or Old Man,
The hoar-green feathery herb, almost a tree,
Growing with rosemary and lavender.
Even to one that knows it well, the names

Half decorate, half perplex, the thing it is:
At least, what that is clings not to the names
In spite of time. And yet I like the names.

The herb itself I like not, but for certain
I love it, as some day the child will love it
Who plucks a feather from the door-side bush
Whenever she goes in or out of the house.
Often she waits there, snipping the tips and shrivelling
The shreds at last on to the path, perhaps
Thinking, perhaps of nothing, till she sniffs
Her fingers and runs off. The bush is still
But half as tall as she, though it is as old;
So well she clips it. Not a word she says;
And I can only wonder how much hereafter
She will remember, with that bitter scent,
Of garden rows, and ancient damson-trees
Topping a hedge, a bent path to a door,
A low thick bush beside the door, and me
Forbidding her to pick.

                    As for myself,
Where first I met the bitter scent is lost.
I, too, often shrivel the grey shreds,
Sniff them and think and sniff again and try
Once more to think what it is I am remembering,
Always in vain. I cannot like the scent,
Yet I would rather give up others more sweet,
With no meaning, than this bitter one.

I have mislaid the key. I sniff the spray
And think of nothing; I see and I hear nothing;
Yet seem, too, to be listening, lying in wait
For what I should, yet never can, remember:
No garden appears, no path, no hoar-green bush
Of Lad's-love, or Old Man, no child beside,
Neither father nor mother, nor any playmate;
Only an avenue, dark, nameless, without end.

The Combe

The Combe was ever dark, ancient and dark.
Its mouth is stopped with bramble, thorn, and briar;
And no one scrambles over the sliding chalk
By beech and yew and perishing juniper
Down the half precipices of its sides, with roots
And rabbit holes for steps. The sun of Winter,
The moon of Summer, and all the singing birds
Except the missel-thrush that loves juniper,
Are quite shut out. But far more ancient and dark
The Combe looks since they killed the badger there,
Dug him out and gave him to the hounds,
That most ancient Briton of English beasts.

In Memoriam (Easter 1915)

The flowers left thick at nightfall in the wood
This Eastertide call into mind the men,
Now far from home, who, with their sweethearts, should
Have gathered them and will do never again.

Aspens

All day and night, save winter, every weather,
Above the inn, the smithy, and the shop,
The aspens at the cross-roads talk together
Of rain, until their last leaves fall from the top.

Out of the blacksmith's cavern comes the ringing
Of hammer, shoe, and anvil; out of the inn
The clink, the hum, the roar, the random singing –
The sounds that for these fifty years have been.

The whisper of the aspens is not drowned,
And over lightless pane and footless road,
Empty as sky, with every other sound
Not ceasing, calls their ghosts from their abode,

A silent smithy, a silent inn, nor fails
In the bare moonlight or the thick-furred gloom,
In tempest or the night of nightingales,
To turn the cross-roads to a ghostly room.

And it would be the same were no house near.
Over all sorts of weather, men, and times,
Aspens must shake their leaves and men may hear
But need not listen, more than to my rhymes.

Whatever wind blows, while they and I have leaves
We cannot other than an aspen be
That ceaselessly, unreasonably grieves,
Or so men think who like a different tree.

Rain

Rain, midnight rain, nothing but the wild rain
On this bleak hut, and solitude, and me
Remembering again that I shall die
And neither hear the rain nor give it thanks
For washing me cleaner than I have been
Since I was born into this solitude.
Blessed are the dead that the rain rains upon:
But here I pray that none whom once I loved
Is dying tonight or lying still awake
Solitary, listening to the rain,
Either in pain or thus in sympathy
Helpless among the living and the dead,
Like a cold water among broken reeds,
Myriads of broken reeds all still and stiff,
Like me who have no love which this wild rain
Has not dissolved except the love of death,
If love it be for what is perfect and
Cannot, the tempest tells me, disappoint.

Thaw

Over the land freckled with snow half-thawed
The speculating rooks at their nests cawed
And saw from elm-tops, delicate as flower of grass,
What we below could not see, Winter pass.

Tall Nettles

Tall nettles cover up, as they have done
These many springs, the rusty harrow, the plough
Long worn out, and the roller made of stone:
Only the elm butt tops the nettles now.

This corner of the farmyard I like most:
As well as any bloom upon a flower
I like the dust on the nettles, never lost
Except to prove the sweetness of a shower.

The Watchers

By the ford at the town's edge
Horse and carter rest:
The carter smokes on the bridge
Watching the water press in swathes about his horse's chest.

From the inn one watches, too,
In the room for visitors
That has no fire, but a view
And many cases of stuffed fish, vermin, and kingfishers.

The sun used to shine

The sun used to shine while we two walked
Slowly together, paused and started
Again, and sometimes mused, sometimes talked
As either pleased, and cheerfully parted

Each night. We never disagreed
Which gate to rest on. The to be
And the late past we gave small heed.
We turned from men or poetry

To rumours of the war remote
Only till both stood disinclined
For aught but the yellow flavorous coat
Of an apple wasps had undermined;

Or a sentry of dark betonies,
The stateliest of small flowers on earth,
At the forest verge; or crocuses
Pale purple as if they had their birth

In sunless Hades fields. The war
Came back to mind with the moonrise
Which soldiers in the east afar
Beheld then. Nevertheless, our eyes

Could as well imagine the Crusades
Or Caesar's battles. Everything
To faintness like those rumours fades –
Like the brook's water glittering

Under the moonlight – like those walks
Now – like us two that took them, and
The fallen apples, all the talks
And silences – like memory's sand

When the tide covers it late or soon,
And other men through other flowers
In those fields under the same moon
Go talking and have easy hours.

As the team's head brass

As the team's head brass flashed out on the turn
The lovers disappeared into the wood.
I sat among the boughs of the fallen elm
That strewed an angle of the fallow, and
Watched the plough narrowing a yellow square
Of charlock. Every time the horses turned
Instead of treading me down, the ploughman leaned
Upon the handles to say or ask a word,
About the weather, next about the war.
Scraping the share he faced towards the wood,
And screwed along the furrow till the brass flashed
Once more.
                    The blizzard felled the elm whose crest
I sat in, by a woodpecker's round hole,
The ploughman said. 'When will they take it away?'
'When the war's over.' So the talk began –
One minute and an interval of ten,
A minute more and the same interval.
'Have you been out?' 'No.' 'And don't want to, perhaps?'
'If I could only come back again, I should.
I could spare an arm. I shouldn't want to lose
A leg. If I should lose my head, why, so,
I should want nothing more.... Have many gone
From here?' 'Yes.' 'Many lost?' 'Yes, a good few.
Only two teams work on the farm this year.
One of my mates is dead. The second day
In France they killed him. It was back in March,
The very night of the blizzard, too. Now if
He had stayed here we should have moved the tree.'
'And I should not have sat here. Everything
Would have been different. For it would have been
Another world.' 'Ay, and a better, though
If we could see all all might seem good.' Then
The lovers came out of the wood again:
The horses started and for the last time
I watched the clods crumble and topple over
After the ploughshare and the stumbling team.

Lights Out

I have come to the borders of sleep,
The unfathomable deep
Forest, where all must lose
Their way, however straight
Or winding, soon or late;
They can not choose.

Many a road and track
That since the dawn's first crack
Up to the forest brink
Deceived the travellers,
Suddenly now blurs,
And in they sink.

Here love ends –
Despair, ambition ends;
All pleasure and all trouble,
Although most sweet or bitter,
Here ends, in sleep that is sweeter
Than tasks most noble.

There is not any book
Or face of dearest look
That I would not turn from now
To go into the unknown
I must enter, and leave, alone,
I know not how.

The tall forest towers:
Its cloudy foliage lowers
Ahead, shelf above shelf:
Its silence I hear and obey
That I may lose my way
And myself.

D.H. LAWRENCE

(1885–1930)

Like Hardy, whose work he studied closely, David Herbert Lawrence is a
novelist-poet whose poetry may be his finest achievement. Lawrence was born
in Eastwood, Nottinghamshire, the fourth son of a coalminer and a former
teacher. His parents' conflicting class-values shaped his literary personality.
Lawrence's most celebrated novel, *Sons and Lovers*, and his first book of poems,
Love Poems and Others, were both published in 1913. In 1911, partly owing
to the threat of TB (from which he was to die), Lawrence ceased to be a
teacher. With his wife Frieda, he began to lead a nomadic life: always seeking
(in Australia, New Mexico and elsewhere) a utopian alternative to the restric-
tions and repressions of England.

Lawrence wrote many kinds of poem, including poems (sometimes in dia-
lect) that recreate the Nottinghamshire of his childhood. 'Piano' is uncannily
akin to Hardy's 'The Self-Unseeing'. However, *Birds, Beasts and Flowers* (1923)
is usually considered his best book. The natural world purges the didacticism
and sexual theorising that can unbalance Lawrence's writings. There is, indeed,
an anthropomorphic element in his animal poems. Yet each poem's rhythm
persuasively mimics a creature's unique qualities, its otherness and place in
the cosmos, while the tone of human address also seems fitted to the occasion.
Lawrence's way of building a poem on subtly paced repetitions was influenced
by the Bible and by Walt Whitman. He criticised both the 'static perfection'
of traditional stanzas, and 'free-versifiers' (like Eliot) who merely 'break the
lovely form of material verse'. He saw his own verse as 'direct utterance from
the instant, whole man'. The living movement of Lawrence's poetry best con-
veys his gospel of sensory 'life': a gospel that has both rejected and absorbed
the nonconformist religion in which he was reared. W.H. Auden, for whom
Lawrence was a 'pilgrim' rather than a 'citizen', calls his messianic approach
to verse and life 'very protestant indeed'. 'Bavarian Gentians' and 'The Ship
of Death' (inspired by Etruscan culture and tombs) are great visionary poems.

Sorrow

Why does the thin grey strand
Floating up from the forgotten
Cigarette between my fingers,
Why does it trouble me?

Ah, you will understand;
When I carried my mother downstairs,
A few times only, at the beginning
Of her soft-foot malady,

I should find, for a reprimand
To my gaiety, a few long grey hairs
On the breast of my coat; and one by one
I watched them float up the dark chimney.

Piano

Softly, in the dusk, a woman is singing to me;
Taking me back down the vista of years, till I see
A child sitting under the piano, in the boom of the tingling strings
And pressing the small, poised feet of a mother who smiles as she sings.

In spite of myself, the insidious mastery of song
Betrays me back, till the heart of me weeps to belong
To the old Sunday evenings at home, with winter outside
And hymns in the cosy parlour, the tinkling piano our guide.

So now it is vain for the singer to burst into clamour
With the great black piano appassionato. The glamour
Of childish days is upon me, my manhood is cast
Down in the flood of remembrance, I weep like a child for the past.

Gloire de Dijon

When she rises in the morning
I linger to watch her;
She spreads the bath-cloth underneath the window
And the sunbeams catch her
Glistening white on the shoulders,
While down her sides the mellow
Golden shadow glows as
She stoops to the sponge, and her swung breasts
Sway like full-blown yellow
Gloire de Dijon roses.

She drips herself with water, and her shoulders
Glisten as silver, they crumple up
Like wet and falling roses, and I listen
For the sluicing of their rain-dishevelled petals.
In the window full of sunlight
Concentrates her golden shadow
Fold on fold, until it glows as
Mellow as the glory roses.

Humming-Bird

I can imagine, in some otherworld
Primeval-dumb, far back
In that most awful stillness, that only gasped and hummed,
Humming-birds raced down the avenues.

Before anything had a soul,
While life was a heave of Matter, half inanimate,
This little bit chipped off in brilliance
And went whizzing through the slow, vast, succulent stems.

I believe there were no flowers then,
In the world where the humming-bird flashed ahead of creation.
I believe he pierced the slow vegetable veins with his long beak.

Probably he was big
As mosses, and little lizards, they say, were once big.
Probably he was a jabbing, terrifying monster.

We look at him through the wrong end of the long telescope of Time,
Luckily for us.

Kangaroo

In the northern hemisphere
Life seems to leap at the air, or skim under the wind
Like stags on rocky ground, or pawing horses, or springy scut-tailed
    rabbits.

Or else rush horizontal to charge at the sky's horizon,
Like bulls or bisons or wild pigs.

Or slip like water slippery towards its ends,
As foxes, stoats, and wolves, and prairie dogs.

Only mice, and moles, and rats, and badgers, and beavers, and
    perhaps bears
Seem belly-plumbed to the earth's mid-navel.
Or frogs that when they leap come flop, and flop to the centre of
    the earth.

But the yellow antipodal Kangaroo, when she sits up,
Who can unseat her, like a liquid drop that is heavy, and just touches
    earth.

The downward drip
The down-urge.
So much denser than cold-blooded frogs.

Delicate mother Kangaroo
Sitting up there rabbit-wise, but huge, plumb-weighted,
And lifting her beautiful slender face, oh! so much more gently and
    finely lined than a rabbit's, or than a hare's,
Lifting her face to nibble at a round white peppermint drop, which
    she loves, sensitive mother Kangaroo.

Her sensitive, long, pure-bred face.
Her full antipodal eyes, so dark,
So big and quiet and remote, having watched so many empty dawns
    in silent Australia.

Her little loose hands, and drooping Victorian shoulders.
And then her great weight below the waist, her vast pale belly
With a thin young yellow little paw hanging out, and straggle of a
    long thin ear, like ribbon,

Like a funny trimming to the middle of her belly, thin little dangle
    of an immature paw, and one thin ear.

Her belly, her big haunches
And, in addition, the great muscular python-stretch of her tail.

There, she shan't have any more peppermint drops.
So she wistfully, sensitively sniffs the air, and then turns, goes off
    in slow sad leaps

On the long flat skis of her legs,
Steered and propelled by that steel-strong snake of a tail.

Stops again, half turns, inquisitive to look back.
While something stirs quickly in her belly, and a lean little face
    comes out, as from a window,
Peaked and a bit dismayed,
Only to disappear again quickly away from the sight of the world,
    to snuggle down in the warmth,
Leaving the trail of a different paw hanging out.

Still she watches with eternal, cocked wistfulness!
How full her eyes are, like the full, fathomless, shining eyes of an
    Australian black-boy
Who has been lost so many centuries on the margins of existence!

She watches with insatiable wistfulness.
Untold centuries of watching for something to come,
For a new signal from life, in that silent lost land of the South.

Where nothing bites but insects and snakes and the sun, small life.
Where no bull roared, no cow ever lowed, no stag cried, no leopard
    screeched, no lion coughed, no dog barked,
But all was silent save for parrots occasionally, in the haunted blue
    bush.

Wistfully watching, with wonderful liquid eyes.
And all her weight, all her blood, dripping sack-wise down towards
    the earth's centre,
And the live little-one taking in its paw at the door of her belly.

Leap then, and come down on the line that draws to the earth's
    deep, heavy centre.

Lizard

A lizard ran out on a rock and looked up, listening
no doubt to the sounding of the spheres.
And what a dandy fellow! the right toss of a chin for you
and swirl of a tail!

If men were as much men as lizards are lizards
they'd be worth looking at.

Bavarian Gentians

Not every man has gentians in his house
in soft September, at slow, sad Michaelmas.

Bavarian gentians, big and dark, only dark
darkening the day-time, torch-like with the smoking blueness of
        Pluto's gloom,
ribbed and torch-like, with their blaze of darkness spread blue
down flattening into points, flattened under the sweep of white day
torch-flower of the blue-smoking darkness, Pluto's dark-blue daze,
black lamps from the halls of Dis, burning dark blue,
giving off darkness, blue darkness, as Demeter's pale lamps give
        off light,
lead me then, lead the way.

Reach me a gentian, give me a torch!
let me guide myself with the blue, forked torch of this flower
down the darker and darker stairs, where blue is darkened on
        blueness
even where Persephone goes, just now, from the frosted September
to the sightless realm where darkness is awake upon the dark
and Persephone herself is but a voice
or a darkness invisible enfolded in the deeper dark
of the arms Plutonic, and pierced with the passion of dense gloom,
among the splendour of torches of darkness, shedding darkness on
        the lost bride and her groom.

The Ship of Death

I

Now it is autumn and the falling fruit
and the long journey towards oblivion.

The apples falling like great drops of dew
to bruise themselves an exit from themselves.

And it is time to go, to bid farewell
to one's own self, and find an exit
from the fallen self.

II

Have you built your ship of death, O have you?
O build your ship of death, for you will need it.

The grim frost is at hand, when the apples will fall
thick, almost thundrous, on the hardened earth.

And death is on the air like a smell of ashes!
Ah! can't you smell it?

And in the bruised body, the frightened soul
finds itself shrinking, wincing from the cold
that blows upon it through the orifices.

III

And can a man his own quietus make
with a bare bodkin?

With daggers, bodkins, bullets, man can make
a bruise or break of exit for his life;
but is that a quietus, O tell me, is it quietus?

Surely not so! for how could murder, even self-murder
ever a quietus make?

IV

O let us talk of quiet that we know,
that we can know, the deep and lovely quiet
of a strong heart at peace!

How can we this, our own quietus, make?

V

Build then the ship of death, for you must take
the longest journey, to oblivion.

And die the death, the long and painful death
that lies between the old self and the new.

Already our bodies are fallen, bruised, badly bruised,
already our souls are oozing through the exit
of the cruel bruise.

Already the dark and endless ocean of the end
is washing in through the breaches of our wounds,
already the flood is upon us.

Oh build your ship of death, your little ark
and furnish it with food, with little cakes, and wine
for the dark flight down oblivion.

VI

Piecemeal the body dies, and the timid soul
has her footing washed away, as the dark flood rises.

We are dying, we are dying, we are all of us dying
and nothing will stay the death-flood rising within us
and soon it will rise on the world, on the outside world.

We are dying, we are dying, piecemeal our bodies are dying
and our strength leaves us,
and our soul cowers naked in the dark rain over the flood,
cowering in the last branches of the tree of our life.

VII

We are dying, we are dying, so all we can do
is now to be willing to die, and to build the ship
of death to carry the soul on the longest journey.

A little ship, with oars and food
and little dishes, and all accoutrements
fitting and ready for the departing soul.

Now launch the small ship, now as the body dies
and life departs, launch out, the fragile soul
in the fragile ship of courage, the ark of faith
with its store of food and little cooking pans
and change of clothes,
upon the flood's black waste
upon the waters of the end
upon the sea of death, where still we sail
darkly, for we cannot steer, and have no port.

There is no port, there is nowhere to go
only the deepening black darkening still
blacker upon the soundless, ungurgling flood
darkness at one with darkness, up and down
and sideways utterly dark, so there is no direction any more.
And the little ship is there; yet she is gone.
She is not seen, for there is nothing to see her by.
She is gone! gone! and yet
somewhere she is there.
Nowhere!

VIII

And everything is gone, the body is gone
completely under, gone, entirely gone.
The upper darkness is heavy on the lower,
between them the little ship
is gone
she is gone.

It is the end, it is oblivion.

IX

And yet out of eternity, a thread
separates itself on the blackness,
a horizontal thread
that fumes a little with pallor upon the dark.

Is it illusion? or does the pallor fume
a little higher?
Ah wait, wait, for there's the dawn,
the cruel dawn of coming back to life
out of oblivion.

Wait, wait, the little ship
drifting, beneath the deathly ashy grey
of a flood-dawn.

Wait, wait! even so, a flush of yellow
and strangely, O chilled wan soul, a flush of rose.

A flush of rose, and the whole thing starts again.

X

The flood subsides, and the body, like a worn sea-shell
emerges strange and lovely.
And the little ship wings home, faltering and lapsing
on the pink flood,
and the frail soul steps out, into her house again
filling the heart with peace.

Swings the heart renewed with peace
even of oblivion.

Oh build your ship of death, oh build it!
for you will need it.
For the voyage of oblivion awaits you.

SIEGFRIED SASSOON
(1886–1967)

Siegfried Sassoon was the son of wealthy Anglo-Jewish parents. Before 1914 he lived a leisured life, golfing, hunting, writing derivative poetry. He joined up on the first day of the Great War, and won a Military Cross which he later renounced. Sassoon had become radicalised by the losses at the Battle of the Somme and by meeting leftwing pacifist intellectuals. His famous protest against the politics of the war – 'A Soldier's Declaration' – was printed in the *Times* and quoted in parliament. To prevent Sassoon from being court-martialled, Robert Graves, a fellow-officer in the Royal Welch Fusiliers, got him admitted to Craiglockhart War Hospital near Edinburgh where the psychological effects of war were treated. There he wrote the poems in *Counter-Attack* (1918), and met and influenced Wilfred Owen. Sassoon returned to action: another expression of solidarity with ordinary soldiers. His most significant postwar writings are memoirs that obsessively revisit his lost generation, partly in an effort to exorcise survivor-guilt. Sassoon's 'Declaration' ends by deploring 'the callous complacence with which the majority of those at home regard the continuance of agonies which they do not share, and which they have not sufficient imagination to realise'. Sassoon's verse-satires attack the ignorance or indifference that sustains both the war and war-rhetoric. His angry mode is complemented by the empathy (in part, homoerotic) which can heighten his usually documentary language. He was well qualified to symbolise, in 'Everyone Sang', the moment of armistice.

'They'

The Bishop tells us: 'When the boys come back
They will not be the same; for they'll have fought
In a just cause: they lead the last attack
On Anti-Christ; their comrades' blood has bought
New right to breed an honourable race,
They have challenged Death and dared him face to face.'

'We're none of us the same!' the boys reply.
For George lost both his legs; and Bill's stone blind;
Poor Jim's shot through the lungs and like to die;
And Bert's gone syphilitic: you'll not find
A chap who's served that hasn't found *some* change.'
And the Bishop said: 'The ways of God are strange!'

The Rear-Guard

(Hindenburg Line, April 1917)

Groping along the tunnel, step by step,
He winked his prying torch with patching glare
From side to side, and sniffed the unwholesome air.

Tins, boxes, bottles, shapes too vague to know;
A mirror smashed, the mattress from a bed;
And he, exploring fifty feet below
The rosy gloom of battle overhead.

Tripping, he grabbed the wall; saw some one lie
Humped at his feet, half-hidden by a rug,
And stooped to give the sleeper's arm a tug.
'I'm looking for headquarters.' No reply.
'God blast your neck!' (For days he'd had no sleep,)
'Get up and guide me through this stinking place.'

Savage, he kicked a soft, unanswering heap,
And flashed his beam across the livid face
Terribly glaring up, whose eyes yet wore
Agony dying hard ten days before;
And fists of fingers clutched a blackening wound.

Alone he staggered on until he found
Dawn's ghost that filtered down a shafted stair
To the dazed, muttering creatures underground
Who hear the boom of shells in muffled sound.
At last, with sweat of horror in his hair,
He climbed through darkness to the twilight air,
Unloading hell behind him step by step.

The Dug-Out

Why do you lie with your legs ungainly huddled,
And one arm bent across your sullen, cold,
Exhausted face? It hurts my heart to watch you,
Deep-shadow'd from the candle's guttering gold;
And you wonder why I shake you by the shoulder;
Drowsy, you mumble and sigh and turn your head...
You are too young to fall asleep for ever;
And when you sleep you remind me of the dead.

Everyone Sang

Everyone suddenly burst out singing;
And I was filled with such delight
As prisoned birds must find in freedom,
Winging wildly across the white
Orchards and dark-green fields; on – on – and out of sight.

Everyone's voice was suddenly lifted;
And beauty came like the setting sun:
My heart was shaken with tears; and horror
Drifted away...O, but Everyone
Was a bird; and the song was wordless; the singing will never
        be done.

EDWIN MUIR

(1887–1959)

Edwin Muir was born on Deerness, Orkney. His family moved to the nearby island of Wyre, and in 1901 to Glasgow. For Muir, this was the loss of Eden, a fall 'into chaos'. His parents and two brothers died, and he once worked in a factory that reduced bones to charcoal. Muir rescued himself by writing criticism; by going to London where he helped to edit the avant-garde journal *The New Age*; and by psychoanalysis. In 1921 he left for the continent with his wife Willa. The Muirs became well-known translators from the German, especially of Kafka (who influenced Muir's poetry). After the war Muir worked for the British Council in Prague and Rome. He had a bad experience back in Scotland as Warden of Newbattle Abbey, a college for mature students. He was beset by anti-creative forces that represented all he hated in Scottish culture.

Muir has made more impression as a critic and translator than as a poet. He began writing poetry when he was 35, and (as he admitted) unreceptive to new techniques. There was also the problem of "Scottish poetry". Muir admired Hugh MacDiarmid's "Synthetic Scots" poems. Yet he never believed that Scots alone could heal the malign effects of John Knox's Calvinist coup which had 'robbed Scotland of all the benefits of the Renaissance', and (with occasional remissions), made the country 'an object-lesson in savage provincialism'. Muir's *Scott and Scotland* (1936) enraged MacDiarmid by arguing that the future of Scottish writing lay in English, and that there was no longer any fruitful distinction to be drawn between the two literatures. Here Muir may also speak for his own dilemmas. Some critics find his "standard English" rather colourless, as they find his allegories lacking in political bite and sensory vividness. Yet Seamus Heaney has recently praised Muir's parables of European history as a neglected model. Muir contemplates 'naked man' in a world of loss, desire and foreboding. 'The Horses' persuades both as an encounter with animals and as a post-nuclear, post-industrial scenario. Here Orkney redeems Glasgow, but not in any simple way.

Orpheus' Dream

And she was there. The little boat
Coasting the perilous isles of sleep,
Zones of oblivion and despair,
Stopped, for Eurydice was there.
The foundering skiff could scarcely keep
All that felicity afloat.

As if we had left earth's frontier wood
Long since and from this sea had won
The lost original of the soul,

The moment gave us pure and whole
Each back to each, and swept us on
Past every choice to boundless good.

Forgiveness, truth, atonement, all
Our love at once – till we could dare
At last to turn our heads and see
The poor ghost of Eurydice
Still sitting in her silver chair,
Alone in Hades' empty hall.

The Horses

Barely a twelvemonth after
The seven days war that put the world to sleep,
Late in the evening the strange horses came.
By then we had made our covenant with silence,
But in the first few days it was so still
We listened to our breathing and were afraid.
On the second day
The radios failed; we turned the knobs; no answer.
On the third day a warship passed us, heading north,
Dead bodies piled on the deck. On the sixth day
A plane plunged over us into the sea. Thereafter
Nothing. The radios dumb;
And still they stand in corners of our kitchens,
And stand, perhaps, turned on, in a million rooms
All over the world. But now if they should speak,
If on a sudden they should speak again,
If on the stroke of noon a voice should speak,
We would not listen, we would not let it bring
That old bad world that swallowed its children quick
At one great gulp. We would not have it again.
Sometimes we think of the nations lying asleep,
Curled blindly in impenetrable sorrow,
And then the thought confounds us with its strangeness.
The tractors lie about our fields; at evening
They look like dank sea-monsters couched and waiting.
We leave them where they are and let them rust:

'They'll moulder away and be like other loam.'
We make our oxen drag our rusty ploughs,
Long laid aside. We have gone back
Far past our fathers' land.
                                        And then, that evening
Late in the summer the strange horses came.
We heard a distant tapping on the road,
A deepening drumming; it stopped, went on again
And at the corner changed to hollow thunder.
We saw the heads
Like a wild wave charging and were afraid.
We had sold our horses in our fathers' time
To buy new tractors. Now they were strange to us
As fabulous steeds set on an ancient shield
Or illustrations in a book of knights.
We did not dare go near them. Yet they waited,
Stubborn and shy, as if they had been sent
By an old command to find our whereabouts
And that long-lost archaic companionship.
In the first moment we had never a thought
That they were creatures to be owned and used.
Among them were some half-a-dozen colts
Dropped in some wilderness of the broken world,
Yet new as if they had come from their own Eden.
Since then they have pulled our ploughs and borne our loads,
But that free servitude still can pierce our hearts.
Our life is changed; their coming our beginning.

I see the image

I see the image of a naked man,
He stoops and picks a smooth stone from the ground,
Turns round and in a wide arc flings it backward
Towards the beginning. What will catch it,
Hand, or paw, or gullet of sea-monster?
He stoops again, turns round and flings a stone
Straight on before him. I listen for its fall,
And hear a ringing on some hidden place
As if against the wall of an iron tower.

T.S. ELIOT

(1888–1965)

Thomas Stearns Eliot wrote the most famous poem of the century, *The Waste Land* (1922). The poem has contexts in his American background as well as its London foreground. Eliot grew up in St Louis, Missouri, but spent long holidays on the east coast. His grandfather, a zealous Unitarian minister from Boston, was a founder of Washington University, St Louis. Religion and education became motifs in Eliot's criticism, as did an ideal of unified tradition. He measured this ideal, at once literary and cultural, against the difficulty of attaining it under modern conditions. Disliking the heterogeneity of American culture, he mythologised what he called 'the mind of Europe'. In 1906 Eliot went to Harvard, and trained as an academic philosopher. But he was converted to poetry by Arthur Symons's *The Symbolist Movement in Literature* (1899), earlier an influence on Yeats. Eliot's moody urban impressions are indebted to Symons's poetry, as well as more directly to French symbolists such as Jules Laforgue. From 1914 Eliot lived in England. He tried, but failed, to join the US navy after America entered the war. Rescued from a job in Lloyds Bank, Eliot founded and edited *The Criterion* (1922-39), and from 1925 had a powerful role with the publishers Faber and Faber. He was awarded the Nobel Prize in 1948.

Critical commentary on *The Waste Land* is often contradictory. On the one hand, critics praise its discontinuity of form and voice; on the other, they try to join up the dots. The poem is seen both as expressing a historical crisis, and as proving the impossibility of expressing anything. Eliot himself states that his personal 'rhythmical grumbling' should not be taken as signifying modern disillusionment. It may be best (as with 'Prufrock') to see *The Waste Land* as a psychological landscape where inner obsessions mesh with outer conditions. As we respond to shifts of sound, rhythm and tone, we pick up Eliot's characteristic notes of nostalgia, desire, ironic distaste, elegy – for the 'buried' war dead, too – and neurosis. His images of sexuality may reflect a nervous breakdown he suffered when his first marriage was failing. His images of culture suggest how his belief in 'the mind of Europe' has been shattered: postwar Europe seems to be out of its mind. The poem's literary quotations and jumbled languages, like its displaced or misplaced people and metaphors of the fragmented body, mourn a lost wholeness. Similarly, *The Waste Land* has been called a 'pre-conversion' poem. Its underlying quest for spiritual meaning can be detected in the 'inexplicable' symbol of 'Magnus Martyr'. In 1928 Eliot termed himself 'classical in literature, royalist in politics, and Anglo-Catholic in religion'. His sequence *Four Quartets* (1943) mystically blends an Anglican version of Englishness with the 'way' to God. Some readers follow George Orwell in preferring Eliot's earlier poetry of 'glowing despair' to his later poetry of 'melancholy faith'.

The Love Song of J. Alfred Prufrock

S'io credessi che mia risposta fosse
a persona che mai tornasse al mondo,
questa fiamma staria senza più scosse.
Ma per ciò che giammai di questo fondo
non tornò vivo alcun, s'i'odo il vero,
senza tema d'infamia ti rispondo.

Let us go then, you and I,
When the evening is spread out against the sky
Like a patient etherised upon a table;
Let us go, through certain half-deserted streets,
The muttering retreats
Of restless nights in one-night cheap hotels
And sawdust restaurants with oyster-shells:
Streets that follow like a tedious argument
Of insidious intent
To lead you to an overwhelming question...
Oh, do not ask, 'What is it?'
Let us go and make our visit.

In the room the women come and go
Talking of Michelangelo.

The yellow fog that rubs its back upon the window-panes,
The yellow smoke that rubs its muzzle on the window-panes,
Licked its tongue into the corners of the evening,
Lingered upon the pools that stand in drains,
Let fall upon its back the soot that falls from chimneys,
Slipped by the terrace, made a sudden leap,
And seeing that it was a soft October night,
Curled once about the house, and fell asleep.

And indeed there will be time
For the yellow smoke that slides along the street
Rubbing its back upon the window-panes;
There will be time, there will be time
To prepare a face to meet the faces that you meet;
There will be time to murder and create,
And time for all the works and days of hands
That lift and drop a question on your plate;
Time for you and time for me,

And time yet for a hundred indecisions,
And for a hundred visions and revisions,
Before the taking of a toast and tea.

    In the room the women come and go
Talking of Michelangelo.

    And indeed there will be time
To wonder, 'Do I dare?' and, 'Do I dare?'
Time to turn back and descend the stair,
With a bald spot in the middle of my hair –
(They will say: 'How his hair is growing thin!')
My morning coat, my collar mounting firmly to the chin,
My necktie rich and modest, but asserted by a simple pin –
(They will say: 'But how his arms and legs are thin!')
Do I dare
Disturb the universe?
In a minute there is time
For decisions and revisions which a minute will reverse.

    For I have known them all already, known them all –
Have known the evenings, mornings, afternoons,
I have measured out my life with coffee spoons;
I know the voices dying with a dying fall
Beneath the music from a farther room.
    So how should I presume?

    And I have known the eyes already, known them all –
The eyes that fix you in a formulated phrase,
And when I am formulated, sprawling on a pin,
When I am pinned and wriggling on the wall,
Then how should I begin
To spit out all the butt-ends of my days and ways?
    And how should I presume?

    And I have known the arms already, known them all –
Arms that are braceleted and white and bare
(But in the lamplight, downed with light brown hair!)
Is it perfume from a dress
That makes me so digress?
Arms that lie along a table, or wrap about a shawl.

And should I then presume?
And how should I begin?

      .   .   .   .

Shall I say, I have gone at dusk through narrow streets
And watched the smoke that rises from the pipes
Of lonely men in shirt-sleeves, leaning out of windows?…

I should have been a pair of ragged claws
Scuttling across the floors of silent seas.

      .   .   .   .

And the afternoon, the evening, sleeps so peacefully!
Smoothed by long fingers,
Asleep…tired…or it malingers,
Stretched on the floor, here beside you and me.
Should I, after tea and cakes and ices,
Have the strength to force the moment to its crisis?
But though I have wept and fasted, wept and prayed,
Though I have seen my head (grown slightly bald) brought in upon
      a platter,
I am no prophet – and here's no great matter;
I have seen the moment of my greatness flicker,
And I have seen the eternal Footman hold my coat, and snicker,
And in short, I was afraid.

And would it have been worth it, after all,
After the cups, the marmalade, the tea,
Among the porcelain, among some talk of you and me,
Would it have been worth while,
To have bitten off the matter with a smile,
To have squeezed the universe into a ball
To roll it towards some overwhelming question,
To say: 'I am Lazarus, come from the dead,
Come back to tell you all, I shall tell you all' –
If one, settling a pillow by her head,
    Should say: 'That is not what I meant at all.
    That is not it, at all.'

And would it have been worth it, after all,
Would it have been worth while,
After the sunsets and the dooryards and the sprinkled streets,

After the novels, after the teacups, after the skirts that trail along
        the floor –
And this, and so much more? –
It is impossible to say just what I mean!
But as if a magic lantern threw the nerves in patterns on a screen:
Would it have been worth while
If one, settling a pillow or throwing off a shawl,
And turning toward the window, should say:
        'That is not it at all,
        That is not what I meant at all.'

                .   .   .   .   .

    No! I am not Prince Hamlet, nor was meant to be;
Am an attendant lord, one that will do
To swell a progress, start a scene or two,
Advise the prince; no doubt, an easy tool,
Deferential, glad to be of use,
Politic, cautious, and meticulous;
Full of high sentence, but a bit obtuse;
At times, indeed, almost ridiculous –
Almost, at times, the Fool.

    I grow old...I grow old...
I shall wear the bottoms of my trousers rolled.

    Shall I part my hair behind? Do I dare to eat a peach?
I shall wear white flannel trousers, and walk upon the beach.
I have heard the mermaids singing, each to each.

I do not think that they will sing to me.

I have seen them riding seaward on the waves
Combing the white hair of the waves blown back
When the wind blows the water white and black.

We have lingered in the chambers of the sea
By sea-girls wreathed with seaweed red and brown
Till human voices wake us, and we drown.

La Figlia Che Piange

O quam te memorem virgo...

Stand on the highest pavement of the stair –
Lean on a garden urn –
Weave, weave the sunlight in your hair –
Clasp your flowers to you with a pained surprise –
Fling them to the ground and turn
With a fugitive resentment in your eyes:
But weave, weave the sunlight in your hair.

So I would have had him leave,
So I would have had her stand and grieve,
So he would have left
As the soul leaves the body torn and bruised,
As the mind deserts the body it has used.
I should find
Some way incomparably light and deft,
Some way we both should understand,
Simple and faithless as a smile and shake of the hand.

She turned away, but with the autumn weather
Compelled my imagination many days,
Many days and many hours:
Her hair over her arms and her arms full of flowers.
And I wonder how they should have been together!
I should have lost a gesture and a pose.
Sometimes these cogitations still amaze
The troubled midnight and the noon's repose.

from The Waste Land

I *The Burial of the Dead*

April is the cruellest month, breeding
Lilacs out of the dead land, mixing
Memory and desire, stirring
Dull roots with spring rain.
Winter kept us warm, covering
Earth in forgetful snow, feeding
A little life with dried tubers.
Summer surprised us, coming over the Starnbergersee
With a shower of rain; we stopped in the colonnade,
And went on in sunlight, into the Hofgarten,
And drank coffee, and talked for an hour.
Bin gar keine Russin, stamm' aus Litauen, echt deutsch.
And when we were children, staying at the arch-duke's,
My cousin's, he took me out on a sled,
And I was frightened. He said, Marie,
Marie, hold on tight. And down we went.
In the mountains, there you feel free.
I read, much of the night, and go south in the winter.

What are the roots that clutch, what branches grow
Out of this stony rubbish? Son of man,
You cannot say, or guess, for you know only
A heap of broken images, where the sun beats,
And the dead tree gives no shelter, the cricket no relief,
And the dry stone no sound of water. Only
There is shadow under this red rock,
(Come in under the shadow of this red rock),
And I will show you something different from either
Your shadow at morning striding behind you
Or your shadow at evening rising to meet you;
I will show you fear in a handful of dust.
    Frisch weht der Wind
    Der Heimat zu
    Mein Irisch Kind,
    Wo weilest du?
'You gave me hyacinths first a year ago;
'They called me the hyacinth girl.'

– Yet when we came back, late, from the hyacinth garden,
Your arms full, and your hair wet, I could not
Speak, and my eyes failed, I was neither
Living nor dead, and I knew nothing,
Looking into the heart of light, the silence.
Oed' und leer das Meer.

Madame Sosostris, famous clairvoyante,
Had a bad cold, nevertheless
Is known to be the wisest woman in Europe,
With a wicked pack of cards. Here, said she,
Is your card, the drowned Phoenician Sailor,
(Those are pearls that were his eyes. Look!)
Here is Belladonna, the Lady of the Rocks,
The lady of situations.
Here is the man with three staves, and here the Wheel,
And here is the one-eyed merchant, and this card,
Which is blank, is something he carries on his back,
Which I am forbidden to see. I do not find
The Hanged Man. Fear death by water.
I see crowds of people, walking round in a ring.
Thank you. If you see dear Mrs Equitone,
Tell her I bring the horoscope myself:
One must be so careful these days.

Unreal City,
Under the brown fog of a winter dawn,
A crowd flowed over London Bridge, so many,
I had not thought death had undone so many.
Sighs, short and infrequent, were exhaled,
And each man fixed his eyes before his feet.
Flowed up the hill and down King William Street,
To where Saint Mary Woolnoth kept the hours
With a dead sound on the final stroke of nine.
There I saw one I knew, and stopped him, crying: 'Stetson!
'You who were with me in the ships at Mylae!
'That corpse you planted last year in your garden,
'Has it begun to sprout? Will it bloom this year?
'Or has the sudden frost disturbed its bed?
'O keep the Dog far hence, that's friend to men,
'Or with his nails he'll dig it up again!
'You! hypocrite lecteur! – mon semblable, – mon frère!'

III *The Fire Sermon*

The river's tent is broken; the last fingers of leaf
Clutch and sink into the wet bank. The wind
Crosses the brown land, unheard. The nymphs are departed.
Sweet Thames, run softly, till I end my song.
The river bears no empty bottles, sandwich papers,
Silk handkerchiefs, cardboard boxes, cigarette ends
Or other testimony of summer nights. The nymphs are departed.
And their friends, the loitering heirs of City directors;
Departed, have left no addresses.
By the waters of Leman I sat down and wept...
Sweet Thames, run softly till I end my song,
Sweet Thames, run softly, for I speak not loud or long.
But at my back in a cold blast I hear
The rattle of the bones, and chuckle spread from ear to ear.

A rat crept softly through the vegetation
Dragging its slimy belly on the bank
While I was fishing in the dull canal
On a winter evening round behind the gashouse
Musing upon the king my brother's wreck
And on the king my father's death before him.
White bodies naked on the low damp ground
And bones cast in a little low dry garret,
Rattled by the rat's foot only, year to year.
But at my back from time to time I hear
The sound of horns and motors, which shall bring
Sweeney to Mrs Porter in the spring.
O the moon shone bright on Mrs Porter
And on her daughter
They wash their feet in soda water
Et O ces voix d'enfants, chantant dans la coupole!

Twit twit twit
Jug jug jug jug jug jug
So rudely forc'd.
Tereu

Unreal City
Under the brown fog of a winter noon
Mr Eugenides, the Smyrna merchant

Unshaven, with a pocket full of currants
C.i.f. London: documents at sight,
Asked me in demotic French
To luncheon at the Cannon Street Hotel
Followed by a weekend at the Metropole.

   At the violet hour, when the eyes and back
Turn upward from the desk, when the human engine waits
Like a taxi throbbing waiting,
I Tiresias, though blind, throbbing between two lives,
Old man with wrinkled female breasts, can see
At the violet hour, the evening hour that strives
Homeward, and brings the sailor home from sea,
The typist home at teatime, clears her breakfast, lights
Her stove, and lays out food in tins.
Out of the window perilously spread
Her drying combinations touched by the sun's last rays,
On the divan are piled (at night her bed)
Stockings, slippers, camisoles, and stays.
I Tiresias, old man with wrinkled dugs
Perceived the scene, and foretold the rest –
I too awaited the expected guest.
He, the young man carbuncular, arrives,
A small house agent's clerk, with one bold stare,
One of the low on whom assurance sits
As a silk hat on a Bradford millionaire.
The time is now propitious, as he guesses,
The meal is ended, she is bored and tired,
Endeavours to engage her in caresses
Which still are unreproved, if undesired.
Flushed and decided, he assaults at once;
Exploring hands encounter no defence;
His vanity requires no response,
And makes a welcome of indifference.
(And I Tiresias have foresuffered all
Enacted on this same divan or bed;
I who have sat by Thebes below the wall
And walked among the lowest of the dead.)
Bestows one final patronising kiss,
And gropes his way, finding the stairs unlit...

She turns and looks a moment in the glass,
Hardly aware of her departed lover;
Her brain allows one half-formed thought to pass:
'Well now that's done: and I'm glad it's over.'
When lovely woman stoops to folly and
Paces about her room again, alone,
She smooths her hair with automatic hand,
And puts a record on the gramophone.

'This music crept by me upon the waters'
And along the Strand, up Queen Victoria Street.
O City city, I can sometimes hear
Beside a public bar in Lower Thames Street,
The pleasant whining of a mandoline
And a clatter and a chatter from within
Where fishmen lounge at noon: where the walls
Of Magnus Martyr hold
Inexplicable splendour of Ionian white and gold.

　　　　　The river sweats
　　　　　Oil and tar
　　　　　The barges drift
　　　　　With the turning tide
　　　　　Red sails
　　　　　Wide
　　　　　To leeward, swing on the heavy spar.
　　　　　The barges wash
　　　　　Drifting logs
　　　　　Down Greenwich reach
　　　　　Past the Isle of Dogs.
　　　　　　　　　Weialala leia
　　　　　　　　　Wallala leialala

　　　　　Elizabeth and Leicester
　　　　　Beating oars
　　　　　The stern was formed
　　　　　A gilded shell
　　　　　Red and gold
　　　　　The brisk swell
　　　　　Rippled both shores
　　　　　Southwest wind
　　　　　Carried down stream
　　　　　The peal of bells

White towers
      Weialala leia
      Wallala leialala

'Trams and dusty trees.
Highbury bore me. Richmond and Kew
Undid me. By Richmond I raised my knees
Supine on the floor of a narrow canoe.'

'My feet are at Moorgate, and my heart
Under my feet. After the event
He wept. He promised "a new start".
I made no comment. What should I resent?'

'On Margate Sands.
I can connect
Nothing with nothing.
The broken fingernails of dirty hands.
My people humble people who expect
Nothing.'
        la la

To Carthage then I came

Burning burning burning burning
O Lord Thou pluckest me out
O Lord Thou pluckest

burning

IV *Death by Water*

Phlebas the Phoenician, a fortnight dead,
Forgot the cry of gulls, and the deep sea swell
And the profit and loss.
              A current under sea
Picked his bones in whispers. As he rose and fell
He passed the stages of his age and youth
Entering the whirlpool.
              Gentile or Jew
O you who turn the wheel and look to windward,
Consider Phlebas, who was once handsome and tall as you.

IVOR GURNEY

(1890–1937)

Ivor Gurney grew up in Gloucester. In 1911 he won an Open Scholarship to study composition at the Royal College of Music. There he set Elizabethan lyrics to music, began to write poetry himself, and took an interest in Englishness as represented by folksong and by the work of Elgar and Vaughan Williams. Gurney had already shown symptoms of schizophrenia, including suicidal tendencies, before he joined the army (the Gloucesters) in 1915. *Severn and Somme* appeared in 1917, *War's Embers* in 1919. During his war-service he was wounded, gassed and shell-shocked. In 1922 he was committed to the City of London Mental Hospital at Dartford, Kent, where he went on writing and composing until his death.

The close textures of Gurney's poetry disturbingly interweave Severn and Somme. They also reflect the obsessive walking of the Gloucestershire hills that marked both his illness and his devotion to the region. Syntactical oddities, like an absence or abundance of definite articles, show the influences of Elizabethan poetry and Gerard Manley Hopkins. Yet the rhythmic discords that Gurney brings to a song ('To His Love') or sonnet ('The Not-Returning') more significantly betray the psychic cost of his belief that the Great War 'must sink into the very foundations and be absorbed'. Beautiful lines are all the more powerful for their sometimes dislocated contexts. Gurney absorbed, too, Edward Thomas's poems. His war-retrospects return Thomas's insights to English landscapes further darkened by his own experience. 'The Mangel-Bury', for example, alludes to Thomas's poem 'Swedes'.

To His Love

He's gone, and all our plans
   Are useless indeed.
We'll walk no more on Cotswold
   Where the sheep feed
   Quietly and take no heed.

His body that was so quick
   Is not as you
Knew it, on Severn river
   Under the blue
   Driving our small boat through.

You would not know him now...
    But still he died
Nobly, so cover him over
    With violets of pride
    Purple from Severn side.

Cover him, cover him soon!
    And with thick-set
Masses of memoried flowers –
    Hide that red wet
    Thing I must somehow forget.

The hoe scrapes earth

The hoe scrapes earth as fine in grain as sand,
I like the swirl of it and the swing in the hand
Of the lithe hoe so clever at craft and grace,
And the friendliness, the clear freedom of the place.

And the green hairs of the wheat on sandy brown.
The draw of eyes toward the coloured town,
The lark ascending slow to a roof of cloud
That cries for the voice of poetry to cry aloud.

Smudgy Dawn

Smudgy dawn scarfed with military colours
Northward, and flowing wider like slow sea water,
Woke in lilac and elm and almost among garden flowers.
Birds a multitude; increasing as it made lighter.
Nothing but I moved by railings there; slept sweeter
Than kings the country folk in thatch or slate shade,
Peace had the grey West, fleece, clouds sure in its power,
Out on much-Severn I thought waves readied for laughter
And the fire-swinger promised behind elm pillars
A day worthy such beginning to come after.

Dawn came not surprising, but later widened
To great space and a sea of many colours
With slate and pink and blue above the frightened
Mud fields soiled and heavy with War's dolours –
And the guns thumped and threatened,
While the bacon frizzled, and the warm incense heightened,
Drifting in bays and dugouts slowly lightened.
First light bringing the thought what familiar star
There was, of town, farm, cottage, over there, over yonder,
And by day before duty settled awhile to
A companionship of good talk, forgetting night's woe.

The Not-Returning

Never comes now the through-and-through clear
Tiredness of body on crisp straw down laid,
Nor the tired thing said
Content before the clean sleep close the eyes,
Or ever resistless rise
Pictures of far country westward, westward out of the sight of the eyes.
Never more delight comes of the roof dark lit
With under-candle flicker nor rich gloom on it,
The limned faces and moving hands shuffling the cards,
The clear conscience, the free mind moving towards
Poetry, friends, the old earthly rewards.
No more they come. No more.
Only the restless searching, the bitter labour,
The going out to watch stars, stumbling blind through the difficult door.

To God

Why have you made life so intolerable
And set me between four walls, where I am able
Not to escape meals without prayer, for that is possible
Only by annoying an attendant. And tonight a sensual
Hell has been put on me, so that all has deserted me

And I am merely crying and trembling in heart
For death, and cannot get it. And gone out is part
Of sanity. And there is dreadful hell within me.
And nothing helps. Forced meals there have been and electricity
And weakening of sanity by influence
That's dreadful to endure. And there is Orders
And I am praying for death, death, death,
And dreadful is the indrawing or out-breathing of breath
Because of the intolerable insults put on my whole soul,
Of the soul loathed, loathed, loathed of the soul.
Gone out every bright thing from my mind.
All lost that ever God himself designed.
Not half can be written of cruelty of man, on man,
Not often such evil guessed as between man and man.

The Mangel-Bury

It was after war; Edward Thomas had fallen at Arras –
I was walking by Gloucester musing on such things
As fill his verse with goodness; it was February; the long house
Straw-thatched of the mangels stretched two wide wings;
And looked as part of the earth heaped up by dead soldiers
In the most fitting place – along the hedge's yet-bare lines.
West spring breathed there early, that none foreign divines.
Across the flat country the rattling of the cart sounded;
Heavy of wood, jingling of iron; as he neared me I waited
For the chance perhaps of heaving at those great rounded
Ruddy or orange things – and right to be rolled and hefted
By a body like mine, soldier still, and clean from water.
Silent he assented; till the cart was drifted
High with those creatures, so right in size and matter.
We threw with our bodies swinging, blood in my ears singing;
His was the thick-set sort of farmer, but well-built –
Perhaps, long before, his blood's name ruled all,
Watched all things for his own. If my luck had so willed
Many questions of lordship I had heard him tell – old
Names, rumours. But my pain to more moving called
And him to some barn business far in the fifteen acre field.

ISAAC ROSENBERG

(1890–1918)

Isaac Rosenberg, son of Jewish immigrants from Eastern Europe, grew up in the East End of London. He left school at 14 to become an apprentice engraver. Later, he received financial help to study art at the Slade School but remained undecided between poetry and art. Edward Marsh, editor of the 'Georgian' anthologies, noticed his poetry. Rosenberg wrote to Marsh in 1916: 'The Homer for this war has yet to be found'. He told another friend that he disliked Rupert Brooke's 'begloried sonnets' because war 'should be approached in a colder way, more abstract, with less of the million feelings everybody feels; or all these should be concentrated in one distinguished emotion'. Rosenberg hated war ('Now is the time to go on an exploring expedition to the North Pole') but in 1915 he enlisted in the Suffolk regiment to help his family out financially. At first he was in a 'Bantam Battalion' for undersized recruits. He was killed near Arras on 1 April 1918. Rosenberg's war poetry seems at once improvisatory and monumental. The intimacy of its dealings with a rat or poppy, the terrible immediacy of 'A man's brains splattered on / A stretcher-bearer's face', occur against an elemental backdrop sculpted by compressed syntax (inversion is a favourite device) and slow-paced lines. His masterpiece 'Dead Man's Dump' concentrates into one symbol 'earth' consumed by violence. A line such as 'None saw their spirits' shadow shake the grass' seems an echo chamber for the entire war.

Break of Day in the Trenches

The darkness crumbles away.
It is the same old druid Time as ever,
Only a live thing leaps my hand,
A queer sardonic rat,
As I pull the parapet's poppy
To stick behind my ear.
Droll rat, they would shoot you if they knew
Your cosmopolitan sympathies.
Now you have touched this English hand
You will do the same to a German
Soon, no doubt, if it be your pleasure
To cross the sleeping green between.
It seems you inwardly grin as you pass
Strong eyes, fine limbs, haughty athletes,
Less chanced than you for life,
Bonds to the whims of murder,
Sprawled in the bowels of the earth,
The torn fields of France.

What do you see in our eyes
At the shrieking iron and flame
Hurled through still heavens?
What quaver – what heart aghast?
Poppies whose roots are in man's veins
Drop, and are ever dropping;
But mine in my ear is safe –
Just a little white with the dust.

Returning, we hear the Larks

Sombre the night is.
And though we have our lives, we know
What sinister threat lurks there.

Dragging these anguished limbs, we only know
This poison-blasted track opens on our camp –
On a little safe sleep.

But hark! joy – joy – strange joy.
Lo! heights of night ringing with unseen larks.
Music showering our upturned list'ning faces.

Death could drop from the dark
As easily as song –
But song only dropped,
Like a blind man's dreams on the sand
By dangerous tides,
Like a girl's dark hair for she dreams no ruin lies there,
Or her kisses where a serpent hides.

Dead Man's Dump

The plunging limbers over the shattered track
Racketed with their rusty freight,
Stuck out like many crowns of thorns,
And the rusty stakes like sceptres old

To stay the flood of brutish men
Upon our brothers dear.

The wheels lurched over sprawled dead
But pained them not, though their bones crunched,
Their shut mouths made no moan,
They lie there huddled, friend and foeman,
Man born of man, and born of woman,
And shells go crying over them
From night till night and now.

Earth has waited for them
All the time of their growth
Fretting for their decay:
Now she has them at last!
In the strength of their strength
Suspended – stopped and held.

What fierce imaginings their dark souls lit
Earth! have they gone into you?
Somewhere they must have gone,
And flung on your hard back
Is their souls' sack,
Emptied of God-ancestralled essences.
Who hurled them out? Who hurled?

None saw their spirits' shadow shake the grass,
Or stood aside for the half used life to pass
Out of those doomed nostrils and the doomed mouth,
When the swift iron burning bee
Drained the wild honey of their youth.

What of us, who flung on the shrieking pyre,
Walk, our usual thoughts untouched,
Our lucky limbs as on ichor fed,
Immortal seeming ever?
Perhaps when the flames beat loud on us,
A fear may choke in our veins
And the startled blood may stop.

The air is loud with death,
The dark air spurts with fire
The explosions ceaseless are.
Timelessly now, some minutes past,

These dead strode time with vigorous life,
Till the shrapnel called 'an end!'
But not to all. In bleeding pangs
Some borne on stretchers dreamed of home,
Dear things, war-blotted from their hearts.

A man's brains splattered on
A stretcher-bearer's face;
His shook shoulders slipped their load,
But when they bent to look again
The drowning soul was sunk too deep
For human tenderness.

They left this dead with the older dead,
Stretched at the cross roads.

Burnt black by strange decay,
Their sinister faces lie
The lid over each eye,
The grass and coloured clay
More motion have than they,
Joined to the great sunk silences.

Here is one not long dead;
His dark hearing caught our far wheels,
And the choked soul stretched weak hands
To reach the living word the far wheels said,
The blood-dazed intelligence beating for light,
Crying through the suspense of the far torturing wheels
Swift for the end to break,
Or the wheels to break,
Cried as the tide of the world broke over his sight.

Will they come? Will they ever come?
Even as the mixed hoofs of the mules,
The quivering-bellied mules,
And the rushing wheels all mixed
With his tortured upturned sight,
So we crashed round the bend,
We heard his weak scream,
We heard his very last sound,
And our wheels grazed his dead face.

HUGH MacDIARMID

(1892–1978)

Hugh MacDiarmid (Christopher Murray Grieve) grew up in Langholm, Dumfriesshire: the 'muckle toon' whose physical and social landscape permeates his poetry. He identified with the Republican, Radical and anti-English traditions of the Scottish Borders. MacDiarmid served with the Royal Army Medical Corps in Salonika and France. After the war he began to write poetry in Scots, and to proclaim 'A New Movement in Scottish Literature'. He became a founder member of the Scottish National Party (1928). In 1933 he went to live on the Shetland island of Whalsay, where he had a nervous breakdown and joined the Communist Party. In 1942 he was conscripted for manual war work. In 1943 he published *Lucky Poet*, a prose epic of his life, talents and campaigns.

At one time expelled from the CP for nationalism, at another from the SNP for communism, MacDiarmid appears riven by contradictions. Yet the most significant split in a career devoted to being 'whaur/ Extremes meet' is that between his didactic later work and the poems he wrote up to 1933. These were published in such volumes as *Sangschaw* (1925), *Penny Wheep* (1926), *A Drunk Man Looks at the Thistle* (1926), *Scots Unbound* (1932) and *Stony Limits* (1934). The selection below mainly represents this intense creative period.

Hugh MacDiarmid's "Synthetic Scots" was revolutionary in mingling often-obsolete dialect words from different Scottish regions. He drew on Jamieson's *Etymological Dictionary of the Scottish Language* (1879–82 edition). This method is neither as 'artificial' nor as 'modernist' as different critics claim. The dictionary words are grafted on to a strong stem: the syntax, idioms and sounds of Langholm speech. MacDiarmid's short lyrics, whose language seems newborn rather than archaic, condense locality and universe, ridiculous and sublime, into a cosmic blend. 'Tarras', a love poem to a bog, which obliquely interprets his reasons for becoming a Scottish nationalist, relishes Scots words as much as the phenomena towards which they point. Relished, too, is the flyting that flays the Langholm bourgeoisie in 'Prayer for a Second Flood'. A range of religious idioms (he once taught a United Free Church – 'Wee Frees' – Sunday school class) condition MacDiarmid's poetry. Such variety of vision and tone is lost in his later manifesto-poems. Yet in 'To a Friend and Fellow-Poet' fresh vocabulary reactivates MacDiarmid's deepest poetic impulses.

Morning

The Day loups up (for she kens richt weel
Owre lang wi' the Nicht she mauna lig)
And plunks the sun i' the lift aince mair
Like a paddle-doo i' the raim-pig.

loups: jumps; *lift:* sky; *paddle-doo:* frog (lit. paddle-dove); *raim-pig:* cream-basin.

The Watergaw

Ae weet forenicht i' the yow-trummle
I saw yon antrin thing,
A watergaw wi' its chitterin' licht
Ayont the on-ding;
An' I thocht o' the last wild look ye gied
Afore ye deed!

There was nae reek i' the laverock's hoose
That nicht – an' nane i' mine;
But I hae thocht o' that foolish licht
Ever sin' syne;
An' I think that mebbe at last I ken
What your look meant then.

Ex vermibus

Gape, gape, gorlin',
For I ha'e a worm
That'll gi'e ye a slee and sliggy sang
Wi' mony a whuram.

Syne i' the lift
Byous spatrils you'll mak',
For a gorlin' wi' worms like this in its wame
Nae airels sall lack.

But owre the tree-taps
Maun flee like a sperk,
Till it hes the haill o' the Heavens alunt
Frae dawin' to derk.

watergaw: stump of rainbow; *ae weet:* one wet; *forenicht:* early evening; *yow-trummle:* cold weather in July after sheep-shearing (lit. ewe tremble); *antrin:* rare; *chitterin':* shivering; *on-ding:* downpour; *reek:* smoke; *laverock:* lark; *sin' syne:* since then.

gorlin': fledgling; *slee:* sly; *sliggy:* cunning; *whuram:* grace-note; *syne:* then; *lift:* sky; *byous:* extraordinary; *spatrils:* musical notes; *wame:* belly; *airels:* tones; *haill:* whole; *alunt:* ablaze.

The Eemis Stane

I' the how-dumb-deid o' the cauld hairst nicht
The warl' like an eemis stane
Wags i' the lift;
An' my eerie memories fa'
Like a yowdendrift.

Like a yowdendrift so's I couldna read
The words cut oot i' the stane
Had the fug o' fame
An' history's hazelraw
No' yirdit thaim.

The Innumerable Christ

Other stars may have their Bethlehem, and their Calvary too.
PROFESSOR J.Y. SIMPSON

Wha kens on whatna Bethlehems
Earth twinkles like a star the nicht,
An' whatna shepherds lift their heids
        In its unearthly licht?

'Yont a' the stars oor een can see
An' farther than their lichts can fly,
I' mony an unco warl' the nicht
        The fatefu' bairnies cry.

I' mony an unco warl' the nicht
The lift gaes black as pitch at noon,
An' sideways on their chests the heids
        O' endless Christs roll doon.

eemis: unsteady; *how-dumb-deid:* hollow dead silent depth; *cauld hairst nicht:* cold
harvest night; *yowdendrift:* blizzard; *fug:* moss; *hazelraw:* lichen; *yirdit:* buried,
earthed; *thaim:* them.

whatna: what kind of; *een:* eyes; *unco:* strange; *lift:* sky.

An' when the earth's as cauld's the mune
An' a' its folk are lang syne deid,
On coontless stars the Babe maun cry
        An' the Crucified maun bleed.

At My Father's Grave

The sunlicht still on me, you row'd in clood,
We look upon each ither noo like hills
Across a valley. I'm nae mair your son.
It is my mind, nae son o' yours, that looks,
And the great darkness o' your death comes up
And equals it across the way.
A livin' man upon a deid man thinks
And ony sma'er thocht's impossible.

Prayer for a Second Flood

There'd ha'e to be nae warnin'. Times ha'e changed
And Noahs are owre numerous nooadays,
(And them the vera folk to benefit maist!)
Knock the feet frae under them, O Lord, wha praise
Your unsearchable ways sae muckle and yet hope
        To keep within knowledgeable scope!

Ding a' their trumpery show to blauds again.
Their measure is the thimblefu' o' Esk in spate.
Like whisky the tittlin' craturs mete oot your poo'ers
Aince a week for bawbees in the kirk-door plate,
– And pit their umbrellas up when they come oot
        If mair than a pulpitfu' o' You's aboot!

row'd: wrapped; *noo:* now.

muckle: much; *ding:* smash; *blauds:* fragments; *tittlin':* prating.

O arselins wi' them! Whummle them again!
Coup them heels-owre-gowdy in a storm sae gundy
That mony a lang fog-theekit face I ken
'll be sooked richt doon under through a cundy
In the High Street, afore you get weel-sterted
   And are still hauf-herted!

Then flush the world in earnest. Let yoursel' gang,
Scour't to the bones, and mak' its marrow holes
Toom as a whistle as they used to be
In days I mind o' ere men fidged wi' souls,
But naething had forgotten you as yet,
   Nor you forgotten it.

Up then and at them, ye Gairds o' Heaven.
The Divine Retreat is owre. Like a tidal bore
Boil in among them; let the lang lugs nourished
On the milk o' the word at last hear the roar
O' human shingle; and replenish the salt o' the earth
   In the place o' their birth.

Tarras

This Bolshevik bog! Suits me doon to the grun'!
For by fike and finnick the world's no' run.
Let fools set store by a simperin' face,
Ithers seek to keep the purale in place
Or grue at vermin – but by heck
The purpose o' life needs them – if us.
Little the bog and the masses reck
O' some dainty-davie or fike-ma-fuss.
Ho for the mother of usk and adder
Spelderin' here in her coal and madder
Faur frae Society's bells and bladder.

---

arselins: backwards; *whummle:* overturn; *coup:* tumble; *heels-owre-gowdy:* head-over-heels; *gundy:* violent; *fog-theekit:* moss-thatched; *cundy:* drain; *toom:* empty; *fidged wi':* worried about; *lugs:* ears.

fike: fuss over trifles; *purale:* the poor; *grue:* shudder; *dainty-davie:* fastidious person; *fike-ma-fuss:* fusspot; *usk:* esk, newt; *spelderin':* sprawling with legs apart; *bladder:* blather.

The fog-wa' splits and a gair is set
O' corbie oats and corcolet
And drulie water like sheepeik seeps
Through the duffie peats, and cranglin' creeps,
Crowdles like a crab, syne cowds awa',
Couthless eneuch, yet cuttedly tae,
Tho' here and there in a sudden swaw
Corky-heidit as if in a playsome way,
But its lichtest kinks are a cowzie sport,
That nocht can cuddum – nocht can sort
For't, endless torsion, riddlin' port.

Ah, woman-fondlin'! What is that to this?
Saft hair to birssy heather, warm kiss
    To cauld black waters' suction.
    Nae ardent breists' erection
But the stark hills'! In what dry-gair-flow
Can I pillow my lowin' cheek here
Wi' nae paps' howe below?
What laithsome parodies appear
O' my body's secrets in this oorie growth
Wi' its peerieweeries a' radgie for scouth
And the haill ratch and rive o' a world uncouth?

Her cautelles! On cods o' crammasy sundew
Or wi' antrin sprigs o' butterwort blue,
Here in a punk-hole, there in a burn,
She gecks to storm and shine in turn,
Trysts wi' this wind and neist wi' that,
Now wi' thunder and syne wi' snaw,
Bare to the banes or wi' birds in her hat,
    – And has bairns by them a',
        – Bairns!

---

fog-wa': moss wall; *gair:* patch; *corbie oats:* black oats; *corcolet:* lichen; *drulie:* muddy; *sheepeik:* sheep-grease; *duffie:* spongy; *cranglin':* winding; *crowdles:* crawls; *cowds:* floats slowly; *couthless:* unkindly; *cuttedly:* laconically; *swaw:* ripple; *corky-heidit:* giddy; *kinks:* twists; *cowzie:* boisterous; *cuddum:* tame, domesticate.

birssy: bristly; *dry-gair-flow:* place where two hills meet; *lowin':* glowing; *howe:* valley; *laithsome:* loathsome; *oorie:* uncanny; *peerieweeries:* very small organisms; *radgie:* randy; *scouth:* free movement; *ratch and rive:* wear and tear.

cautelles: stratagems; *cods:* pillows; *crammasy:* crimson; *antrin:* occasional; *punk-hole:* hole in the moss; *gecks:* looks archly; *neist:* next.

Bycomes o' bogs and gets o' cairns,
Ultimate flow of her flosh and ferns...
The doup of the world is under you here
And, fast in her shochles, she'll find ye,
When you're drawn to where wind and water shear,
Shuttles of glaur, and shot-heuch, to wind ye,
Till you peughle and hoast in the shug-bog there,
While she lies jirblin' wide to the air
And now and then lets a scannachin flare.

Come pledge her in a horse-punckin then!
Loons to a byssim, pock-shakin's o' men,
Needna come vauntin' their poustures to her.
Their paramuddle is whey to her heather.
To gang through her mill they maun pay
Ootsucken multure to the auld vulture,
Nor wi' their flauchter-spades ettle to play,
Withoot thick paikies to gaird their cul-ture!
What's ony schaftmon to this shud moss?
Or pooky-hair to her matted boss?
– Pledge her wha's mou' can relish her floss!

bycomes: illegitimate offspring; gets: bastards; flosh: swamp; doup: hindquarters;
shochles: legs; glaur: soft, oozy mud; shot-heuch: steep bank undermined by water;
peughle and hoast: cough in a stifled manner; shug-bog: quaking bog; jirblin': spill-
ing liquid; scannachin: gleam.

horse-punckin: hole in the mud; loons: boys; byssim: bawd; pock-shakin': youngest,
smallest and weakest of a family; poustures: bodily powers; paramuddle: the red
tripe of cattle; ootsucken multure: mill duties; flauchter-spades: turf-cutting spades;
ettle: try; paikies: protective aprons for turf cutters; cul-ture: pun on 'cull', testicle;
ony: any.

schaftmon: length of fist with thumb extended; shud: coagulated; moss: bog; pooky-
hair: scraggly hair; boss: front of body from chest to loins; floss: the common rush.

To a Friend and Fellow-Poet

It is with the poet as with a guinea worm
Who, to accommodate her teeming progeny
Sacrifices nearly every organ of her body, and becomes
(Her vagina obliterated in her all-else-consuming
Process of uterine expansion, and she still faced
With a grave obstetrical dilemma calling for
Most marvellous contrivance to deposit her prodigious swarm
Where they may find the food they need and have a chance in life)
Almost wholly given over to her motherly task,
Little more than one long tube close-packed with young;
Until from the ruptured bulla, the little circular sore,
You see her dauntless head protrude, and presently, slowly,
A beautiful, delicate, and pellucid tube
Is projected from her mouth, tenses and suddenly spills
Her countless brood in response to a stimulus applied
Not directly to the worm herself, but the skin of her host
With whom she has no organised connection (and that stimulus
O Poets! but cold water!)...The worm's whole musculocutaneous coat
Thus finally functions as a uterus, forcing the uterine tube
With its contents through her mouth. And when the prolapsed
          uterus ruptures
The protruded and now collapsed portion shrivels to a thread
(Alexander Blok's utter emptiness after creating a poem!)
The rapid drying of which effectually and firmly
Closes the wound for the time being...till, later, the stimulus being
          reapplied,
A fresh portion of the uterine tube protrudes, ruptures, and collapses,
Once more ejaculating another seething mass of embryos,
And so the process continues until inch by inch
The entire uterus is expelled and parturition concluded.
Is it not precisely thus we poets deliver our store,
Our whole being the instrument of our suicidal art,
And by the skin of our teeth flype ourselves into fame?

flype: turn inside out.

WILFRED OWEN

(1893–1918)

Wilfred Owen, born in Oswestry, mainly grew up in Birkenhead. Lack of money stopped him from going to university and he worked (1911-13) as assistant to a vicar. This led to a crisis of faith that estranged him from his mother's evangelical Anglicanism, though its influence is transmuted in his war poetry. Owen, for whom 'the fullest, largest liveable life was that of a Poet', had begun to write poetry influenced by Keats. In December 1914 he gave as his only patriotic motivation: 'The sense that I was perpetuating the language in which Keats and the rest of them wrote'. He joined the Artists' Rifles in October 1915, and was later commissioned in the Manchester Regiment. His trench poems are based on four months in France from January 1917. In June he was sent to Craiglockhart War Hospital near Edinburgh suffering from shellshock. In August 1917 he met Siegfried Sassoon there. Owen returned to France, and was killed a week before the Armistice.

Owen's mature poems date from meeting Sassoon, whose example and criticism, Owen said, '*fixed* my Life'. Yet, as Louis MacNeice observes, the war 'could only make [Owen] a poet thanks to the lesser poet whom it broke in him'. His powerfully immediate images reinvent Keats's doctrine of 'Negative Capability', of receptivity to experience. It becomes an art of empathy: Owen termed himself 'a conscientious objector with a very seared conscience'. Like Rosenberg, he turns the trench landscape into an elemental and cosmic space. Here he sets a conflict between a patriarchal God (politicians, generals, the Old Testament ethic used to justify war) and Christ crucified but never redeemed (the suffering soldier). His rhythms, slowed by assonance and consonantal rhyme, seem to enact symbolically both the course of the war and a bleak movement of human consciousness: 'The long, forlorn, relentless trend / From larger day to huger night'. Owen's poems also enact a movement (made explicit in 'Dulce Et Decorum Est') from immediacy and empathy to critique that still challenges every reader. His 'Preface' to the poems he never saw published makes that clear: 'Above all I am not concerned with Poetry. My subject is War, and the pity of War. The Poetry is in the pity. Yet these elegies are to this generation in no sense consolatory. They may be to the next. All a poet can do today is warn. That is why the true Poets must be truthful.'

Anthem for Doomed Youth

What passing-bells for these who die as cattle?
  – Only the monstrous anger of the guns.
  Only the stuttering rifles' rapid rattle
Can patter out their hasty orisons.
No mockeries now for them; no prayers nor bells;
  Nor any voice of mourning save the choirs, –

The shrill, demented choirs of wailing shells;
   And bugles calling for them from sad shires.

What candles may be held to speed them all?
   Not in the hands of boys but in their eyes
Shall shine the holy glimmers of goodbyes.
   The pallor of girls' brows shall be their pall;
Their flowers the tenderness of patient minds,
And each slow dusk a drawing-down of blinds.

I saw his round mouth's crimson deepen as it fell

I saw his round mouth's crimson deepen as it fell,
     Like a sun, in his last deep hour;
Watched the magnificent recession of farewell,
     Clouding, half gleam, half glower,
And a last splendour burn the heavens of his cheek.
     And in his eyes
The cold stars lighting, very old and bleak,
     In different skies.

Dulce Et Decorum Est

Bent double, like old beggars under sacks,
Knock-kneed, coughing like hags, we cursed through sludge,
Till on the haunting flares we turned our backs
And towards our distant rest began to trudge.
Men marched asleep. Many had lost their boots
But limped on, blood-shod. All went lame; all blind;
Drunk with fatigue; deaf even to the hoots
Of tired, outstripped Five-Nines that dropped behind.

Gas! GAS! Quick, boys! – An ecstasy of fumbling,
Fitting the clumsy helmets just in time;
But someone still was yelling out and stumbling,
And flound'ring like a man in fire or lime...
Dim, through the misty panes and thick green light,
As under a green sea, I saw him drowning.

In all my dreams, before my helpless sight,
He plunges at me, guttering, choking, drowning.

If in some smothering dreams you too could pace
Behind the wagon that we flung him in,
And watch the white eyes writhing in his face,
His hanging face, like a devil's sick of sin;
If you could hear, at every jolt, the blood
Come gargling from the froth-corrupted lungs,
Obscene as cancer, bitter as the cud
Of vile, incurable sores on innocent tongues, –
My friend, you would not tell with such high zest
To children ardent for some desperate glory,
The old Lie: Dulce et decorum est
Pro patria mori.

Insensibility

1

Happy are men who yet before they are killed
Can let their veins run cold.
Whom no compassion fleers
Or makes their feet
Sore on the alleys cobbled with their brothers.
The front line withers.
But they are troops who fade, not flowers,
For poets' tearful fooling:
Men, gaps for filling:
Losses, who might have fought
Longer; but no one bothers.

2

And some cease feeling
Even themselves or for themselves.
Dullness best solves
The tease and doubt of shelling,
And Chance's strange arithmetic
Comes simpler than the reckoning of their shilling.
They keep no check on armies' decimation.

3

Happy are these who lose imagination:
They have enough to carry with ammunition.
Their spirit drags no pack.
Their old wounds, save with cold, can not more ache.
Having seen all things red,
Their eyes are rid
Of the hurt of the colour of blood for ever.
And terror's first constriction over,
Their hearts remain small-drawn.
Their senses in some scorching cautery of battle
Now long since ironed,
Can laugh among the dying, unconcerned.

4

Happy the soldier home, with not a notion
How somewhere, every dawn, some men attack,
And many sighs are drained.
Happy the lad whose mind was never trained:
His days are worth forgetting more than not.
He sings along the march
Which we march taciturn, because of dusk,
The long, forlorn, relentless trend
From larger day to huger night.

5

We wise, who with a thought besmirch
Blood over all our soul,
How should we see our task
But through his blunt and lashless eyes?
Alive, he is not vital overmuch;
Dying, not mortal overmuch;
Nor sad, nor proud,
Nor curious at all.
He cannot tell
Old men's placidity from his.

6

But cursed are dullards whom no cannon stuns,
That they should be as stones.
Wretched are they, and mean
With paucity that never was simplicity.
By choice they made themselves immune
To pity and whatever moans in man
Before the last sea and the hapless stars;
Whatever mourns when many leave these shores;
Whatever shares
The eternal reciprocity of tears.

Strange Meeting

It seemed that out of battle I escaped
Down some profound dull tunnel, long since scooped
Through granites which titanic wars had groined.

Yet also there encumbered sleepers groaned,
Too fast in thought or death to be bestirred.
Then, as I probed them, one sprang up, and stared
With piteous recognition in fixed eyes,
Lifting distressful hands, as if to bless.
And by his smile, I knew that sullen hall, –
By his dead smile I knew we stood in Hell.

With a thousand pains that vision's face was grained;
Yet no blood reached there from the upper ground,
And no guns thumped, or down the flues made moan.
'Strange friend,' I said, 'here is no cause to mourn.'
'None,' said that other, 'save the undone years,
The hopelessness. Whatever hope is yours,
Was my life also; I went hunting wild
After the wildest beauty in the world,
Which lies not calm in eyes, or braided hair,
But mocks the steady running of the hour,
And if it grieves, grieves richlier than here.
For by my glee might many men have laughed,
And of my weeping something had been left,

Which must die now. I mean the truth untold,
The pity of war, the pity war distilled.
Now men will go content with what we spoiled,
Or, discontent, boil bloody, and be spilled.
They will be swift with swiftness of the tigress.
None will break ranks, though nations trek from progress.
Courage was mine, and I had mystery,
Wisdom was mine, and I had mastery:
To miss the march of this retreating world
Into vain citadels that are not walled.
Then, when much blood had clogged their chariot-wheels,
I would go up and wash them from sweet wells,
Even with truths that lie too deep for taint.
I would have poured my spirit without stint
But not through wounds; not on the cess of war.
Foreheads of men have bled where no wounds were.

'I am the enemy you killed, my friend.
I knew you in this dark: for so you frowned
Yesterday through me as you jabbed and killed.
I parried; but my hands were loath and cold.
Let us sleep now....'

Futility

Move him into the sun –
Gently its touch awoke him once,
At home, whispering of fields half-sown.
Always it woke him, even in France,
Until this morning and this snow.
If anything might rouse him now
The kind old sun will know.

Think how it wakes the seeds –
Woke once the clays of a cold star.
Are limbs, so dear achieved, are sides
Full-nerved, still warm, too hard to stir?
Was it for this the clay grew tall?
– O what made fatuous sunbeams toil
To break earth's sleep at all?

The Send-Off

Down the close darkening lanes they sang their way
To the siding-shed,
And lined the train with faces grimly gay.

Their breasts were stuck all white with wreath and spray
As men's are, dead.

Dull porters watched them, and a casual tramp
Stood staring hard,
Sorry to miss them from the upland camp.

Then, unmoved, signals nodded, and a lamp
Winked to the guard.

So secretly, like wrongs hushed-up, they went.
They were not ours:
We never heard to which front these were sent;

Nor there if they yet mock what women meant
Who gave them flowers.

Shall they return to beating of great bells
In wild train-loads?
A few, a few, too few for drums and yells,

May creep back, silent, to village wells;
Up half-known roads.

Exposure

Our brains ache, in the merciless iced east winds that knive us...
Wearied we keep awake because the night is silent...
Low, drooping flares confuse our memory of the salient...
Worried by silence, sentries whisper, curious, nervous,
            But nothing happens.

Watching, we hear the mad gusts tugging on the wire,
Like twitching agonies of men among its brambles.
Northward, incessantly, the flickering gunnery rumbles,
Far off, like a dull rumour of some other war.
   What are we doing here?

The poignant misery of dawn begins to grow...
We only know war lasts, rain soaks, and clouds sag stormy.
Dawn massing in the east her melancholy army
Attacks once more in ranks on shivering ranks of grey,
   But nothing happens.

Sudden successive flights of bullets streak the silence.
Less deathly than the air that shudders black with snow,
With sidelong flowing flakes that flock, pause, and renew;
We watch them wandering up and down the wind's nonchalance,
   But nothing happens.

Pale flakes with fingering stealth come feeling for our faces –
We cringe in holes, back on forgotten dreams, and stare, snow-dazed,
Deep into grassier ditches. So we drowse, sun-dozed,
Littered with blossoms trickling where the blackbird fusses,
   – Is it that we are dying?

Slowly our ghosts drag home: glimpsing the sunk fires, glozed
With crusted dark-red jewels; crickets jingle there;
For hours the innocent mice rejoice: the house is theirs;
Shutters and doors, all closed: on us the doors are closed, –
   We turn back to our dying.

Since we believe not otherwise can kind fires burn;
Nor ever suns smile true on child, or field, or fruit.
For God's invincible spring our love is made afraid;
Therefore, not loath, we lie out here; therefore were born,
   For love of God seems dying.

Tonight, this frost will fasten on this mud and us,
Shrivelling many hands, puckering foreheads crisp.
The burying-party, picks and shovels in shaking grasp,
Pause over half-known faces. All their eyes are ice,
   But nothing happens.

CHARLES HAMILTON SORLEY

(1895–1915)

Charles Hamilton Sorley, an officer in the Suffolks, was killed at the Battle of
Loos aged 20. 'What waste!' commented Robert Graves. Sorley had written two
remarkable war poems that anticipate the later protest poetry of Sassoon and
Owen. The first poem ironically slurs the notes of patriotic recruitment-calls. The
second undermines the language of all commemoration. Sorley said of Rupert
Brooke (whose pro-war sonnets his own sonnet criticises): 'He has clothed his
attitude in fine words: but he has taken the sentimental attitude.' While still a
schoolboy at Marlborough, Sorley had attacked the 'finely trained and sweet' voice
of most contemporary writers, and time spent in Germany had inoculated him
against propaganda. He wrote: 'In training to fight for England, I am training to
fight for that deliberate hypocrisy, that terrible middle-class sloth of outlook...
that has marked us out from generation to generation...Indeed I think that after
the war all brave men will renounce their country and confess that they are
strangers and pilgrims on the earth.'

All the hills and vales along

All the hills and vales along
Earth is bursting into song,
And the singers are the chaps
Who are going to die perhaps.
   O sing, marching men,
   Till the valleys ring again.
   Give your gladness to earth's keeping,
   So be glad, when you are sleeping.

Cast away regret and rue,
Think what you are marching to.
Little live, great pass.
Jesus Christ and Barabbas
Were found the same day.
This died, that went his way.
   So sing with joyful breath.
   For why, you are going to death.
   Teeming earth will surely store
   All the gladness that you pour.

Earth that never doubts nor fears,
Earth that knows of death, not tears,
Earth that bore with joyful ease
Hemlock for Socrates,

Earth that blossomed and was glad
'Neath the cross that Christ had,
Shall rejoice and blossom too
When the bullet reaches you.
   Wherefore, men marching
   On the road to death, sing!
   Pour your gladness on earth's head,
   So be merry, so be dead.

From the hills and valleys earth
Shouts back the sound of mirth,
Tramp of feet and lilt of song
Ringing all the road along.
All the music of their going,
Ringing swinging glad song-throwing,
Earth will echo still, when foot
Lies numb and voice mute.
   On marching men, on
   To the gates of death with song.
   Sow your gladness for earth's reaping,
   So you may be glad, though sleeping.
   Strew your gladness on earth's bed,
   So be merry, so be dead.

When you see millions of the mouthless dead

When you see millions of the mouthless dead
Across your dreams in pale battalions go,
Say not soft things as other men have said,
That you'll remember. For you need not so.
Give them not praise. For, deaf, how should they know
It is not curses heaped on each gashed head?
Nor tears. Their blind eyes see not your tears flow.
Nor honour. It is easy to be dead.
Say only this, 'They are dead.' Then add thereto,
'Yet many a better one has died before.'
Then, scanning all the o'ercrowded mass, should you
Perceive one face that you loved heretofore,
It is a spook. None wears the face you knew.
Great death has made all his for evermore.

ROBERT GRAVES
(1895–1985)

Robert Graves grew up in London. His father was the Irish poet Alfred Perceval Graves. His mother instilled strong religious and moral principles that were to make sex initially problematic for Robert. Graves joined the Royal Welch Fusiliers in August 1914 after leaving Charterhouse school. He published war poems but suppressed them later. Despite his closeness to Siegfried Sassoon and admiration for Wilfred Owen, Graves was to write most effectively about the war in his prose memoir *Goodbye to All That* (1929). The memoir is shaped in a way that implies his quest to recover lost faith and transcend traumatic experiences. Between 1925 and 1939 Graves found solace in the strong – or manipulative – personality of the American poet Laura Riding who promoted a series of literary-sexual 'holy circles' with herself at their centre. They lived together in Deyá, Majorca, where Graves mostly lived thereafter. He supported himself by writing fiction, including his well-known *Claudius* novels.

Possibly reinventing his mother's principles and the cult centred on Riding, Graves devised a 'historical grammar of poetic myth': *The White Goddess* (1948, revised 1952, 1961). This work, a bible to some younger poets (such as Ted Hughes), affirms a mystical source of creative power. According to Graves, the Goddess incarnates herself in mortal Muses: a belief that conveniently justified his serial marriages and affairs. Graves's Romantic myth of inspiration seems at odds with his rational wit (as in 'Flying Crooked'), his insistence on craft and revision. He regularly reissued his *Collected Poems* without 'poems that no longer passed muster'. Indeed, his craftsmanship has inspired poets rather different from Hughes (such as Derek Mahon). Like Yeats, he sets up an interplay between syntax and stanza that revitalises traditional forms. Graves's suggestive compression – 'Death became terrible to you and me' – is also achieved by shifts of diction that dramatise shifts of tone. Perhaps the Goddess represents Graves's faith in poetry, his craft the ritual of that faith. The two combine in his influence on the modern love poem.

Love Without Hope

Love without hope, as when the young bird-catcher
Swept off his tall hat to the Squire's own daughter,
So let the imprisoned larks escape and fly
Singing about her head, as she rode by.

Pure Death

We looked, we loved, and therewith instantly
Death became terrible to you and me.
By love we disenthralled our natural terror
From every comfortable philosopher
Or tall, grey doctor of divinity:
Death stood at last in his true rank and order.

It happened soon, so wild of heart were we,
Exchange of gifts grew to a malady:
Their worth rose always higher on each side
Till there seemed nothing but ungivable pride
That yet remained ungiven, and this degree
Called a conclusion not to be denied.

Then we at last bethought ourselves, made shift
And simultaneously this final gift
Gave: each with shaking hands unlocks
The sinister, long, brass-bound coffin-box,
Unwraps pure death, with such bewilderment
As greeted our love's first acknowledgement.

The Christmas Robin

The snows of February had buried Christmas
Deep in the woods, where grew self-seeded
The fir-trees of a Christmas yet unknown,
Without a candle or a strand of tinsel.

Nevertheless when, hand in hand, plodding
Between the frozen ruts, we lovers paused
And 'Christmas trees!' cried suddenly together,
Christmas was there again, as in December.

We velveted our love with fantasy
Down a long vista-row of Christmas trees,
Whose coloured candles slowly guttered down
As grandchildren came trooping round our knees.

But he knew better, did the Christmas robin –
The murderous robin with his breast aglow
And legs apart, in a spade-handle perched:
He prophesied more snow, and worse than snow.

Flying Crooked

The butterfly, a cabbage-white,
(His honest idiocy of flight)
Will never now, it is too late,
Master the art of flying straight,
Yet has – who knows so well as I? –
A just sense of how not to fly:
He lurches here and here by guess
And God and hope and hopelessness.
Even the aerobatic swift
Has not his flying-crooked gift.

Mid-Winter Waking

Stirring suddenly from long hibernation,
I knew myself once more a poet
Guarded by timeless principalities
Against the worm of death, this hillside haunting;
And presently dared open both my eyes.

O gracious, lofty, shone against from under,
Back-of-the-mind-far clouds like towers;
And you, sudden warm airs that blow
Before the expected season of new blossom,
While sheep still gnaw at roots and lambless go –

Be witness that on waking, this mid-winter,
I found her hand in mine laid closely
Who shall watch out the Spring with me.
We stared in silence all around us
But found no winter anywhere to see.

She Tells Her Love While Half Asleep

She tells her love while half asleep,
    In the dark hours,
        With half-words whispered low:
As Earth stirs in her winter sleep
    And puts out grass and flowers
        Despite the snow,
        Despite the falling snow.

Theseus and Ariadne

High on his figured couch beyond the waves
He dreams, in dream recalling her set walk
Down paths of oyster-shell bordered with flowers,
Across the shadowy turf below the vines.
He sighs: 'Deep sunk in my erroneous past
She haunts the ruins and the ravaged lawns.'

Yet still unharmed it stands, the regal house
Crooked with age and overtopped by pines
Where first he wearied of her constancy.
And with a surer foot she goes than when
Dread of his hate was thunder in the air,
When the pines agonised with flaws of wind
And flowers glared up at her with frantic eyes.
Of him, now all is done, she never dreams
But calls a living blessing down upon
What he supposes rubble and rank grass;
Playing the queen to nobler company.

To Juan at the Winter Solstice

There is one story and one story only
That will prove worth your telling,
Whether as learned bard or gifted child;
To it all lines or lesser gauds belong
That startle with their shining
Such common stories as they stray into.

Is it of trees you tell, their months and virtues,
Or strange beasts that beset you,
Of birds that croak at you the Triple will?
Or of the Zodiac and how slow it turns
Below the Boreal Crown,
Prison of all true kings that ever reigned?

Water to water, ark again to ark,
From woman back to woman:
So each new victim treads unfalteringly
The never altered circuit of his fate,
Bringing twelve peers as witness
Both to his starry rise and starry fall.

Or is it of the Virgin's silver beauty,
All fish below the thighs?
She in her left hand bears a leafy quince;
When with her right she crooks a finger, smiling,
How may the King hold back?
Royally then he barters life for love.

Or of the undying snake from chaos hatched,
Whose coils contain the ocean,
Into whose chops with naked sword he springs,
Then in black water, tangled by the reeds,
Battles three days and nights,
To be spewed up beside her scalloped shore?

Much snow is falling, winds roar hollowly,
The owl hoots from the elder,
Fear in your heart cries to the loving-cup:
Sorrow to sorrow as the sparks fly upward.
The log groans and confesses:
There is one story and one story only.

Dwell on her graciousness, dwell on her smiling,
Do not forget what flowers
The great boar trampled down in ivy time.
Her brow was creamy as the crested wave,
Her sea-grey eyes were wild
But nothing promised that is not performed.

The White Goddess

All saints revile her, and all sober men
Ruled by the God Apollo's golden mean –
In scorn of which we sailed to find her
In distant regions likeliest to hold her
Whom we desired above all things to know,
Sister of the mirage and echo.

It was a virtue not to stay,
To go our headstrong and heroic way
Seeking her out at the volcano's head,
Among pack ice, or where the track had faded
Beyond the cavern of the seven sleepers:
Whose broad high brow was white as any leper's,
Whose eyes were blue, with rowan-berry lips,
With hair curled honey-coloured to white hips.

Green sap of Spring in the young wood a-stir
Will celebrate the Mountain Mother,
And every song-bird shout awhile for her;
But we are gifted, even in November
Rawest of seasons, with so huge a sense
Of her nakedly worn magnificence
We forget cruelty and past betrayal,
Heedless of where the next bright bolt may fall.

AUSTIN CLARKE

(1896–1974)

Austin Clarke grew up in Dublin. At University College Dublin he studied Irish under Douglas Hyde (the main mover in the Gaelic Revival) and English under Thomas MacDonagh, a poet executed for his role in the Easter Rising. Clarke succeeded to MacDonagh's lectureship. It has been speculated that a complex sense of guilt, as well as problems with Catholicism, triggered his breakdown in 1919. His long poem *Mnemosyne Lay in Dust* (1966) revisits this period. Clarke lost his lectureship in 1921, and became a freelance writer and reviewer based in England. In 1937 he returned to Ireland. After *Night and Morning* (1938) Clarke published no poetry for 17 years. Then he specialised in satirical poems that attacked the Irish state for permitting the repressive Catholic Church to dictate its ethos. The selection below suggests, however, that Clarke's most valuable poems are his early lyrics. He was strongly, perhaps too strongly, influenced by Yeats and the Irish Literary Revival. But, unlike Clarke's many verse-plays on legendary themes, his lyrics have original and distinctive rhythms. This is partly due to his imitation of Gaelic assonantal poetry. He writes: 'Assonance...takes the clapper from the bell of rhyme. In simple patterns, the tonic word at the end of the line is supported by a vowel-rhyme in the middle of the next line.' Some cadences also carry Clarke's idealistic desire to create a spiritual provenance for the new state. The pre-Norman 'Celtic-Romanesque' period of the Irish Church could be imagined as a pre-lapsarian weave of Irish landscape, Irish art and, above all, life-affirming religion that did not seek to 'Burn Ovid with the rest'.

Secrecy

Had we been only lovers from a book
That holy men who had a hand in heaven
Illuminated: in a yellow wood,
Where crimson beast and bird are clawed with gold
And, wound in branches, hunt or hawk themselves,
Sun-woman, I would hide you as the ring
Of his own shining fetters that the snake,
Who is the wood itself, can never find.

The Lost Heifer

When the black herds of the rain were grazing
In the gap of the pure cold wind
And the watery hazes of the hazel
Brought her into my mind,
I thought of the last honey by the water
That no hive can find.

Brightness was drenching through the branches
When she wandered again,
Turning the silver out of dark grasses
Where the skylark had lain,
And her voice coming softly over the meadow
Was the mist becoming rain.

Pilgrimage

When the far south glittered
Behind the grey beaded plains,
And cloudier ships were bitted
Along the pale waves,
The showery breeze – that plies
A mile from Ara – stood
And took our boat on sand:
There by dim wells the women tied
A wish on thorn, while rainfall
Was quiet as the turning of books
In the holy schools at dawn.

Grey holdings of rain
Had grown less with the fields,
As we came to that blessed place
Where hail and honey meet.
O Clonmacnoise was crossed
With light: those cloistered scholars,
Whose knowledge of the gospel
Is cast as metal in pure voices,
Were all rejoicing daily,

And cunning hands with cold and jewels
Brought chalices to flame.

Loud above the grassland,
In Cashel of the towers,
We heard with the yellow candles
The chanting of the hours,
White clergy saying High Mass,
A fasting crowd at prayer,
A choir that sang before them;
And in stained glass the holy day
Was sainted as we passed
Beyond that chancel where the dragons
Are carved upon the arch.

Treasured with chasuble,
Sun-braided, rich-cloak'd wine cup,
We saw, there, iron handbells,
Great annals in the shrine
A high-king bore to battle:
Where, from the branch of Adam,
The noble forms of language –
Brighter than green or blue enamels
Burned in white bronze – embodied
The wings and fiery animals
Which veil the chair of God.

Beyond a rocky townland
And that last tower where ocean
Is dim as haze, a sound
Of wild confession rose:
Black congregations moved
Around the booths of prayer
To hear a saint reprove them;
And from his boat he raised a blessing
To souls that had come down
The holy mountain of the west
Or wailed still in the cloud.

Light in the tide of Shannon
May ride at anchor half
The day and, high in spar-top
Or leather sails of their craft,

Wine merchants will have sleep;
But on a barren isle,
Where Paradise is praised
At daycome, smaller than the sea-gulls,
We heard white Culdees pray
Until our hollow ship was kneeling
Over the longer waves.

The Planter's Daughter

When night stirred at sea
And the fire brought a crowd in,
They say that her beauty
Was music in mouth
And few in the candlelight
Thought her too proud,
For the house of the planter
Is known by the trees.

Men that had seen her
Drank deep and were silent,
The women were speaking
Wherever she went –
As a bell that is rung
Or a wonder told shyly,
And O she was the Sunday
In every week.

Penal Law

Burn Ovid with the rest. Lovers will find
A hedge-school for themselves and learn by heart
All that the clergy banish from the mind,
When hands are joined and head bows in the dark.

BASIL BUNTING

(1900–1985)

Basil Bunting was born in Newcastle, and brought up as a Quaker. In 1918 he spent six months in prison as a conscientious objector. In 1923 he met Ezra Pound and followed him to Rapallo where he also became friendly with Louis Zukofsky. Bunting's induction into Poundian "modernism" was complete when Pound included 50 pages of his poetry in the *Active Anthology* (1933). For almost 30 years Bunting lived mainly abroad. This included war-service in Persia with the RAF. In 1952 he returned permanently to Northumberland. In 1966 he published his most celebrated work, *Briggflatts*, whose name comes from a small hamlet in the Pennines. This long poem spans Bunting's cosmopolitanism and localism, his modernist techniques and Wordsworthian poetic hinterland. He evokes the poem's autobiographical genesis as: 'Peggy Greenbank and her whole ambience, the Rawthey valley, the fells of Lunedale, the Viking inheritance all spent save the faint smell of it, the ancient Quaker life accepted without thought and without suspicion that it might seem eccentric: and what happens when one deliberately thrusts love aside, as I then did – it has its revenge.' Like other parts of the poem, the first section (the only stanzaic section) reflects Bunting's interest in links between poetic and musical composition. The sounds of individual words, assonance, repetition, and an echo of Anglo-Saxon alliterative metre bring alive the 'whole ambience': the 'madrigal' of the River Rawthey, the counterpoint of mason's 'mallet' and 'lark's twitter', of 'fellside bleat, / hide-and-seek peewit'. Bunting distinguished his 'sonata' from the multivocal structures of Pound and Zukofsky: 'I prefer to let the poem be shaped by the fact that only one voice is ever really audible at a time.' For Thom Gunn, *Briggflatts* does more than other long modernist poems to effect 'some kind of reconciliation with our beginnings'.

from Briggflatts

I

Brag, sweet tenor bull,
descant on Rawthey's madrigal,
each pebble its part
for the fells' late spring.
Dance tiptoe, bull,
black against may.
Ridiculous and lovely
chase hurdling shadows
morning into noon.
May on the bull's hide
and through the dale
furrows fill with may,
paving the slowworm's way.

A mason times his mallet
to a lark's twitter,
listening while the marble rests,
lays his rule
at a letter's edge,
fingertips checking,
till the stone spells a name
naming none,
a man abolished.
Painful lark, labouring to rise!
The solemn mallet says:
In the grave's slot
he lies. We rot.

Decay thrusts the blade,
wheat stands in excrement
trembling. Rawthey trembles.
Tongue stumbles, ears err
for fear of spring.
Rub the stone with sand,
wet sandstone rending
roughness away. Fingers
ache on the rubbing stone.
The mason says: Rocks
happen by chance.
No one here bolts the door,
love is so sore.

Stone smooth as skin,
cold as the dead they load
on a low lorry by night.
The moon sits on the fell
but it will rain.
Under sacks on the stone
two children lie,
hear the horse stale,
the mason whistle,
harness mutter to shaft,
felloe to axle squeak,
rut thud the rim,
crushed grit.

Stocking to stocking, jersey to jersey,
head to a hard arm,
they kiss under the rain,
bruised by their marble bed.
In Garsdale, dawn;
at Hawes, tea from the can.
Rain stops, sacks
steam in the sun, they sit up.
Copper-wire moustache,
sea-reflecting eyes
and Baltic plainsong speech
declare: By such rocks
men killed Bloodaxe.

Fierce blood throbs in his tongue,
lean words.
Skulls cropped for steel caps
huddle round Stainmore.
Their becks ring on limestone,
whisper to peat.
The clogged cart pushes the horse downhill.
In such soft air
they trudge and sing,
laying the tune frankly on the air.
All sounds fall still,
fellside bleat,
hide-and-seek peewit.

Her pulse their pace,
palm countering palm,
till a trench is filled,
stone white as cheese
jeers at the dale.
Knotty wood, hard to rive,
smoulders to ash;
smell of October apples.
The road again,
at a trot.
Wetter, warmed, they watch
the mason meditate
on name and date.

Rain rinses the road,
the bull streams and laments.
Sour rye porridge from the hob
with cream and black tea,
meat, crust and crumb.
Her parents in bed
the children dry their clothes.
He has untied the tape
of her striped flannel drawers
before the range. Naked
on the pricked rag mat
his fingers comb
thatch of his manhood's home.

Gentle generous voices weave
over bare night
words to confirm and delight
till bird dawn.
Rainwater from the butt
she fetches and flannel
to wash him inch by inch,
kissing the pebbles.
Shining slowworm part of the marvel.
The mason stirs:
Words!
Pens are too light.
Take a chisel to write.

Every birth a crime,
every sentence life.
Wiped of mould and mites
would the ball run true?
No hope of going back.
Hounds falter and stray,
shame deflects the pen.
Love murdered neither bleeds nor stifles
but jogs the draftsman's elbow.
What can he, changed, tell
her, changed, perhaps dead?
Delight dwindles. Blame
stays the same.

Brief words are hard to find,
shapes to carve and discard:
Bloodaxe, king of York,
king of Dublin, king of Orkney.
Take no notice of tears;
letter the stone to stand
over love laid aside lest
insufferable happiness impede
flight to Stainmore,
to trace
lark, mallet,
becks, flocks
and axe knocks.

Dung will not soil the slowworm's
mosaic. Breathless lark
drops to nest in sodden trash;
Rawthey truculent, dingy.
Drudge at the mallet, the may is down,
fog on fells. Guilty of spring
and spring's ending
amputated years ache after
the bull is beef, love a convenience.
It is easier to die than to remember.
Name and date
split in soft slate
a few months obliterate.

STEVIE SMITH

(1902–1971)

Florence Margaret Smith was nicknamed 'Stevie' because her fringe resembled that of the jockey Steve Donaghue. Aged three, she moved with her mother and sister to her aunt's home in Palmers Green, a North London outer suburb. She lived in this 'house of female habitation' for the rest of her life. She also stayed in the same job: spending 30 years as private secretary to the magazine publishers Sir George Newnes and Sir Neville Pearson. During the 1930s Smith published two novels, including *Novel on Yellow Paper* (1936), and two books of poems: *A Good Time Was Had By All* (1937) and *Tender Only To One* (1938). Yet her reputation grew unevenly, although her distinctively voiced readings later became famous. Critics were puzzled by Smith's false-naive style; her strange cast of characters; the childlike drawings that accompanied certain poems; her indifference to literary hierarchy or fashion; the sudden switches from comedy to theology, from doggerel to dirge, from waving to drowning. The selection below may support Philip Larkin's judgment that her poems 'speak with the authority of sadness'. Their attitude to other kinds of authority (male included) deserves the overused adjective 'subversive'. In 1960 Smith wrote of the Muse: 'She is an Angel, very strong…The human creature is alone in his carapace. Poetry is a strong way out. The passage out that she blasts is often in splinters, covered with blood; but she can come out softly. Poetry is very light-fingered, she is like the god Hermes in my poem "The Ambassador"… Also she is like the horse Hermes is riding, this animal is dangerous…'

The Abominable Lake

Deep in the still mysterious waters of the lake a world lies drowned.
How sombre and sad the silent world in the womb of the lake,
Not the reflection of Tellus, not the arch of heaven
Lies in the waters of the abominable lake,
But an earth and a heaven beyond the dominion of Time,
Beyond the soft sensual touch of the seasonal flow
And the inviolable sequence of midnight and noon.
Poor world, my heart breaks for your sealed inarticulate woe,
And the tears that are frozen in yours melt to flood in my eyes,
Overflow and descend and impinge on the waters of the lake
And shatter at once the form of the silent world.
But the teardrops mingle, the waters shudder and close,
And again and again the sad world is revealed to my sight.
Then I know, and the knowledge transfixes my sensitive heart,
Not my tears, nor my prayers, nor my gold shall encompass at last
A freedom unthought, manumission unhoped, undesired.

Infelice

Walking swiftly with a dreadful duchess,
He smiled too briefly, his face was pale as sand,
He jumped into a taxi when he saw me coming,
Leaving me alone with a private meaning,
He loves me so much, my heart is singing.
Later at the Club when I rang him in the evening
They said: Sir Rat is dining, is dining, is dining,
No Madam, he left no message, ah how his silence speaks,
He loves me too much for words, my heart is singing.
The Pullman seats are here, the tickets for Paris, I am waiting,
Presently the telephone rings, it is his valet speaking,
Sir Rat is called away, to Scotland, his constituents,
(Ah the dreadful duchess, but he loves me best)
Best pleasure to the last, my heart is singing.
One night he came, it was four in the morning,
Walking slowly upstairs, he stands beside my bed,
Dear darling, lie beside me, it is too cold to stand speaking,
He lies down beside me, his face is like the sand,
He is in a sleep of love, my heart is singing.
Sleeping softly softly, in the morning I must wake him,
And waking he murmurs, I only came to sleep.
The words are so sweetly cruel, how deeply he loves me,
I say them to myself alone, my heart is singing.
Now the sunshine strengthens, it is ten in the morning,
He is so timid in love, he only needs to know,
He is my little child, how can he come if I do not call him,
I will write and tell him everything, I take the pen and write:
I love you so much, my heart is singing.

The Ambassador

Underneath the broad hat is the face of the Ambassador
He rides on a white horse through hell looking two ways.
Doors open before him and shut when he has passed.
He is master of the mysteries and in the market place
He is known. He stole the trident, the girdle,

The sword, the sceptre and many mechanical instruments.
Thieves honour him. In the underworld he rides carelessly.
Sometimes he rises into the air and flies silently.

Not Waving but Drowning

Nobody heard him, the dead man,
But still he lay moaning:
I was much further out than you thought
And not waving but drowning.

Poor chap, he always loved larking
And now he's dead
It must have been too cold for him his heart gave way,
They said.

Oh, no no no, it was too cold always
(Still the dead one lay moaning)
I was much too far out all my life
And not waving but drowning.

I Remember

It was my bridal night I remember,
An old man of seventy-three
I lay with my young bride in my arms,
A girl with t.b.
It was wartime, and overhead
The Germans were making a particularly heavy raid on Hampstead.
What rendered the confusion worse, perversely
Our bombers had chosen that moment to set out for Germany.
Harry, do they ever collide?
I do not think it has ever happened,
Oh my bride, my bride.

God the Eater

There is a god in whom I do not believe
Yet to this god my love stretches,
This god whom I do not believe in is
My whole life, my life and I am his.

Everything that I have of pleasure and pain
(Of pain, of bitter pain and men's contempt)
I give this god for him to feed upon
As he is my whole life and I am his.

When I am dead I hope that he will eat
Everything I have been and have not been
And crunch and feed upon it and grow fat
Eating my life all up as it is his.

Oh grateful colours, bright looks!

The grass is green
The tulip is red
A ginger cat walks over
The pink almond petals on the flower bed.
Enough has been said to show
It is life we are talking about. Oh
Grateful colours, bright looks! Well, to go
On. Fabricated things too – front doors and gates,
Bricks, slates, paving stones – are coloured
And as it has been raining and is sunny now
They shine. Only that puddle
Which, reflecting the height of the sky
Quite gives one a feeling of vertigo, shows
No colour, is a negative. Men!
Seize colours quick, heap them up while you can.
But perhaps it is a false tale that says
The landscape of the dead
Is colourless.

PATRICK KAVANAGH

(1904–1967)

Patrick Kavanagh grew up in the townland of Mucker, Inniskeen, Co. Monaghan (one of the Ulster counties that became part of the Irish state). He left school at 13 to work on the family farm. Like John Clare, he was inspired by his surroundings and educated himself in poetry. Like Clare, too, he had difficult relations with the literary metropolis. In 1939 Kavanagh moved to Dublin: 'the worst mistake of my life'. He met Dublin writers who, in the aftermath of the Irish Revival, were 'trying to be peasants'. Hence the anger that drives his long poem *The Great Hunger* (1942), which centres on the restricted life actually lived by small farmers. Neither country nor city could fulfil Kavanagh's needs. He represents his aesthetic core, his Muse of place, his 'whitethorn hedges', as a sanctuary from both. After 1939 his positive Inniskeen poems are poems of retrospect, compensation and nostalgia. Kavanagh's autobiographical prose, as in *The Green Fool* (1938), also reflects these psychic and cultural splits.

Kavanagh's affiliation to small-farm Catholic Ireland has been contrasted with Yeats's affiliation to Coole Park. Up to a point he is the 'peasant' who 'writes back'. For Seamus Heaney, he 'raised the inhibited energies of a sub-culture to the power of a cultural resource'. Yet Kavanagh criticised the effects of Irish nationalism on poetry, and learned from the concreteness of English pastoral. He was also able to integrate visionary Romanticism (Wordsworth) with his Catholic sense of the material world as manifesting God (immanence). 'A Christmas Childhood' traces an almost medieval cosmic harmony. Like the father's melodion, the poem orchestrates the townland. Much quoted is Kavanagh's statement (in 'The Parish and the Universe') that: 'The parochial mentality...is never in any doubt about the social and artistic validity of his parish.' The sonnet cheekily called 'Epic' makes the same point. Kavanagh's local microcosms greatly influenced the manner in which poets such as Seamus Heaney and Paul Muldoon make poems from their own experience of rural Catholic Ulster. But his achievement faces several ways from its various border-lands. For Paul Durcan, in the Irish Republic, his 'spiritual courage' and intensity of social anger have been more important.

Inniskeen Road: July Evening

The bicycles go by in twos and threes –
There's a dance in Billy Brennan's barn tonight,
And there's the half-talk code of mysteries
And the wink-and-elbow language of delight.
Half-past eight and there is not a spot
Upon a mile of road, no shadow thrown
That might turn out a man or woman, not
A footfall tapping secrecies of stone.

I have what every poet hates in spite
Of all the solemn talk of contemplation.
Oh, Alexander Selkirk knew the plight
Of being king and government and nation.
A road, a mile of kingdom, I am king
Of banks and stones and every blooming thing.

Shancoduff

My black hills have never seen the sun rising,
Eternally they look north towards Armagh.
Lot's wife would not be salt if she had been
Incurious as my black hills that are happy
When dawn whitens Glassdrummond chapel.

My hills hoard the bright shillings of March
While the sun searches in every pocket.
They are my Alps and I have climbed the Matterhorn
With a sheaf of hay for three perishing calves
In the field under the Big Forth of Rocksavage.

The sleety winds fondle the rushy beards of Shancoduff
While the cattle-drovers sheltering in the Featherna Bush
Look up and say: 'Who owns them hungry hills
That the water-hen and snipe must have forsaken?
A poet? Then by heavens he must be poor.'
I hear and is my heart not badly shaken?

Spraying the Potatoes

The barrels of blue potato-spray
Stood on a headland of July
Beside an orchard wall where roses
Were young girls hanging from the sky.

The flocks of green potato-stalks
Were blossom spread for sudden flight,
The Kerr's Pinks in a frivelled blue,
The Arran Banners wearing white.

And over that potato-field
A lazy veil of woven sun.
Dandelions growing on headlands, showing
Their unloved hearts to everyone.

And I was there with the knapsack sprayer
On the barrel's edge poised. A wasp was floating
Dead on a sunken briar leaf
Over a copper-poisoned ocean.

The axle-roll of a rut-locked cart
Broke the burnt stick of noon in two.
An old man came through a corn-field
Remembering his youth and some Ruth he knew.

He turned my way. 'God further the work.'
He echoed an ancient farming prayer.
I thanked him. He eyed the potato-drills.
He said: 'You are bound to have good ones there.'

We talked and our talk was a theme of kings,
A theme for strings. He hunkered down
In the shade of the orchard wall. O roses
The old man dies in the young girl's frown.

And poet lost to potato-fields,
Remembering the lime and copper smell
Of the spraying barrels he is not lost
Or till blossomed stalks cannot weave a spell.

from A Christmas Childhood

My father played the melodion
Outside at our gate;
There were stars in the morning east
And they danced to his music.

Across the wild bogs his melodion called
To Lennons and Callans.
As I pulled on my trousers in a hurry
I knew some strange thing had happened.

Outside in the cow-house my mother
Made the music of milking;
The light of her stable-lamp was a star
And the frost of Bethlehem made it twinkle.

A water-hen screeched in the bog,
Mass-going feet
Crunched the wafer-ice on the pot-holes,
Somebody wistfully twisted the bellows wheel.

My child poet picked out the letters
On the grey stone,
In silver the wonder of a Christmas townland,
The winking glitter of a frosty dawn.

Cassiopeia was over
Cassidy's hanging hill,
I looked and three whin bushes rode across
The horizon – the Three Wise Kings.

An old man passing said:
'Can't he make it talk' –
The melodion. I hid in the doorway
And tightened the belt of my box-pleated coat.

I nicked six nicks on the door-post
With my penknife's big blade –
There was a little one for cutting tobacco.
And I was six Christmases of age.

My father played the melodion,
My mother milked the cows,
And I had a prayer like a white rose pinned
On the Virgin Mary's blouse.

Consider the Grass Growing

Consider the grass growing
As it grew last year and the year before,
Cool about the ankles like summer rivers
When we walked on a May evening through the meadows
To watch the mare that was going to foal.

Kerr's Ass

We borrowed the loan of Kerr's big ass
To go to Dundalk with butter,
Brought him home the evening before the market
An exile that night in Mucker.

We heeled up the cart before the door,
We took the harness inside –
The straw-stuffed straddle, the broken breeching
With bits of bull-wire tied;

The winkers that had no choke-band,
The collar and the reins...
In Ealing Broadway, London Town
I name their several names

Until a world comes to life –
Morning, the silent bog,
And the god of imagination waking
In a Mucker fog.

Innocence

They laughed at one I loved –
The triangular hill that hung
Under the Big Forth. They said
That I was bounded by the whitethorn hedges

Of the little farm and did not know the world.
But I knew that love's doorway to life
Is the same doorway everywhere.

Ashamed of what I loved
I flung her from me and called her a ditch
Although she was smiling at me with violets.

But now I am back in her briary arms
The dew of an Indian Summer morning lies
On bleached potato-stalks –
What age am I?

I do not know what age I am,
I am no mortal age;
I know nothing of women,
Nothing of cities,
I cannot die
Unless I walk outside these whitethorn hedges.

Epic

I have lived in important places, times
When great events were decided: who owned
That half a rood of rock, a no-man's land
Surrounded by our pitchfork-armed claims.
I heard the Duffys shouting 'Damn your soul'
And old McCabe stripped to the waist, seen
Step the plot defying blue cast-steel –
'Here is the march along these iron stones'.
That was the year of the Munich bother. Which
Was most important? I inclined
To lose my faith in Ballyrush and Gortin
Till Homer's ghost came whispering to my mind
He said: I made the *Iliad* from such
A local row. Gods make their own importance.

NORMAN CAMERON

(1905–1953)

Norman Cameron was born in Bombay, educated in Edinburgh and at Oxford University. He spent some time in Majorca with Robert Graves and Laura Riding, then worked in London as an advertising copywriter (he invented 'Night Starvation' for Horlicks). Cameron spent the Second World War as a civilian propagandist attached to military units abroad. An elusive yet convivial personality, he formed his style early, and any resemblance to Graves suggests affinity rather than imitation. Although Cameron's output was small, he should be seen not as an occasional poet but as wary of writing without an impulse. He said: 'I write a poem because I think it wants to be written'. Certainly his compact structures (they hover around sonnet-length) seem flung well free of their author. Even 'Meeting My Former Self ' places an objectively intriguing riddle in the foreground. 'Green, Green is El Aghir' conjures an oasis by highlighting refrain, consonantal rhyme, French words that suggest "civilisation". Any symbolism of war and peace is subtly pressed. Cameron influenced his generation (he contributed to Geoffrey Grigson's 1930s magazine *New Verse*) by offering the poem as a coolly intricate, yet not passionless, object. He uses myth or parable to penetrate shadowy 'crannies'.

Central Europe

Despite their boastful Margraves and their flags
The inland years – fat peasants winterbound,
Stunned by the heat of their enormous stoves,
Whimpering fear of baleful gods and wolves –
Have set a bloody darkness in their souls.
Still they can see, fixed amid this red haze
Of swimming particles, the forest-faces,
Come, following the deeper shade, to town.

They need a wind bringing up gulls and salt,
Sailors and nabobs with new foreign gifts,
To blow their crannies free of ancient fear.

Fight with a Water-Spirit

Though many men had passed the ford, not one
Had ever seen that jeering water-ghost
Denying their true conquest of the stream.
But I, who saw him smile behind a stone,
Stopped, challenged him to justify his boast.
Then came the fight, exhausting as a dream,
With stuff not quite impalpable. He sank,
Sighing, at last, in a small shrinking pile.
But my victorious paean changed to fright
To see once more the pale curve of his flank
There in the water, and his endless smile
Broaden behind the stone. No use to fight.
Better to give the place a holy name,
Go on with less ambition than I came.

Meeting My Former Self

Meeting my former self in a nostalgia
Of confident, confiding recognition,
Offering him an island in the Atlantic –
Half-way, I said, from Tenerife to England.
Great cliffs of chalk slope from the fishing-village
Up to the lighthouse. Rum sold free of duty.
Only the fishermen and lighthouse-keeper
Besides ourselves. Drinking the rum, card-playing
And walking in the wastes of stone and cactus
And meeting the mail-steamer once a fortnight.
– But these inducements pitifully withered
At his embarrassed look. Turning to welcome
A friend he had acquired since our last meeting,
Not known to me, he spoke of other matters;
And I was weeping and humiliated.

Green, Green is El Aghir

Sprawled on the crates and sacks in the rear of the truck,
I was gummy-mouthed from the sun and the dust of the track,
And the two Arab soldiers I'd taken on as hitch-hikers
At a torrid petrol-dump, had been there on their hunkers
Since early morning. I said, in a kind of French
'On m'a dit, qu'il y a une belle source d'eau fraîche,
Plus loin, à El Aghir'...

               It was eighty more kilometres
Until round a corner we heard a splashing of waters,
And there, in a green, dark street, was a fountain with two faces
Discharging both ways, from full-throated faucets
Into basins, thence into troughs and thence into brooks.
Our negro corporal driver slammed his brakes,
And we yelped and leapt from the truck and went at the double
To fill our bidons and bottles and drink and dabble.
Then, swollen with water, we went to an inn for wine.
The Arabs came, too, though their faith might have stood between.
'After all,' they said, 'it's a boisson,' without contrition.

Green, green is El Aghir. It has a railway-station,
And the wealth of its soil has borne many another fruit,
A mairie, a school and an elegant Salle de Fêtes.
Such blessings, as I remarked, in effect, to the waiter,
Are added unto them that have plenty of water.

Wörther See

Would that wars might end for all soldiers like this:
Swimming, rowing, sailing, deep walks in the woods;
Landscapes rich in vines and maize, flowers and fruit;
Natives clean and honest, plump, wooable girls;
Food well-cooked and varied, camp discipline light;
No more danger, boredom, dirt, weariness, din;
Pride in battles won, the world's gratitude earned;
Ease in which to stretch the cramped limbs of the soul:
Would that wars might end for all soldiers like this.

WILLIAM EMPSON

(1906–1984)

William Empson's influence as a poet has been disproportionate to his small output. Born in Yorkshire, he was precociously brilliant. At Cambridge he studied under I.A. Richards, author of *Principles of Literary Criticism* (1925). When only 24, Empson published his influential critical work *Seven Types of Ambiguity*. In the 1930s he lectured in Japan and China. After the war, during which he organised propaganda broadcasts to China, he returned there as Professor of English at Peking University and experienced the Communist takeover. In 1953 he became Professor of English Literature at Sheffield. Empson might seem to follow some precepts of T.S. Eliot. His poetry is 'difficult', allied to a complex critical sense of 'tradition', and influenced – more centrally than Eliot's – by John Donne. Yet he writes in traditional stanzas ('Missing Dates' vies with Dylan Thomas's 'Do not go gentle into that good night' as the most famous villanelle of the century). Also, his poetry may be less 'impersonal' (another doctrine of Eliot's) than some critics maintain. Certainly it owes something to the 'objectivity' that Cambridge criticism tried to transfer from Cambridge science. Two poems below begin 'There is', and proceed to elaborate an image that appears detached from the speaker. But the argument of both 'Homage to the British Museum' and 'Note on Local Flora' has a more than intellectual music. Their verbal intensity – 'I knew the Phoenix was a vegetable' – suggests that Empson, as he implied in a well-known article, did 'learn a style from a despair'. His irony belies a 'thirst' for spiritual meaning. 'Let it go' may be both a painful glimpse behind the scenes and a farewell to poetry. Empson's aesthetic was at odds with the overt socio-political focus of much 1930s poetry. Yet he concentrates the decade's deepest concerns. At one level, his 'British Museum' symbolises the condition of England. Keith Douglas may have learned from the way in which an effect like 'at the points formally stressed' stands back 'formally' from experience to convey its essence. Empson's influence extends to the poets of Philip Larkin's generation and beyond.

Camping Out

And now she cleans her teeth into the lake:
Gives it (God's grace) for her own bounty's sake
What morning's pale and the crisp mist debars:
Its glass of the divine (that will could break)
Restores, beyond nature: or lets Heaven take
(Itself being dimmed) her pattern, who half awake
Milks between rocks a straddled sky of stars.

Soap tension the star pattern magnifies.
Smoothly Madonna through-assumes the skies
Whose vaults are opened to achieve the Lord.

No, it is we soaring explore galaxies,
Our bullet boat light's speed by thousands flies.
Who moves so among stars their frame unties;
See where they blur, and die, and are outsoared.

Homage to the British Museum

There is a Supreme God in the ethnological section;
A hollow toad shape, faced with a blank shield.
He needs his belly to include the Pantheon,
Which is inserted through a hole behind.
At the navel, at the points formally stressed, at the organs of sense,
Lice glue themselves, dolls, local deities,
His smooth wood creeps with all the creeds of the world.

Attending there let us absorb the cultures of nations
And dissolve into our judgement all their codes.
Then, being clogged with a natural hesitation
(People are continually asking one the way out),
Let us stand here and admit that we have no road.
Being everything, let us admit that is to be something,
Or give ourselves the benefit of the doubt;
Let us offer our pinch of dust all to this God,
And grant his reign over the entire building.

Note on Local Flora

There is a tree native in Turkestan,
Or further east towards the Tree of Heaven,
Whose hard cold cones, not being wards to time,
Will leave their mother only for good cause;
Will ripen only in a forest fire;
Wait, to be fathered as was Bacchus once,
Through men's long lives, that image of time's end.
I knew the Phoenix was a vegetable.
So Semele desired her deity
As this in Kew thirsts for the Red Dawn.

Missing Dates

Slowly the poison the whole blood stream fills.
It is not the effort nor the failure tires.
The waste remains, the waste remains and kills.

It is not your system or clear sight that mills
Down small to the consequence a life requires;
Slowly the poison the whole blood stream fills.

They bled an old dog dry yet the exchange rills
Of young dog blood gave but a month's desires;
The waste remains, the waste remains and kills.

It is the Chinese tombs and the slag hills
Usurp the soil, and not the soil retires.
Slowly the poison the whole blood stream fills.

Not to have fire is to be a skin that shrills.
The complete fire is death. From partial fires
The waste remains, the waste remains and kills.

It is the poems you have lost, the ills
From missing dates, at which the heart expires.
Slowly the poison the whole blood stream fills.
The waste remains, the waste remains and kills.

Let it go

It is this deep blankness is the real thing strange.
    The more things happen to you the more you can't
        Tell or remember even what they were.

The contradictions cover such a range.
    The talk would talk and go so far aslant.
        You don't want madhouse and the whole thing there.

W.H. AUDEN

(1907–1973)

Wystan Hugh Auden was so influential in the 1930s that some critics name a whole poetic generation after him. Auden grew up near Birmingham, and studied English at Oxford. His *Poems* (1930) and Michael Roberts's anthology *New Signatures* (1932) seemed to announce a new poetic movement with a leader who was taking poetry in a left-wing direction. Auden's chief disciples, Stephen Spender and Cecil Day Lewis, misread his early poetry as a call for revolution. In fact, it was conditioned by a complex of factors: rebellion against his middle-class public school background, homosexual alienation, nine months in Berlin, anxiety about England ('this island now'), psychoanalysis, Marxism, youthful anarchism. Perhaps Auden's greatest appeal was the panache with which his poetry of highly concentrated statement grabbed words and images from the full range of modern living: politics, science, technology, popular culture, the city. He gave traditional forms contemporary excitement, as in his long poem 'Letter to Lord Byron' which identifies with its 'gay and witty' recipient. Geoffrey Grigson writes that Auden's 'volubility' broke 'a terror of the word' imposed by Eliot.

Anti-Fascist, rather than Communist, Auden believed in civilisation: 'the just city'. To map its whereabouts, and signpost its absence, he specialises in allegorical landscapes where private neurosis merges into public crisis. That applies to 'Through the Looking-Glass', a love poem with a utopian conclusion. The climax of Auden's politically engaged allegories was 'Spain' (1937). But brief experience of the Spanish Civil War (he was alarmed by the ruined churches) made him realise the snags involved in projecting 'Our fever's menacing shapes' on to other people's wars. He left behind his false position as leader of the literary Left when he and Christopher Isherwood sailed for America in January 1939. In 1946 Auden became a US citizen.

Auden's departure for America was criticised then (as dodging the war) and affects his reputation now. Philip Larkin, whose juvenilia imitate Auden's deft handling of sonnet-form and abstract diction, says: 'At one stroke he lost his key subject and emotion – Europe and the fear of war – and abandoned his audience together with their common dialect and concerns.' But Auden's end-of-the-30s poems are powerful because they dramatise his conflicts about art and politics, as does his prose-work 'The Prolific and the Devourer': 'The voice of the Tempter: "Unless you take part in the class struggle, you cannot become a major writer".' His elegy for Yeats and 'September 1, 1939' (the date when Hitler invaded Poland) combine intensified images of historical 'offence' with moral language that heralds his commitment to Anglicanism. Auden went on arguing with himself about poetry even after he ceased to believe in its directly political effect. Does it just survive in 'the valley of its saying'? 'In Praise of Limestone' (1948), in which Auden allegorises his own imaginative landscape, obliquely claims that he is still doing his 'worldly duty' as a poet. The poem's formal brilliance, its fusion of abstract argument with sensory impact, itself vindicates his fertile invention and serious subversion. Auden's influence has been prolific, too. It can be detected, for instance, in Larkin; in Derek Mahon's delicate blends of private and public address; in James Fenton's strategies as a political poet.

Through the Looking-Glass

The earth turns over, our side feels the cold,
And life sinks choking in the wells of trees;
The ticking heart comes to a standstill, killed,
The icing on the pond waits for the boys.
Among the holly and the gifts I move,
The carols on the piano, the glowing hearth,
All our traditional sympathy with birth,
Put by your challenge to the shifts of love.

Your portrait hangs before me on the wall,
And there what view I wish for I shall find,
The wooded or the stony, though not all
The painter's gifts can make its flatness round;
Through each blue iris greet the heaven of failures,
That mirror world where Logic is reversed,
Where age becomes the handsome child at last,
The glass wave parted for the country sailors.

There move the enormous comics, drawn from life –
My father as an Airedale and a gardener,
My mother chasing letters with a knife.
You are not present as a character;
(Only the family have speaking parts).
You are a valley or a river-bend,
The one an aunt refers to as a friend,
The tree from which the weasel racing starts.

Behind me roars that other world it matches,
Love's daytime kingdom which I say you rule,
His total state where all must wear your badges,
Keep order perfect as a naval school.
Noble emotions, organised and massed,
Line the straight flood-lit tracks of memory
To cheer your image as it flashes by,
All lust at once informed on and suppressed.

Yours is the only name expressive there,
And family affection speaks in cypher.
Lay-out of hospital and street and square
That comfort to its homesick children offer,
As I, their author, stand between these dreams,

Unable to choose either for a home,
Your would-be lover who has never come
In a great bed at midnight to your arms.

Such dreams are amorous; they are indeed:
But no one but myself is loved in these,
While time flies on above the dreamer's head,
Flies on, flies on, and with your beauty flies,
And pride succeeds to each succeeding state,
Still able to buy up the life within,
License no liberty except his own,
Order the fireworks after the defeat.

Language of moderation cannot hide: –
My sea is empty and its waves are rough;
Gone from the map the shore where childhood played,
Tight-fisted as a peasant, eating love;
Lost in my wake the archipelago,
Islands of self through which I sailed all day
Planting a pirate's flag, a generous boy;
And lost my way to action and to you.

Lost if I steer. Tempest and tide may blow
Sailor and ship past the illusive reef,
And I yet land to celebrate with you
The birth of natural order and true love:
With you enjoy the untransfigured scene,
My father down the garden in his gaiters,
My mother at her bureau writing letters,
Free to our favours, all our titles gone.

On This Island

Look, stranger, on this island now
The leaping light for your delight discovers,
Stand stable here
And silent be,
That through the channels of the ear
May wander like a river
The swaying sound of the sea.

Here at a small field's ending pause
Where the chalk wall falls to the foam and its tall ledges
Oppose the pluck
And knock of the tide,
And the shingle scrambles after the suck-
-ing surf, and a gull lodges
A moment on its sheer side.

Far off like floating seeds the ships
Diverge on urgent voluntary errands,
And this full view
Indeed may enter
And move in memory as now these clouds do,
That pass the harbour mirror
And all the summer through the water saunter.

Musée des Beaux Arts

About suffering they were never wrong,
The Old Masters: how well they understood
Its human position; how it takes place
While someone else is eating or opening a window or just walking
          dully along;
How, when the aged are reverently, passionately waiting
For the miraculous birth, there always must be
Children who did not specially want it to happen, skating
On a pond at the edge of the wood:
They never forgot
That even the dreadful martyrdom must run its course
Anyhow in a corner, some untidy spot
Where the dogs go on with their doggy life and the torturer's horse
Scratches its innocent behind on a tree.

In Brueghel's *Icarus*, for instance: how everything turns away
Quite leisurely from the disaster; the ploughman may
Have heard the splash, the forsaken cry,
But for him it was not an important failure; the sun shone
As it had to on the white legs disappearing into the green
Water; and the expensive delicate ship that must have seen
Something amazing, a boy falling out of the sky,
Had somewhere to get to and sailed calmly on.

Gare du Midi

A nondescript express in from the South,
Crowds round the ticket barrier, a face
To welcome which the mayor has not contrived
Bugles or braid: something about the mouth
Distracts the stray look with alarm and pity.
Snow is falling. Clutching a little case,
He walks out briskly to infect a city
Whose terrible future may have just arrived.

Epitaph on a Tyrant

Perfection, of a kind, was what he was after,
And the poetry he invented was easy to understand;
He knew human folly like the back of his hand,
And was greatly interested in armies and fleets;
When he laughed, respectable senators burst with laughter,
And when he cried the little children died in the streets.

Edward Lear

Left by his friend to breakfast alone on the white
Italian shore, his Terrible Demon arose
Over his shoulder; he wept to himself in the night,
A dirty landscape-painter who hated his nose.

The legions of cruel inquisitive They
Were so many and big like dogs: he was upset
By Germans and boats; affection was miles away:
But guided by tears he successfully reached his Regret.

How prodigious the welcome was. Flowers took his hat
And bore him off to introduce him to the tongs;
The demon's false nose made the table laugh; a cat
Soon had him waltzing madly, let him squeeze her hand;
Words pushed him to the piano to sing comic songs;

And children swarmed to him like settlers. He became a land.

In Memory of W.B. Yeats
(d. Jan. 1939)

I

He disappeared in the dead of winter:
The brooks were frozen, the air-ports almost deserted,
And snow disfigured the public statues;
The mercury sank in the mouth of the dying day.
O all the instruments agree
The day of his death was a dark cold day.

Far from his illness
The wolves ran on through the evergreen forests,
The peasant river was untempted by the fashionable quays;
By mourning tongues
The death of the poet was kept from his poems.

But for him it was his last afternoon as himself,
An afternoon of nurses and rumours;
The provinces of his body revolted,
The squares of his mind were empty,
Silence invaded the suburbs,
The current of his feeling failed: he became his admirers.

Now he is scattered among a hundred cities
And wholly given over to unfamiliar affections;
To find his happiness in another kind of wood
And be punished under a foreign code of conscience.
The words of a dead man
Are modified in the guts of the living.

But in the importance and noise of to-morrow
When the brokers are roaring like beasts on the floor of the Bourse,
And the poor have the sufferings to which they are fairly accustomed,
And each in the cell of himself is almost convinced of his freedom;
A few thousand will think of this day
As one thinks of a day when one did something slightly unusual.

O all the instruments agree
The day of his death was a dark cold day.

2

You were silly like us: your gift survived it all;
The parish of rich women, physical decay,
Yourself; mad Ireland hurt you into poetry.
Now Ireland has her madness and her weather still,
For poetry makes nothing happen: it survives
In the valley of its saying where executives
Would never want to tamper; it flows south
From ranches of isolation and the busy griefs,
Raw towns that we believe and die in; it survives,
A way of happening, a mouth.

3

Earth, receive an honoured guest;
William Yeats is laid to rest:
Let the Irish vessel lie
Emptied of its poetry.

Time that is intolerant
Of the brave and innocent,
And indifferent in a week
To a beautiful physique,

Worships language and forgives
Everyone by whom it lives;
Pardons cowardice, conceit,
Lays its honours at their feet.

Time that with this strange excuse
Pardoned Kipling and his views,
And will pardon Paul Claudel,
Pardons him for writing well.

In the nightmare of the dark
All the dogs of Europe bark,
And the living nations wait,
Each sequestered in its hate;

Intellectual disgrace
Stares from every human face,
And the seas of pity lie
Locked and frozen in each eye.

Follow, poet, follow right
To the bottom of the night,
With your unconstraining voice
Still persuade us to rejoice;

With the farming of a verse
Make a vineyard of the curse,
Sing of human unsuccess
In a rapture of distress;

In the deserts of the heart
Let the healing fountain start,
In the prison of his days
Teach the free man how to praise.

September 1, 1939

I sit in one of the dives
On Fifty-Second Street
Uncertain and afraid
As the clever hopes expire
Of a low dishonest decade:
Waves of anger and fear
Circulate over the bright
And darkened lands of the earth,
Obsessing our private lives;
The unmentionable odour of death
Offends the September night.

Accurate scholarship can
Unearth the whole offence
From Luther until now
That has driven a culture mad,
Find what occurred at Linz,
What huge imago made
A psychopathic god:
I and the public know
What all schoolchildren learn,
Those to whom evil is done
Do evil in return.

Exiled Thucydides knew
All that a speech can say
About Democracy,
And what dictators do,
The elderly rubbish they talk
To an apathetic grave;
Analysed all in his book,
The enlightenment driven away,
The habit-forming pain,
Mismanagement and grief:
We must suffer them all again.

Into this neutral air
Where blind skyscrapers use
Their full height to proclaim
The strength of Collective Man,
Each language pours its vain
Competitive excuse:
But who can live for long
In an euphoric dream;
Out of the mirror they stare,
Imperialism's face
And the international wrong.

Faces along the bar
Cling to their average day:
The lights must never go out,
The music must always play,
All the conventions conspire
To make this fort assume

The furniture of home;
Lest we should see where we are,
Lost in a haunted wood,
Children afraid of the night
Who have never been happy or good.

The windiest militant trash
Important Persons shout
Is not so crude as our wish:
What mad Nijinsky wrote
About Diaghilev
Is true of the normal heart;
For the error bred in the bone
Of each woman and each man
Craves what it cannot have,
Not universal love
But to be loved alone.

From the conservative dark
Into the ethical life
The dense commuters come,
Repeating their morning vow,
'I *will* be true to the wife,
I'll concentrate more on my work',
And helpless governors wake
To resume their compulsory game:
Who can release them now,
Who can reach the deaf,
Who can speak for the dumb?

All I have is a voice
To undo the folded lie,
The romantic lie in the brain
Of the sensual man-in-the-street
And the lie of Authority
Whose buildings grope the sky:
There is no such thing as the State
And no one exists alone;
Hunger allows no choice
To the citizen or the police;
We must love one another or die.

Defenceless under the night
Our world in stupor lies;
Yet, dotted everywhere,
Ironic points of light
Flash out wherever the Just
Exchange their messages:
May I, composed like them
Of Eros and of dust,
Beleaguered by the same
Negation and despair,
Show an affirming flame.

In Praise of Limestone

If it form the one landscape that we, the inconstant ones,
    Are consistently homesick for, this is chiefly
Because it dissolves in water. Mark these rounded slopes
    With their surface fragrance of thyme and, beneath,
A secret system of caves and conduits; hear the springs
    That spurt out everywhere with a chuckle,
Each filling a private pool for its fish and carving
    Its own little ravine whose cliffs entertain
The butterfly and the lizard; examine this region
    Of short distances and definite places:
What could be more like Mother or a fitter background
    For her son, the flirtatious male who lounges
Against a rock in the sunlight, never doubting
    That for all his faults he is loved; whose works are but
Extensions of his power to charm? From weathered outcrop
    To hill-top temple, from appearing waters to
Conspicuous fountains, from a wild to a formal vineyard,
    Are ingenious but short steps that a child's wish
To receive more attention than his brothers, whether
    By pleasing or teasing, can easily take.

Watch, then, the band of rivals as they climb up and down
    Their steep stone gennels in twos and threes, at times
Arm in arm, but never, thank God, in step; or engaged
    On the shady side of a square at midday in

Voluble discourse, knowing each other too well to think
     There are any important secrets, unable
To conceive a god whose temper-tantrums are moral
     And not to be pacified by a clever line
Or a good lay: for, accustomed to a stone that responds,
     They have never had to veil their faces in awe
Of a crater whose blazing fury could not be fixed;
     Adjusted to the local needs of valleys
Where everything can be touched or reached by walking,
     Their eyes have never looked into infinite space
Through the lattice-work of a nomad's comb; born lucky,
     Their legs have never encountered the fungi
And insects of the jungle, the monstrous forms and lives
     With which we have nothing, we like to hope, in common.
So, when one of them goes to the bad, the way his mind works
     Remains comprehensible: to become a pimp
Or deal in fake jewellery or ruin a fine tenor voice
     For effects that bring down the house, could happen to all
But the best and the worst of us...
                                        That is why, I suppose,
     The best and worst never stayed here long but sought
Immoderate soils where the beauty was not so external,
     The light less public and the meaning of life
Something more than a mad camp. 'Come!' cried the granite wastes,
     'How evasive is your humour, how accidental
Your kindest kiss, how permanent is death.' (Saints-to-be
     Slipped away sighing.) 'Come!' purred the clays and gravels,
'On our plains there is room for armies to drill; rivers
     Wait to be tamed and slaves to construct you a tomb
In the grand manner: soft as the earth is mankind and both
     Need to be altered.' (Intendant Caesars rose and
Left, slamming the door.) But the really reckless were fetched
     By an older colder voice, the oceanic whisper:
'I am the solitude that asks and promises nothing;
     That is how I shall set you free. There is no love;
There are only the various envies, all of them sad.'

     They were right, my dear, all those voices were right
And still are; this land is not the sweet home that it looks,
     Nor its peace the historical calm of a site
Where something was settled once and for all: A backward
     And dilapidated province, connected
To the big busy world by a tunnel, with a certain

Seedy appeal, is that all it is now? Not quite:
It has a worldly duty which in spite of itself
    It does not neglect, but calls into question
All the Great Powers assume; it disturbs our rights. The poet,
    Admired for his earnest habit of calling
The sun the sun, his mind Puzzle, is made uneasy
    By these marble statues which so obviously doubt
His antimythological myth; and these gamins,
    Pursuing the scientist down the tiled colonnade
With such lively offers, rebuke his concern for Nature's
    Remotest aspects: I, too, am reproached, for what
And how much you know. Not to lose time, not to get caught,
    Not to be left behind, not, please! to resemble
The beasts who repeat themselves, or a thing like water
    Or stone whose conduct can be predicted, these
Are our Common Prayer, whose greatest comfort is music
    Which can be made anywhere, is invisible,
And does not smell. In so far as we have to look forward
    To death as a fact, no doubt we are right: But if
Sins can be forgiven, if bodies rise from the dead,
    These modifications of matter into
Innocent athletes and gesticulating fountains,
    Made solely for pleasure, make a further point:
The blessed will not care what angle they are regarded from,
    Having nothing to hide. Dear, I know nothing of
Either, but when I try to imagine a faultless love
    Or the life to come, what I hear is the murmur
Of underground streams, what I see is a limestone landscape.

LOUIS MacNEICE

(1907–1963)

Louis MacNeice grew up in Carrickfergus where his father (later a bishop) was
Church of Ireland (Anglican) Rector. His mother's illness and early death
condition the nightmare scenarios in MacNeice's poetry, together with its
counter-impulse towards an 'incorrigibly plural' flow of perception, sensation
and language. MacNeice was educated at Marlborough and Oxford. During
the 1930s he taught Classics at Birmingham University and Bedford College,
London. In December 1940, after a year in America, he returned to London so
as not to 'miss history' and the Blitz. He joined the BBC where he worked for
20 years as a writer-producer of radio features and plays. MacNeice died of
pneumonia after going down potholes to record sound-effects for his radio-
play *Persons from Porlock*.

Often overshadowed by Auden during the 1930s, MacNeice now appears
just as distinctive and influential. He learned from Auden's public voice, but is
more inclined to let images, especially of the contemporary city, embody his
critique. MacNeice rejected Marxist slogan-poetry, insisting: 'The poet is a
maker, not a retail trader'. Thus his long poem *Autumn Journal* (1939), an end-
of-the-30s epic, filters the Munich crisis through 'reportage, metaphysics,
ethics, lyrical emotion, autobiography, nightmare' (his own words). From an
Irish angle, MacNeice can be seen as absorbing Yeats's lyrical drama of mor-
tality and history, while exposing it to modernity, popular culture and demotic
language. 'Dublin' echoes 'Easter 1916' as MacNeice links the city's troubled
past, the impending Second World War and the conflicts experienced by Irish
Protestants. Yet the city that 'will not / Have' him becomes his mirror.

In the late 1950s, MacNeice began to write what he called 'parable' poetry
'relying more on syntax and bony feature than on bloom or frill or the floating
image'. Here, for instance, urban images (like transport) figure not as sensation
or reportage but as emblems of the human journey or quest. Particularly in his
last two collections, *Solstices* (1961) and *The Burning Perch* (1963), MacNeice
poses his habitual questions about the self in the world, love and death, by
basing a poem's structure on peculiarities of syntax, idiom, refrain. The plural
refrains of 'Reflections' create a perceptual maze. MacNeice's aesthetic com-
plexity is bound up with his cultural and religious background. Hence the
variety of his impact on later poets from Northern Ireland. Derek Mahon's
'In Carrowdore Churchyard' and Ciaran Carson's 'Snow' illustrate the point.

Mayfly

Barometer of my moods today, mayfly,
Up and down one among a million, one
The same at best as the rest of the jigging mayflies,
One only day of May alive beneath the sun.

The yokels tilt their pewters and the foam
Flowers in the sun beside the jewelled water.
Daughter of the South, call the sunbeams home
To nest between your breasts. The kingcups
Ephemeral are gay gulps of laughter.

Gulp of yellow merriment; cackle of ripples;
Lips of the river that pout and whisper round the reeds.
The mayfly flirting and posturing over the water
Goes up and down in the lift so many times for fun.

'When we are grown up we are sure to alter
Much for the better, to adopt solider creeds;
The kingcup will cease proffering his cup
And the foam will have blown from the beer and the heat no longer
        dance
And the lift lose fascination and the May
Change her tune to June – but the trouble with us mayflies
Is that we never have the chance to be grown up.'

They never have the chance, but what of time they have
They stretch out taut and thin and ringing clear;
So we, whose strand of life is not much more,
Let us too make our time elastic and
Inconsequently dance above the dazzling wave.

Nor put too much on the sympathy of things,
The dregs of drink, the dried cups of flowers,
The pathetic fallacy of the passing hours
When it is we who pass them – hours of stone,
Long rows of granite sphinxes looking on.

It is we who pass them, we the circus masters
Who make the mayflies dance, the lapwings lift their crests;
The show will soon shut down, its gay-rags gone,
But when this summer is over let us die together,
I want always to be near your breasts.

Birmingham

Smoke from the train-gulf hid by hoardings blunders upward, the
    brakes of cars
Pipe as the policeman pivoting round raises his flat hand, bars
With his figure of a monolith Pharaoh the queue of fidgety machines
(Chromium dogs on the bonnet, faces behind the triplex screens).
Behind him the streets run away between the proud glass of shops,
Cubical scent-bottles artificial legs arctic foxes and electric mops,
But beyond this centre the slumward vista thins like a diagram:
There, unvisited, are Vulcan's forges who doesn't care a tinker's damn.

Splayed outwards through the suburbs houses, houses for rest
Seducingly rigged by the builder, half-timbered houses with lips pressed
So tightly and eyes staring at the traffic through bleary haws
And only a six-inch grip of the racing earth in their concrete claws;
In these houses men as in a dream pursue the Platonic Forms
With wireless and cairn terriers and gadgets approximating to the
    fickle norms
And endeavour to find God and score one over the neighbour
By climbing tentatively upward on jerry-built beauty and sweated
    labour.

The lunch hour: the shops empty, shopgirls' faces relax
Diaphanous as green glass, empty as old almanacs
As incoherent with ticketed gewgaws tiered behind their heads
As the Burne-Jones windows in St Philip's broken by crawling leads;
Insipid colour, patches of emotion, Saturday thrills
(This theatre is sprayed with 'June') – the gutter take our old playbills,
Next weekend it is likely in the heart's funfair we shall pull
Strong enough on the handle to get back our money; or at any rate it
    is possible.

On shining lines the trams like vast sarcophagi move
Into the sky, plum after sunset, merging to duck's egg, barred with mauve
Zeppelin clouds, and Pentecost-like the cars' headlights bud
Out from sideroads and the traffic signals, crème-de-menthe or bull's
    blood,
Tell one to stop, the engine gently breathing, or to go on
To where like black pipes of organs in the frayed and fading zone
Of the West the factory chimneys on sullen sentry will all night wait
To call, in the harsh morning, sleep-stupid faces through the daily gate.

Snow

The room was suddenly rich and the great bay-window was
Spawning snow and pink roses against it
Soundlessly collateral and incompatible:
World is suddener than we fancy it.

World is crazier and more of it than we think,
Incorrigibly plural. I peel and portion
A tangerine and spit the pips and feel
The drunkenness of things being various.

And the fire flames with a bubbling sound for world
Is more spiteful and gay than one supposes –
On the tongue on the eyes on the ears in the palms of one's hands –
There is more than glass between the snow and the huge roses.

Dublin

Grey brick upon brick,
Declamatory bronze
On sombre pedestals –
O'Connell, Grattan, Moore –
And the brewery tugs and the swans
On the balustraded stream
And the bare bones of a fanlight
Over a hungry door
And the air soft on the cheek
And porter running from the taps
With a head of yellow cream
And Nelson on his pillar
Watching his world collapse.

This was never my town,
I was not born nor bred
Nor schooled here and she will not
Have me alive or dead
But yet she holds my mind

With her seedy elegance,
With her gentle veils of rain
And all her ghosts that walk
And all that hide behind
Her Georgian façades –
The catcalls and the pain,
The glamour of her squalor,
The bravado of her talk.

The lights jig in the river
With a concertina movement
And the sun comes up in the morning
Like barley-sugar on the water
And the mist on the Wicklow hills
Is close, as close
As the peasantry were to the landlord,
As the Irish to the Anglo-Irish,
As the killer is close one moment
To the man he kills,
Or as the moment itself
Is close to the next moment.

She is not an Irish town
And she is not English,
Historic with guns and vermin
And the cold renown
Of a fragment of Church Latin,
Of an oratorical phrase.
But oh the days are soft,
Soft enough to forget
The lesson better learnt,
The bullet on the wet
Streets, the crooked deal,
The steel behind the laugh,
The Four Courts burnt.

Fort of the Dane,
Garrison of the Saxon,
Augustan capital
Of a Gaelic nation,
Appropriating all
The alien brought,
You give me time for thought

And by a juggler's trick
You poise the toppling hour –
O greyness run to flower,
Grey stone, grey water,
And brick upon grey brick.

Meeting Point

Time was away and somewhere else,
There were two glasses and two chairs
And two people with the one pulse
(Somebody stopped the moving stairs):
Time was away and somewhere else.

And they were neither up nor down;
The stream's music did not stop
Flowing through heather, limpid brown,
Although they sat in a coffee shop
And they were neither up nor down.

The bell was silent in the air
Holding its inverted poise –
Between the clang and clang a flower,
A brazen calyx of no noise:
The bell was silent in the air.

The camels crossed the miles of sand
That stretched around the cups and plates;
The desert was their own, they planned
To portion out the stars and dates:
The camels crossed the miles of sand.

Time was away and somewhere else.
The waiter did not come, the clock
Forgot them and the radio waltz
Came out like water from a rock:
Time was away and somewhere else.

Her fingers flicked away the ash
That bloomed again in tropic trees:
Not caring if the markets crash
When they had forests such as these,
Her fingers flicked away the ash.

God or whatever means the Good
Be praised that time can stop like this,
That what the heart has understood
Can verify in the body's peace
God or whatever means the Good.

Time was away and she was here
And life no longer what it was,
The bell was silent in the air
And all the room one glow because
Time was away and she was here.

Death of an Actress

I see from the paper that Florrie Forde is dead —
Collapsed after singing to wounded soldiers,
At the age of sixty-five. The American notice
Says no doubt all that need be said

About this one-time chorus girl; whose role
For more than forty stifling years was giving
Sexual, sentimental, or comic entertainment,
A gaudy posy for the popular soul.

Plush and cigars: she waddled into the lights,
Old and huge and painted, in velvet and tiara,
Her voice gone but around her head an aura
Of all her vanilla-sweet forgotten vaudeville nights.

With an elephantine shimmy and a sugared wink
She threw a trellis of Dorothy Perkins roses
Around an audience come from slum and suburb
And weary of the tea-leaves in the sink;

Who found her songs a rainbow leading west
To the home they never had, to the chocolate Sunday
Of boy and girl, to cowslip time, to the never-
Ending weekend Islands of the Blest.

In the Isle of Man before the war before
The present one she made a ragtime favourite
of 'Tipperary', which became the swan-song
Of troop-ships on a darkened shore;

And during Munich sang her ancient quiz
Of *Where's Bill Bailey?* and the chorus answered,
Muddling through and glad to have no answer:
Where's Bill Bailey? How do *we* know where he is!

Now on a late and bandaged April day
In a military hospital Miss Florrie
Forde has made her positively last appearance
And taken her bow and gone correctly away.

Correctly. For she stood
For an older England, for children toddling
Hand in hand while the day was bright. Let the wren and robin
Gently with leaves cover the Babes in the Wood.

Night Club

After the legshows and the brandies
And all the pick-me-ups for tired
Men there is a feeling
Something more is required.

The lights go down and eyes
Look up across the room;
Salome comes in, bearing
The head of God knows whom.

Reflections

The mirror above my fireplace reflects the reflected
Room in my window; I look in the mirror at night
And see two rooms, the first where left is right
And the second, beyond the reflected window, corrected
But there I am standing back to my back. The standard
Lamp comes thrice in my mirror, twice in my window,
The fire in the mirror lies two rooms away through the window,
The fire in the window lies one room away down the terrace,
My actual room stands sandwiched between confections
Of night and lights and glass and in both directions
I can see beyond and through the reflections the street lamps
At home outdoors where my indoors rooms lie stranded,
Where a taxi perhaps will drive in through the bookcase
Whose books are not for reading and past the fire
Which gives no warmth and pull up by my desk
At which I cannot write since I am not lefthanded.

Soap Suds

This brand of soap has the same smell as once in the big
House he visited when he was eight: the walls of the bathroom open
To reveal a lawn where a great yellow ball rolls back through a hoop
To rest at the head of a mallet held in the hands of a child.

And these were the joys of that house: a tower with a telescope;
Two great faded globes, one of the earth, one of the stars;
A stuffed black dog in the hall; a walled garden with bees;
A rabbit warren; a rockery; a vine under glass; the sea.

To which he has now returned. The day of course is fine
And a grown-up voice cries Play! The mallet slowly swings,
Then crack, a great gong booms from the dog-dark hall and the ball
Skims forward through the hoop and then through the next and then

Through hoops where no hoops were and each dissolves in turn
And the grass has grown head-high and an angry voice cries Play!
But the ball is lost and the mallet slipped long since from the hands
Under the running tap that are not the hands of a child.

Charon

The conductor's hands were black with money:
Hold on to your ticket, he said, the inspector's
Mind is black with suspicion, and hold on to
That dissolving map. We moved through London,
We could see the pigeons through the glass but failed
To hear their rumours of wars, we could see
The lost dog barking but never knew
That his bark was as shrill as a cock crowing,
We just jogged on, at each request
Stop there was a crowd of aggressively vacant
Faces, we just jogged on, eternity
Gave itself airs in revolving lights
And then we came to the Thames and all
The bridges were down, the further shore
Was lost in fog, so we asked the conductor
What we should do. He said: Take the ferry
Faute de mieux. We flicked the flashlight
And there was the ferryman just as Virgil
And Dante had seen him. He looked at us coldly
And his eyes were dead and his hands on the oar
Were black with obols and varicose veins
Marbled his calves and he said to us coldly:
If you want to die you will have to pay for it.

JOHN HEWITT
(1907–1987)

John Hewitt was born in Belfast and brought up as a Methodist. He lived in Belfast all his life apart from 1957-72, when he directed the Herbert Art Gallery and Museum in Coventry. This followed his failure to be appointed Director of the Belfast Museum and Art Gallery where he had worked since leaving Queen's University, Belfast in 1930. His left-wing politics, internationalist outlook and criticism of the unionist regime deprived him of a job in which he might have applied his ideas about Ulster 'regional' culture. Hewitt's regionalism drew on theorists of community such as Lewis Mumford. It was prompted by desire to bridge the Northern Irish sectarian and political divide, by Scottish and Welsh literary movements, and by pursuit of 'a native mode' for his own poetry. He realised the far-reaching literary implications of the fact that 'Ulster's position in this island involves us in problems and cleavages for which we can find no counterpart elsewhere in the British archipelago'. From 1969 the "Troubles" exposed the limits of 'Ulster, considered as a region and not as the symbol of any particular creed'. Yet Hewitt's ideas interested the young Seamus Heaney, and they underlie current approaches to 'cultural diversity' in Northern Ireland. His impact as a cultural thinker and father of subsequent "Northern Irish poetry" has exceeded the impact of his own poetry. Yet his large, often discursive body of work includes intense and moving effects. This is particularly so when he revisits the problem of writing poetry: the variables of its landscape or language, the gap between life's 'substance' and its poetic 'shadow'. 'A Local Poet' is a self-elegy in which the weaver-poets who wrote in Ulster Scots constitute a touchstone.

Landscape

For a countryman the living landscape is
a map of kinship at one level,
at another, just below this, a chart of use,
never at any level a fine view:
sky is a handbook of labour or idleness;
wind in one airt is the lapping of hay,
in another a long day at turf on the moss;
landscape is families, and a lone man
boiling a small pot, and letters once a year;
it is also, underpinning this, good corn
and summer grazing for sheep free of scab
and fallow acres waiting for the lint.
So talk of weather is also talk of life,
and life is man and place and these have names.

airt: point of the compass; *lapping:* rolling into bundles; *moss:* bog; *lint:* flax.

Substance and Shadow

There is a bareness in the images
I temper time with in my mind's defence;
they hold their own, their stubborn secrecies;
no use to rage against their reticence:
a gannet's plunge, a heron by a pond,
a last rook homing as the sun goes down,
a spider squatting on a bracken-frond,
and thistles in a cornsheaf's tufted crown,
a boulder on a hillside, lichen-stained,
the sparks of sun on dripping icicles,
their durable significance contained
in texture, colour, shape, and nothing else.
All these are sharp, spare, simple, native to
this small republic I have charted out
as the sure acre where my sense is true,
while round its boundaries sprawl the screes of doubt.

My lamp lights up the kettle on the stove
and throws its shadow on the whitewashed wall,
like some Assyrian profile with, above,
a snake, or bird-prowed helmet crested tall;
but this remains a shadow; when I shift
the lamp or move the kettle it is gone,
the substance and the shadow break adrift
that needed bronze to lock them, bronze or stone.

Gloss, on the difficulties of translation

Across Loch Laig
the yellow-billed blackbird
whistles from the blossomed whin.

Not, as you might expect,
a Japanese poem, although
it has the seventeen
syllables of the haiku.
Ninth-century Irish, in fact,

from a handbook on metrics,
the first written reference
to my native place.

In forty years of verse
I have not inched much further.
I may have matched the images;
but the intricate wordplay
of the original – assonance,
rime, alliteration –
is beyond my grasp.

To begin with, I should
have to substitute
golden for *yellow*
and *gorse* for *whin,*
this last is the word we use
on both sides of Belfast Lough.

A Local Poet

He followed their lilting stanzas
through a thousand columns or more,
and scratched for the splintered couplets
in the cracks on the cottage floor,
for his Rhyming Weavers fell silent
when they flocked through the factory door.

He'd imagined a highway of heroes
and stepped aside on the grass
to let Cuchulain's chariot through,
and the Starry Ploughmen pass;
but he met the Travelling Gunman
instead of the Galloglass.

And so, with luck, for a decade
down the widowed years ahead,
the pension which crippled his courage
will keep him in daily bread,
while he mourns for his mannerly verses
that had left so much unsaid.

ROBERT GARIOCH
(1909–1981)

Robert Garioch Sutherland grew up in Edinburgh, and studied at Edinburgh
University. Conscripted in 1941, he spent most of the war as a prisoner. This
experience inspired a memoir, *Two Men and a Blanket*, and an allegorical poem,
'The Wire'. Garioch worked as a teacher in England (1946-59) and Edinburgh
– 'Elegy' suggests his problems with that profession. Unassuming, critical,
independent-minded, Garioch never pushed himself, but is now seen as central
to modern Scottish poetry. For Edwin Morgan, the serious and comic aspects
of his work are linked by 'a certain existential terror, half-veiled'.

Garioch did not get on with Hugh MacDiarmid whose politics and later
poetry he thought confused: 'it seems that in poetry one is not expected (by
Scots obsequious critics) to write sense (provided that one is a Great Man)'.
They differed, too, in their approach to Scots. For MacDiarmid, precursors
like Robert Fergusson or Robert Burns had become unreachable (owing to
Kailyard imitation and sentiment), whereas Garioch found a tradition for his
own poetry there. Nor did he follow MacDiarmid into Synthetic Scots, priding
himself on his ear for living vernacular. He translated many sonnets by the
19th-century Italian poet Giuseppe Belli, giving Edinburgh speech and point to
Belli's dialect-critiques of Rome. The poems below illustrate Garioch's versa-
tility: the satirical alertness that spares neither 'bienlie men' nor (in 'Sisyphus')
workers; the passion capable of rewriting (in 'Ghaisties') Marvell's 'To His
Coy Mistress'; the unusual angle on war; the refusal to limit the potentiality
of Scots, as when he combines it with classical myth and metre (hexameters)
to create a striking modern parable.

Ghaisties

Cauld are the ghaisties in yon kirkyaird,
    and cauld the airms
that they mell wi the mists of the timm breists of their loves;
at the heid of their bed cauld angels staund on guaird,
    and marble doves.
They ken-na the fear of Gode, as they sleep ayont sin,
    nor the terror of man,
and there's nane but the angels to glunch at their trueloves' chairms,
yet they lang for the reek of the creeshie swat frae the skin
    and the grup of a haun.

mell: mix; *timm:* empty; *ayont:* beyond; *glunch:* look sour; *creeshie:* greasy.

But we in the warld are alowe
wi the glawmer of bluid-reid flame
that loups to the bluid in yer tongue's tip as it tingles on mine,
        and the howe
of the back we love wi our finger-nebbs, and the wame,
brent-white, wi a flush aneath like cramosie wine,
hou it curves to meet my ain!
        O, ma sonsie frow,
whit tho the flesh be bruckle, and fiends be slee,
the joys of the solid earth we'll pree or they dwine,
we'll lauch at daith, and man, and the fiend, aa three,
        afore we dee.

My Faither Sees Me

My faither sees me throu the gless;
why is he out there in the mirk?
His luik gaes throu me like a dirk,
and mine throu his, baith merciless.

Taen-up aa wi my affairs,
what I maun spend, what I maun hain,
I saw throu the black shiny pane;
he tuik me geynear unawares.

I see him, by the winnock-bar,
yerkan his heid as I yerk mine;
luik maikan luik in double line,
ilk of the ither is made war.

---

alowe: on fire; *loups:* jumps; *howe:* hollow; *finger-nebbs:* fingertips; *wame:* belly;
brent-white: quite white; *cramosie:* crimson; *sonsie:* buxom; *frow:* lusty woman;
bruckle: frail; *slee:* sly; *pree:* prove; *or:* before; *dwine:* fade.

aa: entirely; *hain:* save; *geynear:* almost; *winnock-bar:* window-bar; *yerk:* jerk;
maikan: matching; *ilk:* each; *war:* aware.

Yon luik has flasht frae my faither's een
in Edinbrugh, and hou faur hyne
in Sutherland, and hou lang syne
in Stromness, Dornoch, Aberdeen?

I beik about my cosy, bricht,
fluorescent electric warld.
He sees me yet, yon norland yarl;
I steik my shutters guid and ticht.

Sisyphus

Bumpity doun in the corrie gaed whuddran the pitiless whun stane.
Sisyphus, pechan and sweitan, disjaskit, forfeuchan and broun'd-aff,
sat on the heather a hanlawhile, houpan the Boss didna spy him,
seein the terms of his contract includit nae mention of tea-breaks,
syne at the muckle big scunnersom boulder he trauchlit aince mair.
Ach! hou kenspeckle it was, that he ken'd ilka spreckle and blotch
    on't.
Heavin awa at its wecht, he manhaunnlit the bruitt up the brae-face,
takkan the easiest gait he had fand in a fudder of dour years,
haudan awa frae the craigs had affrichtit him maist in his youth-heid,
feelin his years aa the same, he gaed cannily, tenty of slipped discs.
Eftir an hour and a quarter he warslit his wey to the brae's heid,
hystit his boulder richt up on the tap of the cairn – and it stude
    there!
streikit his length on the chuckie-stanes, houpan the Boss wadna
    spy him,
had a wee look at the scenery, feenisht a pie and a cheese-piece.
Whit was he thinkin about, that he jist gied the boulder a wee shove?
Bumpity doun in the corrie gaed whuddran the pitiless whun stane,
Sisyphus dodderan eftir it, shair of his cheque at the month's end.

een: eyes; *hyne:* away; *beik:* bask; *norland:* north-country; *yarl:* fellow; *steik:* fasten.

whuddran: thudding; *whun:* hard; *pechan:* panting; *disjaskit:* fed up; *forfeuchan:*
exhausted; *hanlawhile:* short time; *syne:* then; *scunnersom:* hateful; *trauchlit:*
laboured; *kenspeckle:* familiar; *spreckle:* mark; *gait:* way; *fudder:* great number;
tenty: wary; *warslit:* wrestled; *hystit:* hoisted; *streikit:* stretched; *chuckie-stanes:*
pebbles; *shair:* sure.

During a Music Festival

Cantie in seaside simmer on the dunes,
I fling awa my dowp of cigarette
whaur bairns hae biggit castles out of sand
and watch the reik rise frae the parapet.

Suddenlike I am back in Libya;
yon's the escarpment, and a bleizan plane,
the wee white speck that feeds the luift wi reik,
dirkins a horror-pictur on my brain.

And aye the reik bleeds frae the warld's rim
as it has duin frae Babylon and Troy,
London, Bonn, Edinbro, time eftir time.
And great Beethoven sang a Hymn to Joy.

Elegy

They are lang deid, folk that I used to ken,
their firm-set lips aa mowdert and agley,
sherp-tempert een rusty amang the cley:
they are baith deid, thae wycelike, bienlie men,

heidmaisters, that had been in pouer for ten
or twenty year afore fate's taiglie wey
brocht me, a young, weill-harnit, blate and fey
new-cleckit dominie, intill their den.

Ane tellt me it was time I learnt to write –
round-haund, he meant – and saw about my hair:
I mind of him, beld-heidit, wi a kyte.

Ane sneerit quarterly – I cuidna square
my savings bank – and sniftert in his spite.
Weill, gin they arena deid, it's time they were.

cantie: cheerful; *dowp:* butt; *biggit:* built; *reik:* smoke; *dirkins:* darkens.

mowdert: mouldering; *agley:* awry; *een:* eyes; *wycelike:* sensible; *bienlie:* comfortable;
taiglie: tangled; *weill-harnit:* intelligent; *blate:* shy; *new-cleckit:* just-hatched;
dominie: schoolmaster; *kyte:* paunch; *sniftert:* snuffled; *gin:* if.

NORMAN MACCAIG

(1910–1996)

Norman MacCaig grew up in Edinburgh, but had family links with the island of Scalpay (off Harris). He often visited Assynt, Sutherland, where his Highlands poems are set. MacCaig studied Classics at Edinburgh University, and this influenced his later stress on clear formal shapes. Seeing the Gaelic tradition as 'classical', too, he attacked Celticist visions of 'chaps twangling harps while their ladies are away marrying seals'. MacCaig underwent his own 'long haul towards lucidity' after publishing two collections in the Romantic style favoured by the 1940s 'Apocalyptic' movement. A pacifist, he refused to fight in the Second World War. This may have cost him promotion during his 30 year career as a primary school teacher. Meanwhile, MacCaig became central to Edinburgh's postwar literary life. From 1972 to 1978 he was Reader in Poetry at Stirling University. MacCaig has been criticised as both over-prolific and over-neat: unwilling to push his striking images further. Yet Don Paterson writes that 'reading his *Collected Poems* is like tipping out a bucket of gemstones on the carpet'. In 'Stag in a neglected hayfield' MacCaig builds an elegiac intensity. In 'So many summers' the stanzaic movement carries the cumulative weight of mortality. The clarity of MacCaig's best poems, in which the Highlands are usually his vulnerable Muse, pivots on an observer whose psyche is fully absorbed into the scene.

Summer farm

Straws like tame lightnings lie about the grass
And hang zigzag on hedges. Green as glass
The water in the horse-trough shines.
Nine ducks go wobbling by in two straight lines.

A hen stares at nothing with one eye,
Then picks it up. Out of an empty sky
A swallow falls and, flickering through
The barn, dives up again into the dizzy blue.

I lie, not thinking, in the cool, soft grass,
Afraid of where a thought might take me – as
This grasshopper with plated face
Unfolds his legs and finds himself in space.

Self under self, a pile of selves I stand
Threaded on time, and with metaphysic hand
Lift the farm like a lid and see
Farm within farm, and in the centre, me.

Fetching cows

The black one, last as usual, swings her head
And coils a black tongue round a grass-tuft. I
Watch her soft weight come down, her split feet spread.

In front, the others swing and slouch; they roll
Their great Greek eyes and breathe out milky gusts
From muzzles black and shiny as wet coal.

The collie trots, bored, at my heels, then plops
Into the ditch. The sea makes a tired sound
That's always stopping though it never stops.

A haycart squats prickeared against the sky.
Hay breath and milk breath. Far out in the West
The wrecked sun founders though its colours fly.

The collie's bored. There's nothing to control…
The black cow is two native carriers
Bringing its belly home, slung from a pole.

Sleeping compartment

I don't like this, being carried sideways
through the night. I feel wrong and helpless – like
a timber broadside in a fast stream.

Such a way of moving may suit
that odd snake the sidewinder
in Arizona: but not me in Perthshire.

I feel at rightangles to everything,
a crossgrain in existence. – It scrapes
the top of my head and my footsoles.

To forget outside is no help either –
then I become a blockage
in the long gut of the train.

I try to think I'm an Alice in Wonderland
mountaineer bivouacked
on a ledge five feet high.

It's no good. I go sidelong.
I rock sideways... I draw in my feet
to let Aviemore pass.

So many summers

Beside one loch, a hind's neat skeleton,
Beside another, a boat pulled high and dry:
Two neat geometries drawn in the weather:
Two things already dead and still to die.

I passed them every summer, rod in hand,
Skirting the bright blue or the spitting gray,
And, every summer, saw how the bleached timbers
Gaped wider and the neat ribs fell away.

Time adds one malice to another one –
Now you'd look very close before you knew
If it's the boat that ran, the hind went sailing.
So many summers, and I have lived them too.

Stag in a neglected hayfield

He's not in his blazing red yet. His antlers
Are a foot that'll be a spreading yard.
The field was a hayfield: now a heifer
And two cows graze there and no dog barks.

That's the outward scene. The inner –
A mountain forgotten, a remembered man.
The deer will return to the hill: but stiller
Than the stone above them are the scything hands.

In memoriam

On that stormy night
a top branch broke off
on the biggest tree in my garden.

It's still up there. Though its leaves
are withered black among the green
the living branches
won't let it fall.

Blue tit on a string of peanuts

A cubic inch of some stars
weighs a hundred tons – Blue tit,
who could measure the power
of your tiny spark of energy? Your hair-thin legs
(one north-east, one due west) support
a scrap of volcano, four inches
of hurricane: and, seeing me, you make the sound
of a grain of sawdust being sawn
by the minutest of saws.

R.S. THOMAS
(1913–2000)

Ronald Stuart Thomas, born in Cardiff, grew up in Holyhead. He studied
Classics at University College, Bangor. From 1936 to 1978 he ministered as
an Anglican priest in Wales. Not a native speaker, he learned Welsh, and the
language haunts this 'Anglo-Welsh' poet who is also a Welsh nationalist. 'This
devilish bilingualism!' he once exclaimed. He published an autobiography in
Welsh, *Neb* ('No-one'), in 1985, later translated into English by Jason Walford
Davies as part of his *Autobiographies* (1997).

During the 1940s Thomas urged that Anglo-Welsh writers should learn
from the Irish Revival and Scottish Renaissance. His postwar cultural national-
ism associated England (and South Wales) with the bad things about modernity.
He argued that Welsh heritage and experience should foster poetry 'different
from that of the essentially urban-minded English poets'. Thomas's anger about
the depopulated Welsh hill country led him to invent 'Iago Prytherch': a far-
mer who represents a dying culture together with the restrictive effects of non-
conformism, isolation and hard labour. Prytherch functions as a scapegoat for
Thomas's disappointment in Wales, and 'The Gap in the Hedge', which reflects
on his own need for Prytherch, may be the most telling poem in the series.

The selection below represents Thomas as primarily a religious poet. His
Collected Poems (1993) cumulatively suggests that he voices the human spirit
scanning Nature for the face of God. In the Introduction to his *Penguin Book
of Religious Verse* (1963), he says: 'it is not necessarily the poems couched in
conventionally religious language that convey the truest religious experience'.
Thomas writes in a cryptic, crystalline shorthand that generates mystery in
its 'gaps'. To quote 'Via Negativa', it is a poetry of 'the place where we go /
Seeking'.

January

The fox drags its wounded belly
Over the snow, the crimson seeds
Of blood burst with a mild explosion,
Soft as excrement, bold as roses.

Over the snow that feels no pity,
Whose white hands can give no healing,
The fox drags its wounded belly.

The Gap in the Hedge

That man, Prytherch, with the torn cap,
I saw him often, framed in the gap
Between two hazels with his sharp eyes,
Bright as thorns, watching the sunrise
Filling the valley with its pale yellow
Light, where the sheep and the lambs went haloed
With grey mist lifting from the dew.
Or was it a likeness that the twigs drew
With bold pencilling upon that bare
Piece of the sky? For he's still there
At early morning, when the light is right
And I look up suddenly at a bird's flight.

The Cat and the Sea

It is a matter of a black cat
On a bare cliff top in March
Whose eyes anticipate
The gorse petals;

The formal equation of
A domestic purr
With the cold interiors
Of the sea's mirror.

A Blackbird Singing

It seems wrong that out of this bird,
Black, bold, a suggestion of dark
Places about it, there yet should come
Such rich music, as though the notes'
Ore were changed to a rare metal
At one touch of that bright bill.

You have heard it often, alone at your desk
In a green April, your mind drawn
Away from its work by sweet disturbance
Of the mild evening outside your room.

A slow singer, but loading each phrase
With history's overtones, love, joy
And grief learned by his dark tribe
In other orchards and passed on
Instinctively as they are now,
But fresh always with new tears.

Via Negativa

Why no! I never thought other than
That God is that great absence
In our lives, the empty silence
Within, the place where we go
Seeking, not in hope to
Arrive or find. He keeps the interstices
In our knowledge, the darkness
Between stars. His are the echoes
We follow, the footprints he has just
Left. We put our hands in
His side hoping to find
It warm. We look at people
And places as though he had looked
At them, too; but miss the reflection.

Moorland

It is beautiful and still;
                  the air rarefied
as the interior of a cathedral

expecting a presence. It is where, also,
        the harrier occurs,
materialising from nothing, snow-

soft, but with claws of fire,
        quartering the bare earth
for the prey that escapes it;

hovering over the incipient
        scream, here a moment, then
not here, like my belief in God.

A Marriage

We met
        under a shower
of bird-notes.
        Fifty years passed,
love's moment
        in a world in
servitude to time.
        She was young;
I kissed with my eyes
        closed and opened
them on her wrinkles.
        'Come,' said death,
choosing her as his
        partner for
the last dance. And she,
        who in life
had done everything
        with a bird's grace,
opened her bill now
        for the shedding
of one sigh no
        heavier than a feather.

HENRY REED

(1914–1986)

Henry Reed was born in Birmingham, and attended Birmingham University at a time when Louis MacNeice's presence as lecturer in Classics helped to create a lively literary milieu. A homosexual, Reed reinvented himself as more upper-class than he actually was. He found Italy and London less constricting than Birmingham. He translated Leopardi and Montale, and Italy provides the title of the only collection he published during his lifetime: *A Map of Verona* (1946). In 1941 Reed was conscripted into the Royal Army Ordnance Corps: hence 'Lessons of the War'. In 1942 he was transferred to the Government Code and Cypher School at Bletchley. After the war he made a reputation as a radio playwright. 'Naming of Parts' (a poem featured in Dylan Thomas's public performances) and 'Judging Distances' maximise Reed's gifts for mimicry and dramatic speech. He engineers a moving as well as satirical collision between languages of authority and subversion (poetry), landscapes of war and peace. (The 'lovers' of Hardy's 'In Time of "The Breaking of Nations"' and Edward Thomas's 'As the team's head brass' reappear.) 'Hiding Beneath the Furze' has absorbed the allegorical and folk idioms that Auden updated during the 1930s. Yet Reed's parable of war's recurrence distinctively blends political terror with psychic shock.

Hiding Beneath the Furze
(Autumn 1939)

Hiding beneath the furze as they passed him by,
    He drowned their talk with the noise of his own heart,
And faltering, came at last to the short hot road
    With the flat white cottage under the rowan trees:
And this can never happen, ever again.

Before his fever drowned him, he stumbled in,
    And the old woman rose, and said in the dialect, 'Enter'.
He entered, and drank, and hearing his fever roaring,
    Surrendered himself to its sweating luxuries:
And this can never happen, ever again.

There were bowls of milk, and (after such hunger) bread.
    Here was the night he had longed for on the highway.
Strange, that his horror could dance so gaily in sunlight,
    And rescue and peace be here in the smoky dark:
And this can never happen, ever again.

When he awoke, he found his pursuers had been,
　　But the woman had lied, and easily deceived them.
She had never questioned his right – for who so childish
　　Could ever do wrong? 'He is my son,' she had said:
And this can never happen, ever again.

The days passed into weeks, and the newspapers came,
　　And he saw that the world was safe, and his name unmentioned.
He could return to the towns and his waiting friends,
　　The evil captain had fled defeated to Norway:
And this can never happen, ever again.

And this can never happen, ever again.
　　He stands on the icy pier and waits to depart,
The town behind him is lightless, his friends are dead,
　　The captain will set his spies in his very heart,
And the fever is gone that rocked inside his head.

from **Lessons of the War**

1 *Naming of Parts*

Today we have naming of parts. Yesterday,
We had daily cleaning. And tomorrow morning,
We shall have what to do after firing. But today,
Today we have naming of parts. Japonica
Glistens like coral in all of the neighbouring gardens,
　　　　And today we have naming of parts.

This is the lower sling swivel. And this
Is the upper sling swivel, whose use you will see,
When you are given your slings. And this is the piling swivel,
Which in your case you have not got. The branches
Hold in the gardens their silent, eloquent gestures,
　　　　Which in our case we have not got.

This is the safety-catch, which is always released
With an easy flick of the thumb. And please do not let me
See anyone using his finger. You can do it quite easy
If you have any strength in your thumb. The blossoms
Are fragile and motionless, never letting anyone see
      Any of them using their finger.

And this you can see is the bolt. The purpose of this
Is to open the breech, as you see. We can slide it
Rapidly backwards and forwards: we call this
Easing the spring. And rapidly backwards and forwards
The early bees are assaulting and fumbling the flowers:
      They call it easing the Spring.

They call it easing the Spring: it is perfectly easy
If you have any strength in your thumb: like the bolt,
And the breech, and the cocking-piece, and the point of balance,
Which in our case we have not got; and the almond-blossom
Silent in all of the gardens and the bees going backwards and forwards,
      For today we have naming of parts.

2 *Judging Distances*

Not only how far away, but the way that you say it
Is very important. Perhaps you may never get
The knack of judging a distance, but at least you know
How to report on a landscape: the central sector,
The right of arc and that, which we had last Tuesday,
      And at least you know

That maps are of time, not place, so far as the army
Happens to be concerned – the reason being,
Is one which need not delay us. Again, you know
There are three kinds of tree, three only, the fir and the poplar,
And those which have bushy tops to; and lastly
      That things only seem to be things.

A barn is not called a barn, to put it more plainly,
Or a field in the distance, where sheep may be safely grazing.
You must never be over-sure. You must say, when reporting:
At five o'clock in the central sector is a dozen
Of what appear to be animals; whatever you do,
      Don't call the bleeders *sheep*.

I am sure that's quite clear; and suppose, for the sake of example,
The one at the end, asleep, endeavours to tell us
What he sees over there to the west, and how far away,
After first having come to attention. There to the west,
On the fields of summer the sun and the shadows bestow
  Vestments of purple and gold.

The still white dwellings are like a mirage in the heat,
And under the swaying elms a man and a woman
Lie gently together. Which is, perhaps, only to say
That there is a row of houses to the left of arc,
And that under some poplars a pair of what appear to be humans
  Appear to be loving.

Well that, for an answer, is what we might rightly call
Moderately satisfactory only, the reason being,
Is that two things have been omitted, and those are important.
The human beings, now: in what direction are they,
And how far away, would you say? And do not forget
  There may be dead ground in between.

There may be dead ground in between; and I may not have got
The knack of judging a distance; I will only venture
A guess that perhaps between me and the apparent lovers
(Who, incidentally, appear by now to have finished)
At seven o'clock from the houses, is roughly a distance
  Of about one year and a half.

DYLAN THOMAS
(1914–1953)

Dylan Thomas called himself 'unnational', 'a border case': 'Regarded in England as a Welshman (and a waterer of England's milk), and in Wales as an Englishman...I should be living in a small private leper-house in Hereford or Shropshire, one foot in Wales and my vowels in England.' Thomas grew up in Swansea, where his father was Senior English Master at the Grammar School. Elocution lessons explain the English 'vowels' of the resonant voice in which he later gave readings of poetry. A talented broadcaster, Thomas wrote the famous radio-play *Under Milk Wood*. His Welsh base became Laugharne, Carmarthenshire, where 'Over Sir John's hill' is set. Thomas died during an American reading tour. Alcohol may not have been wholly to blame.

The "Welshness" of Thomas's poetry consists, first, in its religious intensity. He creates a life-affirming version of Welsh nonconformism (Chapel) with its tradition of eloquent preaching and passionate hymn-singing. Secondly, he has absorbed two contrasting landscapes: Swansea, his 'ugly lovely' 'sea town', and the "Welsh Wales" of his childhood holidays in Carmarthenshire. 'Fern Hill' reconstructs that Eden as a poetic source which identifies the physical world with the music of language. Thomas's earlier poetry is less relaxed and 'tuneful'. Criticised for letting his unconscious 'flow', he replied that his poems were, rather, 'hewn' ('After the funeral' refers to its own 'hewn voice, gesture and psalm').This claim is borne out by Thomas's obsessively worked worksheets. In poems such as 'The force that through the green fuse' he does more than 'load every rift with ore', as Keats advised. He tries to say everything at once about life and death, womb and world, spirit and flesh, eternity and time. His poetry is also 'driven' by his effort to exorcise a sense of the body's sinfulness. He said: 'I hold a beast, an angel, and a madman in me'. At times, Thomas's cadences float free of a content whose obscurities resist analysis. Yet the 'force' and ambition of his work had an incalculable effect on later poetry. His readings, as well as poems, re-emphasised poetry's primary appeal to the ear. Louis MacNeice says: 'When his first work appeared it was astonishingly new, and yet went back to the oldest of our roots.' His influence on Ted Hughes can be sensed from the cosmic bird-fable, 'Over Sir John's hill', where Thomas combines an intricate stanza with rhythms closer to free verse.

The force that through the green fuse drives the flower

The force that through the green fuse drives the flower
Drives my green age; that blasts the roots of trees
Is my destroyer.
And I am dumb to tell the crooked rose
My youth is bent by the same wintry fever.

The force that drives the water through the rocks
Drives my red blood; that dries the mouthing streams
Turns mine to wax.
And I am dumb to mouth unto my veins
How at the mountain spring the same mouth sucks.

The hand that whirls the water in the pool
Stirs the quicksand; that ropes the blowing wind
Hauls my shroud sail.
And I am dumb to tell the hanging man
How of my clay is made the hangman's lime.

The lips of time leech to the fountain head;
Love drips and gathers, but the fallen blood
Shall calm her sores.
And I am dumb to tell a weather's wind
How time has ticked a heaven round the stars.

And I am dumb to tell the lover's tomb
How at my sheet goes the same crooked worm.

After the funeral
(in memory of Ann Jones)

After the funeral, mule praises, brays,
Windshake of sailshaped ears, muffle-toed tap
Tap happily of one peg in the thick
Grave's foot, blinds down the lids, the teeth in black,
The spittled eyes, the salt ponds in the sleeves,
Morning smack of the spade that wakes up sleep,
Shakes a desolate boy who slits his throat
In the dark of the coffin and sheds dry leaves,
That breaks one bone to light with a judgment clout,
After the feast of tear-stuffed time and thistles
In a room with a stuffed fox and a stale fern,
I stand, for this memorial's sake, alone
In the snivelling hours with dead, humped Ann
Whose hooded, fountain heart once fell in puddles
Round the parched worlds of Wales and drowned each sun
(Though this for her is a monstrous image blindly

Magnified out of praise; her death was a still drop;
She would not have me sinking in the holy
Flood of her heart's fame; she would lie dumb and deep
And need no druid of her broken body).
But I, Ann's bard on a raised hearth, call all
The seas to service that her wood-tongued virtue
Babble like a bellbuoy over the hymning heads,
Bow down the walls of the ferned and foxy woods
That her love sing and swing through a brown chapel,
Bless her bent spirit with four, crossing birds.
Her flesh was meek as milk, but this skyward statue
With the wild breast and blessed and giant skull
Is carved from her in a room with a wet window
In a fiercely mourning house in a crooked year.
I know her scrubbed and sour humble hands
Lie with religion in their cramp, her threadbare
Whisper in a damp word, her wits drilled hollow,
Her fist of a face died clenched on a round pain;
And sculptured Ann is seventy years of stone.
These cloud-sopped, marble hands, this monumental
Argument of the hewn voice, gesture and psalm,
Storm me forever over her grave until
The stuffed lung of the fox twitch and cry Love
And the strutting fern lay seeds on the black sill.

Once it was the colour of saying

Once it was the colour of saying
Soaked my table the uglier side of a hill
With a capsized field where a school sat still
And a black and white patch of girls grew playing;
The gentle seaslides of saying I must undo
That all the charmingly drowned arise to cockcrow and kill.
When I whistled with mitching boys through a reservoir park
Where at night we stoned the cold and cuckoo
Lovers in the dirt of their leafy beds,
The shade of their trees was a word of many shades
And a lamp of lightning for the poor in the dark;
Now my saying shall be my undoing,
And every stone I wind off like a reel.

Twenty-four years

Twenty-four years remind the tears of my eyes.
(Bury the dead for fear that they walk to the grave in labour.)
In the groin of the natural doorway I crouched like a tailor
Sewing a shroud for a journey
By the light of the meat-eating sun.
Dressed to die, the sensual strut begun,
With my red veins full of money,
In the final direction of the elementary town
I advance for as long as forever is.

Do not go gentle into that good night

Do not go gentle into that good night,
Old age should burn and rave at close of day;
Rage, rage against the dying of the light.

Though wise men at their end know dark is right,
Because their words had forked no lightning they
Do not go gentle into that good night.

Good men, the last wave by, crying how bright
Their frail deeds might have danced in a green bay,
Rage, rage against the dying of the light.

Wild men who caught and sang the sun in flight,
And learn, too late, they grieved it on its way,
Do not go gentle into that good night.

Grave men, near death, who see with blinding sight
Blind eyes could blaze like meteors and be gay,
Rage, rage against the dying of the light.

And you, my father, there on the sad height,
Curse, bless, me now with your fierce tears, I pray.
Do not go gentle into that good night.
Rage, rage against the dying of the light.

Among those Killed in the Dawn Raid
was a Man Aged a Hundred

When the morning was waking over the war
He put on his clothes and stepped out and he died,
The locks yawned loose and a blast blew them wide,
He dropped where he loved on the burst pavement stone
And the funeral grains of the slaughtered floor.
Tell his street on its back he stopped a sun
And the craters of his eyes grew springshoots and fire
When all the keys shot from the locks, and rang.
Dig no more for the chains of his grey-haired heart.
The heavenly ambulance drawn by a wound
Assembling waits for the spade's ring on the cage.
O keep his bones away from that common cart,
The morning is flying on the wings of his age
And a hundred storks perch on the sun's right hand.

Fern Hill

Now as I was young and easy under the apple boughs
About the lilting house and happy as the grass was green,
        The night above the dingle starry,
            Time let me hail and climb
        Golden in the heydays of his eyes,
And honoured among wagons I was prince of the apple towns
And once below a time I lordly had the trees and leaves
            Trail with daisies and barley
        Down the rivers of the windfall light.

And as I was green and carefree, famous among the barns
About the happy yard and singing as the farm was home,
        In the sun that is young once only,
            Time let me play and be
        Golden in the mercy of his means,
And green and golden I was huntsman and herdsman, the calves
Sang to my horn, the foxes on the hills barked clear and cold,
            And the sabbath rang slowly
        In the pebbles of the holy streams.

All the sun long it was running, it was lovely, the hay
Fields high as the house, the tunes from the chimneys, it was air
    And playing, lovely and watery
        And fire green as grass.
    And nightly under the simple stars
As I rode to sleep the owls were bearing the farm away,
All the moon long I heard, blessed among stables, the nightjars
    Flying with the ricks, and the horses
        Flashing into the dark.

And then to awake, and the farm, like a wanderer white
With the dew, come back, the cock on his shoulder: it was all
    Shining, it was Adam and maiden,
        The sky gathered again
    And the sun grew round that very day.
So it must have been after the birth of the simple light
In the first, spinning place, the spellbound horses walking warm
    Out of the whinnying green stable
        On to the fields of praise.

And honoured among foxes and pheasants by the gay house
Under the new made clouds and happy as the heart was long,
    In the sun born over and over,
        I ran my heedless ways,
    My wishes raced through the house high hay
And nothing I cared, at my sky blue trades, that time allows
In all his tuneful turning so few and such morning songs
    Before the children green and golden
        Follow him out of grace,

Nothing I cared, in the lamb white days, that time would take me
Up to the swallow thronged loft by the shadow of my hand,
    In the moon that is always rising,
        Nor that riding to sleep
    I should hear him fly with the high fields
And wake to the farm forever fled from the childless land.
Oh as I was young and easy in the mercy of his means,
        Time held me green and dying
    Though I sang in my chains like the sea.

Over Sir John's hill

Over Sir John's hill,
The hawk on fire hangs still;
In a hoisted cloud, at drop of dusk, he pulls to his claws
And gallows, up the rays of his eyes the small birds of the bay
And the shrill child's play
Wars
Of the sparrows and such who swansing, dusk, in wrangling hedges.
And blithely they squawk
To fiery tyburn over the wrestle of elms until
The flash the noosed hawk
Crashes, and slowly the fishing holy stalking heron
In the river Towy below bows his tilted headstone.

Flash, and the plumes crack,
And a black cap of jack-
Daws Sir John's just hill dons, and again the gulled birds hare
To the hawk on fire, the halter height, over Towy's fins,
In a whack of wind.
There
Where the elegiac fisherbird stabs and paddles
In the pebbly dab filled
Shallow and sedge, and 'dilly dilly,' calls the loft hawk,
'Come and be killed,'
I open the leaves of the water at a passage
Of psalms and shadows among the pincered sandcrabs prancing

And read, in a shell,
Death clear as a buoy's bell:
All praise of the hawk on fire in hawk-eyed dusk be sung,
When his viperish fuse hangs looped with flames under the brand
Wing, and blest shall
Young
Green chickens of the bay and bushes cluck, 'dilly dilly,
Come let us die.'
We grieve as the blithe birds, never again, leave shingle and elm,
The heron and I,
I young Aesop fabling to the near night by the dingle
Of eels, saint heron hymning in the shell-hung distant

Crystal harbour vale
Where the sea cobbles sail,
And wharves of water where the walls dance and the white cranes stilt.
It is the heron and I, under judging Sir John's elmed
Hill, tell-tale the knelled
Guilt
Of the led-astray birds whom God, for their breast of whistles,
Have mercy on,
God in his whirlwind silence save, who marks the sparrows hail,
For their souls' song.
Now the heron grieves in the weeded verge. Through windows
Of dusk and water I see the tilting whispering

Heron, mirrored, go,
As the snapt feathers snow,
Fishing in the tear of the Towy. Only a hoot owl
Hollows, a grassblade blown in cupped hands, in the looted elms.
And no green cocks or hens
Shout
Now on Sir John's hill. The heron, ankling the scaly
Lowlands of the waves,
Makes all the music; and I who hear the tune of the slow,
Wear-willow river, grave,
Before the lunge of the night, the notes on this time-shaken
Stone for the sake of the souls of the slain birds sailing.

ALUN LEWIS

(1915-1944)

Alun Lewis grew up in Cwmaman, a mining village in Mid-Glamorgan. He studied history at University College of Wales, Aberystwyth. Lewis hated industrialisation, the conditions endured by colliers, repressive nonconformism. Undecided between literature and social commitment ('generally flummoxed with so many irons all stuck into an empty grate'), he tried schoolteaching and wrote short stories and poems. In 1942 *The Last Inspection*, a collection of stories, and *Raiders' Dawn*, a collection of poems, were published. In 1940 Lewis had cut the Gordian knot of his indecisions by volunteering for the army. He was critical of the army's ethos, but eager for experience and action. In India with the South Wales Borderers, he wrote: 'I'll never be just English or just Welsh again.' In March 1944 he died in Burma 'accidentally wounded by a pistol shot'. Some critics connect these circumstances with Lewis's imaginative conflict between death-wish and life-wish, idealism and fatalism. 'All Day It Has Rained...', full of quotations from Edward Thomas (including 'Rain'), identifies with Thomas's brooding 'On death and beauty'. Lewis's talent was still maturing when he died, as some over-emphatic rhymes and over-Romantic phrases show. Nonetheless, his poles of love and war, belonging ('We made the universe to be our home') and relinquishment, dramatise an intensive quest for meaning.

All Day It Has Rained...

All day it has rained, and we on the edge of the moors
Have sprawled in our bell-tents, moody and dull as boors,
Groundsheets and blankets spread on the muddy ground
And from the first grey wakening we have found
No refuge from the skirmishing fine rain
And the wind that made the canvas heave and flap
And the taut wet guy-ropes ravel out and snap.
All day the rain has glided, wave and mist and dream,
Drenching the gorse and heather, a gossamer stream
Too light to stir the acorns that suddenly
Snatched from their cups by the wild south-westerly
Pattered against the tent and our upturned dreaming faces.
And we stretched out, unbuttoning our braces,
Smoking a Woodbine, darning dirty socks,
Reading the Sunday papers – I saw a fox
And mentioned it in the note I scribbled home; –
And we talked of girls, and dropping bombs on Rome,

And thought of the quiet dead and the loud celebrities
Exhorting us to slaughter, and the herded refugees;
– Yet thought softly, morosely of them, and as indifferently
As of ourselves or those whom we
For years have loved, and will again
Tomorrow maybe love; but now it is the rain
Possesses us entirely, the twilight and the rain.

And I can remember nothing dearer or more to my heart
Than the children I watched in the woods on Saturday
Shaking down burning chestnuts for the schoolyard's merry play,
Or the shaggy patient dog who followed me
By Sheet and Steep and up the wooded scree
To the Shoulder o' Mutton where Edward Thomas brooded long
On death and beauty – till a bullet stopped his song.

Goodbye

So we must say Goodbye, my darling,
And go, as lovers go, for ever;
Tonight remains, to pack and fix on labels
And make an end of lying down together.

I put a final shilling in the gas,
And watch you slip your dress below your knees
And lie so still I hear your rustling comb
Modulate the autumn in the trees.

And all the countless things I shall remember
Lay mummy-cloths of silence round my head;
I fill the carafe with a drink of water;
You say 'We paid a guinea for this bed,'

And then, 'We'll leave some gas, a little warmth
For the next resident, and these dry flowers,'
And turn your face away, afraid to speak
The big word, that Eternity is ours.

Your kisses close my eyes and yet you stare
As though God struck a child with nameless fears;
Perhaps the water glitters and discloses
Time's chalice and its limpid useless tears.

Everything we renounce except our selves;
Selfishness is the last of all to go;
Our sighs are exhalations of the earth,
Our footprints leave a track across the snow.

We made the universe to be our home,
Our nostrils took the wind to be our breath,
Our hearts are massive towers of delight,
We stride across the seven seas of death.

Yet when all's done you'll keep the emerald
I placed upon your finger in the street;
And I will keep the patches that you sewed
On my old battledress tonight, my sweet.

W.S. GRAHAM

(1918–1986)

William Sydney Graham was born in Greenock. At 14 he began an engineering apprenticeship on Clydeside. He went to evening classes in art and literature, and spent a year at Newbattle Abbey, the Scottish college for mature students. He refused to be conscripted, but an ulcer and factory work saved him from prosecution. By now he was writing poems influenced by Dylan Thomas. From 1943, Graham lived mainly in Cornwall, ultimately at Madron, Penzance. A full-time poet, often hard-up, he was closely associated with painters of the St Ives School. Graham's proximity to avant-garde painting and admiration for James Joyce promoted a self-consciousness about his medium which can become excessive. 'Notes on a Poetry of Release' (1946) anticipates both his problems as a poet and his finest achievements: 'The most difficult thing for me to remember is that a poem is made of words and not of the expanding heart, the overflowing soul, or the sensitive observer. A poem is made of words... Each word changes every time it is brought to life. Each single word uttered twice becomes a new word each time. You cannot twice bring the same word into sound...The poem begins to form from the first intention. But the intention is already breaking into another...Even the poet as a man who searches continually is a new searcher with his direction changing at every step.' Sometimes Graham's concern with how language, itself unstable, can represent the unstable self in an unstable world produces rather abstract poetry, even in the celebrated title-poem of *The Nightfishing* (1955). The selection below highlights some extraordinary later work. Here Graham's alertness to the provisionality of words also dramatises 'the expanding heart, the overflowing soul'. The tender poems, mostly in the present tense, to his (dead) father and (living) wife present haunting dream-landscapes where the boundary between memory and experience, presence and absence, seems to dissolve. Mysterious breaks or breaths occur between the deceptively simple statements or questions. Here Graham's Heraclitean idea of language as always flowing ('You cannot twice bring the same word into sound') finds its form. Similarly, 'The Stepping Stones', at one level a poem about poetry, involves the reader in changes of direction 'at every step'.

To Alexander Graham

Lying asleep walking
Last night I met my father
Who seemed pleased to see me.
He wanted to speak. I saw
His mouth saying something
But the dream had no sound.

We were surrounded by
Laid-up paddle steamers
In The Old Quay in Greenock.
I smelt the tar and the ropes.

It seemed that I was standing
Beside the big iron cannon
The tugs used to tie up to
When I was a boy. I turned
To see Dad standing just
Across the causeway under
That one lamp they keep on.

He recognised me immediately.
I could see that. He was
The handsome, same age
With his good brows as when
He would take me on Sundays
Saying we'll go for a walk.

Dad, what am I doing here?
What is it I am doing now?
Are you proud of me?
Going away, I knew
You wanted to tell me something.

You stopped and almost turned back
To say something. My father,
I try to be the best
In you you give me always.

Lying asleep turning
Round in the quay-lit dark
It was my father standing
As real as life. I smelt
The quay's tar and the ropes.

I think he wanted to speak.
But the dream had no sound.
I think I must have loved him.

The Stepping Stones

I have my yellow boots on to walk
Across the shires where I hide
Away from my true people and all
I can't put easily into my life.

So you will see I am stepping on
The stones between the runnels getting
Nowhere nowhere. It is almost
Embarrassing to be alive alone.

Take my hand and pull me over from
The last stone on to the moss and
The three celandines. Now my dear
Let us go home across the shires.

To My Wife at Midnight

1

Are you to say goodnight
And turn away under
The blanket of your delight?

Are you to let me go
Alone to sleep beside you
Into the drifting snow?

Where we each reach,
Sleeping alone together,
Nobody can touch.

Is the cat's window open?
Shall I turn into your back?
And what is to happen?

What is to happen to us
And what is to happen to each
Of us asleep in our places?

2

I mean us both going
Into sleep at our ages
To sleep and get our fairing.

They have all gone home.
Night beasts are coming out.
The black wood of Madron

Is just waking up.
I hear the rain outside
To help me to go to sleep.

Nessie, dont let my soul
Skip and miss a beat
And cause me to fall.

3

Are you asleep I say
Into the back of your neck
For you not to hear me.

Are you asleep? I hear
Your heart under the pillow
Saying my dear my dear

My dear for all it's worth.
Where is the dun's moor
Which began your breath?

4

Ness, to tell you the truth
I am drifting away
Down to fish for the saithe.

Is the cat's window open?
The weather is on my shoulder
And I am drifting down

Into O can you hear me
Among your Dunsmuir Clan?
Are you coming out to play?

5

Did I behave badly
On the field at Culloden?
I lie sore-wounded now

By all activities, and
The terrible acts of my time
Are only a distant sound.

With responsibility
I am drifting off
Breathing regularly

Into my younger days
To play the games of Greenock
Beside the sugar-house quays.

6

Nessie Dunsmuir, I say
Wheesht wheesht to myself
To help me now to go

Under into somewhere
In the redcoat rain.
Buckle me for the war.

Are you to say goodnight
And kiss me and fasten
My drowsy armour tight?

My dear camp-follower,
Hap the blanket round me
And tuck in a flower.

Maybe from my sleep
In the stoure at Culloden
I'll see you here asleep

In your lonely place.

saithe: pollock, a type of cod; *stoure:* strife.

KEITH DOUGLAS

(1920–1944)

When Keith Douglas was killed during the Allied invasion of Normandy, he left behind poetry whose major importance is still being realised. Douglas calls his ancestry 'Scottish and pre-Revolution French'. As a schoolboy at Christ's Hospital, London, he already published poems. At Merton College, Oxford, he was encouraged by Edmund Blunden, a soldier-poet of the Great War. Partly owing to a broken love affair, partly owing to a constant desire to be where the action was, Douglas joined up when war was declared. In 1941 he went to Palestine as an officer in the Nottinghamshire Sherwood Rangers. His vivid prose account of the North African Campaign, *Alamein to Zem Zem* (1946), updates the 1930s theme of 'journey to a war'. Douglas's poetry, too, moved on. In a different way from Dylan Thomas, he reasserted poetry's cosmic scope. 'Time Eating' and 'The Marvel' are Shakespearean in their rich interlacing of love and death, the body and time, the globe and its creatures, creativity and destruction, 'material and abstract' language. Yet – as 'Cairo Jag' underlines – history is part of that larger, richer picture, and war has changed the meaning of political poetry. In 'Poets in This War' (1943) Douglas criticises supposedly political poets for being 'curiously unable to react', and 'the nation's public character' for remaining 'as absurdly ignorant and reactionary as ever'. A year later he wrote: 'For me, it is simply a case of fighting *against* the Nazi regime'.

Douglas was as wary of repeating the trench poets ('hell cannot be let loose twice') as of repeating the 1930s. He could move on because he adjusted his language and imagery to the historical moment, to the poetic moment. Douglas's belief that 'every word must work for its keep' became a means of critique: 'my object…is to write true things, significant things in words each of which works for its place in a line. My rhythms…are carefully chosen to enable the poems to be *read* as significant speech'. 'Words' implies that language without this ethic leads to prison-camps. To keep words alive by rhythmic changes of tack that resist predictable melody is a form of ethical vigilance. Yet while Douglas's rhythms keep moving, they also hold his gaze. The swordfish's eye, used as 'a powerful enlarging glass', the hand's 'translation of forms', are images for his poetry: for a formal distancing that enables us first to see, then feel. Douglas's talent as a visual artist shapes his poetry's self-image as a lens or spectacle. His desert arena, although less hellish than the trench landscape, is an equally macabre cosmic theatre. 'How to Kill' rewrites Owen's 'Strange Meeting' for that theatre. Douglas returns to the action of killing the enemy and identifies it with his poem's procedure. For Ted Hughes, a great admirer, all his work is a 'balancing act in words, which draws the reader into the same imperilled concentration as Douglas's own'.

Time Eating

Ravenous Time has flowers for his food
at Autumn – yet can cleverly make good
each petal: devours animals and men,
but for ten dead he can create ten.

If you enquire how secretly you've come
to mansize from the bigness of a stone
it will appear it's his art made you rise
so gradually to your proper size.

But while he makes he eats: the very part
where he began, even the elusive heart
Time's ruminative tongue will wash
and slow juice masticate all flesh.

That volatile huge intestine holds
material and abstract in its folds:
thought and ambition melt, and even the world
will alter, in that catholic belly curled.

But Time, who ate my love, you cannot make
such another. You who can remake
the lizard's tail and the bright snakeskin
cannot, cannot. That you gobbled in
too quick: and though you brought me from a boy
you can make no more of me, only destroy.

The Marvel

A baron of the sea, the great tropic
swordfish, spreadeagled on the thirsty deck
where sailors killed him, in the bright Pacific

yielded to the sharp enquiring blade
the eye which guided him and found his prey
in the dim country where he was a lord;

which is an instrument forged in semi-darkness
yet taken from the corpse of this strong traveller
becomes a powerful enlarging glass

reflecting the unusual sun's heat.
With it a sailor writes on the hot wood
the name of a harlot in his last port.

For it is one most curious device
of many, kept by the interesting waves –
and I suppose the querulous soft voice

of mariners who rotted into ghosts
digested by the gluttonous tides
could recount many. Let them be your hosts

and take you where their forgotten ships lie
with fishes going over the tall masts –
all this emerges from the burning eye.

And to engrave that word the sun goes through
with the power of the sea,
writing her name and a marvel too.

The Hand

The hand is perfect in itself – the five
fingers though changing attitude depend
on a golden point, the imaginary true focal
to which infinities of motion and shape are yoked.
There is no beginning to the hand, no end,
and the bone retains its proportion in the grave.

I can transmute this hand, changing each
finger to a man or a woman, and the hills
behind, drawn in their relation:
and to more than men, women, hills, by alteration
of symbols standing for the fingers, for the whole hand,
this alchemy is not difficult to teach,

this making a set of pictures; this drawing
shapes within the shapes of the hand –
an ordinary translation of forms. But hence,
try to impose arguments
whose phrases, each upon a digit, tend
to the centre of reasoning, the mainspring.

To do this is drilling the mind, still a recruit,
for the active expeditions of his duty
when he must navigate alone the wild
cosmos, as the Jew wanders the world:
and we, watching the tracks of him at liberty
like the geometry of feet
upon a shore, constructed in the sand,
look for the proportions, the form of an immense hand.

Cairo Jag

Shall I get drunk or cut myself a piece of cake,
a pasty Syrian with a few words of English
or the Turk who says she is a princess – she dances
apparently by levitation? Or Marcelle, Parisienne
always preoccupied with her dull dead lover:
she has all the photographs and his letters
tied in a bundle and stamped *Décedé* in mauve ink.
All this takes place in a stink of jasmin.

But there are the streets dedicated to sleep
stenches and the sour smells, the sour cries
do not disturb their application to slumber
all day, scattered on the pavement like rags
afflicted with fatalism and hashish. The women
offering their children brown-paper breasts
dry and twisted, elongated like the skull,
Holbein's signature. But this stained white town
is something in accordance with mundane conventions –
Marcelle drops her Gallic airs and tragedy
suddenly shrieks in Arabic about the fare

with the cabman, links herself so
with the somnambulists and legless beggars:
it is all one, all as you have heard.

But by a day's travelling you reach a new world
the vegetation is of iron
dead tanks, gun barrels split like celery
the metal brambles have no flowers or berries
and there are all sorts of manure, you can imagine
the dead themselves, their boots, clothes and possessions
clinging to the ground, a man with no head
has a packet of chocolate and a souvenir of Tripoli.

Words

Words are my instruments but not my servants;
by the white pillar of a prince I lie in wait
for them. In what the hour or the minute invents,
in a web formally meshed or inchoate,
these fritillaries are come upon, trapped:
hot-coloured, or the cold scarabs a thousand years
old, found in cerements and unwrapped.
The catch and the ways of catching are diverse.
For instance this stooping man, the bones of whose face are
like the hollow birds' bones, is a trap for words.
And the pockmarked house bleached by the glare
whose insides war has dried out like gourds
attracts words. There are those who capture them
in hundreds, keep them prisoners in black
bottles, release them at exercise and clap them back.
But I keep words only a breath of time
turning in the lightest of cages – uncover
and let them go: sometimes they escape for ever.

Desert Flowers

Living in a wide landscape are the flowers –
Rosenberg I only repeat what you were saying –
the shell and the hawk every hour
are slaying men and jerboas, slaying

the mind: but the body can fill
the hungry flowers and the dogs who cry words
at nights, the most hostile things of all.
But that is not new. Each time the night discards

draperies on the eyes and leaves the mind awake
I look each side of the door of sleep
for the little coin it will take
to buy the secret I shall not keep.

I see men as trees suffering
or confound the detail and the horizon.
Lay the coin on my tongue and I will sing
of what the others never set eyes on.

Vergissmeinnicht

Three weeks gone and the combatants gone
returning over the nightmare ground
we found the place again, and found
the soldier sprawling in the sun.

The frowning barrel of his gun
overshadowing. As we came on
that day, he hit my tank with one
like the entry of a demon.

Look. Here in the gunpit spoil
the dishonoured picture of his girl
who has put: *Steffi. Vergissmeinnicht*
in a copybook gothic script.

We see him almost with content,
abased, and seeming to have paid
and mocked at by his own equipment
that's hard and good when he's decayed.

But she would weep to see today
how on his skin the swart flies move;
the dust upon the paper eye
and the burst stomach like a cave.

For here the lover and killer are mingled
who had one body and one heart.
And death who had the soldier singled
has done the lover mortal hurt.

How to Kill

Under the parabola of a ball,
a child turning into a man,
I looked into the air too long.
The ball fell in my hand, it sang
in the closed fist: *Open Open*
Behold a gift designed to kill.

Now in my dial of glass appears
the soldier who is going to die.
He smiles, and moves about in ways
his mother knows, habits of his.
The wires touch his face: I cry
NOW. Death, like a familiar, hears

and look, has made a man of dust
of a man of flesh. This sorcery
I do. Being damned, I am amused
to see the centre of love diffused
and the waves of love travel into vacancy.
How easy it is to make a ghost.

The weightless mosquito touches
her tiny shadow on the stone,
and with how like, how infinite
a lightness, man and shadow meet.
They fuse. A shadow is a man
when the mosquito death approaches.

On a Return from Egypt

To stand here in the wings of Europe
disheartened, I have come away
from the sick land where in the sun lay
the gentle sloe-eyed murderers
of themselves, exquisites under a curse;
here to exercise my depleted fury.

For the heart is a coal, growing colder
when jewelled cerulean seas change
into grey rocks, grey water-fringe,
sea and sky altering like a cloth
till colour and sheen are gone both:
cold is an opiate of the soldier.

And all my endeavours are unlucky explorers
come back, abandoning the expedition;
the specimens, the lilies of ambition
still spring in their climate, still unpicked:
but time, time is all I lacked
to find them, as the great collectors before me.

The next month, then, is a window
and with a crash I'll split the glass.
Behind it stands one I must kiss,
person of love or death
a person or a wraith,
I fear what I shall find.

EDWIN MORGAN

(*born* 1920)

Edwin Morgan grew up in Glasgow. His studies were interrupted by the Second World War. At first he registered as a conscientious objector, but then volunteered for the Royal Army Medical Corps which took him to the Middle East. From 1947 to 1980 he lectured in English at Glasgow University. During the 1960s Morgan experienced a sexual and artistic liberation. He was able to admit his homosexuality, and became excited by the experimental work of poets in North and South America. He says in the 'Epilogue' to his *Collected Poems* (1990): 'At forty I woke up, saw it was day, / found there was love, heard a new beat, heard Beats, / sent airmail solidarity to Saõ / Paolo's poetic-concrete revolution'. Morgan translated Russian "Futurist" poets, such as Mayakovsky, and Italian and Hungarian poetry. Tom Leonard sums up his synthesis of the local and foreign by calling him 'Cultural attaché to the legendary city of Morganiana, said to exist behind a door marked "Morgan" in an unobtrusive block of flats off Great Western Road'.

Morgan's concrete poems are not just a way of highlighting poetry as shapes on a page. They also depend on sound-effects. 'Clydesdale' interweaves a refrain-word with rhyming compound-words that suggest plough-horses' movement and environment. What Morgan admires in Mayakovsky is his 'acutely inventive use of word and sound in every device of onomatopoeia, alliteration, assonance and dissonance, pun and palindrome'. 'Canedolia', which inventively translates 'Caledonia', Scotland, into a sound-collage, plays similar tricks. Scottish place-names are twisted and combined so as to imply the country's qualities. Morgan's *Collected Poems* (1990) displays a prolific and various poet who has also written free verse ('The Unspoken') and many sonnets. His experimentalism, like his interest in science and science fiction, does not detach his poetry from Glasgow. The spirit of the Scottish intellectual polymath breathes in Morgan's discovery 'that you can write poetry about anything. You really can! The world, history, society, everything in it, pleads to become a voice, voices.' 'Foundation' is a manifesto along these lines.

Chinese Cat

p m r k g n i a o u
p m r k g n i a o
p m r k n i a o
p m r n i a o
p m r i a o
p m i a o
m i a o
m a o

Clydesdale

go
    fetlocksnow
                go
                    gullfurrow
                                go
go
    brassglow
                go
                    sweatflow
                                go
go
    plodknow
                go
                    clodshow
                                go
go
    leatherbelow
                go
                    potatothrow
                                go
go
    growfellow
                go
                    crowfollow
                                go
go
    Balerno
                go
                    Palermo
                                whoa

Aberdeen Train

Rubbing a glistening circle
on the steamed-up window I framed
a pheasant in a field of mist.

The sun was a great red thing somewhere low,
struggling with the milky scene. In the furrows
a piece of glass winked into life,
hypnotised the silly dandy; we
hooted past him with his head cocked,
contemplating a bottle-end.
And this was the last of October,
a Chinese moment in the Mearns.

Canedolia
an off-concrete Scotch fantasia

oa! hoy! awe! ba! mey!

who saw?
rhu saw rum. garve saw smoo. nigg saw tain. lairg saw lagg.
rigg saw eigg. largs saw haggs. tongue saw luss. mull saw yell.
stoer saw strone. drem saw muck. gask saw noss. unst saw cults.
echt saw banff. weem saw wick. trool saw twatt.

how far?
from largo to lunga from joppa to skibo from ratho to shona from
ulva to minto from tinto to tolsta from soutra to marsco from
braco to barra from alva to stobo from fogo to fada from gigha to
gogo from kelso to stroma from hirta to spango.

what is it like there?
och it's freuchie, it's faifley, it's wamphray, it's frandy, it's
sliddery.

what do you do?
we foindle and fungle, we bonkle and meigle and maxpoffle. we
scotstarvit, armit, wormit, and even whifflet. we play at crossstobs,
leuchars, gorbals, and finfan. we scavaig, and there's aye a bit of
tilquhilly. if it's wet, treshnish and mishnish.

what is the best of the country?
blinkbonny! airgold! thundergay!

and the worst?
scrishven, shiskine, scrabster, and snizort.

listen! what's that?
catacol and wauchope, never heed them.

tell us about last night
well, we had a wee ferintosh and we lay on the quiraing. it was
pure strontian!

but who was there?
petermoidart and craigenkenneth and cambusputtock and
ecclemuchty and corriehulish and balladolly and altnacanny and
clauchanvrechan and stronachlochan and auchenlachar and
tighnacrankie and tilliebruaich and killieharra and invervannach and
achnatudlem and machrishellach and inchtamurchan and
auchterfechan and kinlochculter and ardnawhallie and
invershuggle.

and what was the toast?
schiehallion! schiehallion! schiehallion!

The Unspoken

When the troopship was pitching round the Cape
in '41, and there was a lull in the night uproar of seas and winds,
          and a sudden full moon
swung huge out of the darkness like the world it is,
and we all crowded onto the wet deck, leaning on the rail, our arms
          on each other's shoulders, gazing at the savage outcrop of
          great Africa,
and Tommy Cosh started singing 'Mandalay' and we joined in
          with our raucous chorus of the unforgettable song,
and the dawn came up like thunder like that moon drawing the
          water of our yearning
though we were going to war, and left us exalted,
that was happiness,
but it is not like that.

When the television newscaster said
the second sputnik was up, not empty
but with a small dog on board,
a half-ton treasury of life orbiting a thousand miles above the thin
            television masts and mists of November,
in clear space, heard, observed,
the faint far heartbeat sending back its message
steady and delicate,
and I was stirred by a deep confusion of feelings,
got up, stood with my back to the wall and my palms pressed hard
            against it, my arms held wide
as if I could spring from this earth –
not loath myself to go out that very day where Laika had shown man,
felt my cheeks burning with old Promethean warmth
rekindled – ready –
covered my face with my hands, seeing only an animal
strapped in a doomed capsule, but the future
was still there, cool and whole like the moon,
waiting to be taken, smiling even
as the dog's bones and the elaborate casket of aluminium
glow white and fuse in the arc of re-entry,
and I knew what I felt was history,
its thrilling brilliance came down,
came down,
comes down on us all, bringing pride and pity,
but it is not like that.

But Glasgow days and grey weathers, when the rain
beat on the bus shelter and you leaned slightly against me, and the
            back of your hand touched my hand in the shadows, and
            nothing was said,
when your hair grazed mine accidentally as we talked in a café,
            yet not quite accidentally,
when I stole a glance at your face as we stood in a doorway and
            found I was afraid
of what might happen if I should never see it again,
when we met, and met, in spite of such differences in our lives,
and did the common things that in our feeling
became extraordinary, so that our first kiss
was like the winter morning moon, and as you shifted in my arms
it was the sea changing the shingle that changes it
as if for ever (but we are bound by nothing, but like smoke
to mist or light in water we move, and mix) –

O then it was a story as old as war or man,
and although we have not said it we know it,
and although we have not claimed it we do it,
and although we have not vowed it we keep it,
without a name to the end.

Foundation

'What would you put in the foundation-stone
for future generations?' 'A horseshoe,
a ballet shoe, a horseshoe crab, a sea-horse,
a sheriff's star, a pacemaker, a tit's egg, a tomato,
a ladybird, a love-letter, a laugh-track, a yo-yo,
a microtektite, a silicon chip, a chip pan,
a Rembrandt, a Reinhardt, a Reinhardt jigsaw – '
'That's some foundation-stone – ' ' – a hovercraft,
a manta ray, a bulldozer, a windjammer,
a planetarium, an oilrig, a Concorde, a cornfield,
a gannetry, a hypermarket, a continental shelf,
a brace of asteroids, a spiral nebula – '
'Why don't you take my question seriously – ?'
' – a black hole, a dream, a conceptual universe,
no, make it a dozen conceptual universes
laid tail to head like sardines in a tin
and poured all over with lovely oil
of poetry: seal it; solder the key.'

PHILIP LARKIN

(1922–1985)

In 'I Remember, I Remember' Philip Larkin represents his youth in Coventry as a non-event. He inverts Dylan Thomas's 'Fern Hill' and satirises several Romantic notions of a poet's 'seedtime' (Wordsworth). Larkin's adulthood also appears humdrum: after leaving wartime Oxford he became a university librarian, chiefly in Belfast (1950-55) and Hull. Yet his *Selected Letters* (1992) and Andrew Motion's biography (1993) point to a disturbed inner life in which sexual obsession is a recurrent theme. This should not have surprised readers of *The Less Deceived* (1955), *The Whitsun Weddings* (1964) and *High Windows* (1974). In some ways, Larkin is a late-Romantic lyric poet whose ideal of beauty (in women and art) is shadowed by mortality and driven by neurosis. In 'I Remember, I Remember' ' "You look as if you wished the place in Hell" ' hints at unhappiness – 'Nothing' – as his real poetic source. For Larkin, 'what you imagine makes you dissatisfied with what you experience, and may even lead you to neglect it'. 'Deceptions' empathises not only with the 'ruined' girl, but with the rapist's passage from 'desire' to desolation.

A contrasting poem 'Wedding Wind' (whose female persona may help Larkin to celebrate fulfilment) draws on Lawrence's images of sexuality. Lawrence and Yeats influenced the visionary element that precariously survives in Larkin's work, although he found Hardy's 'sadness' more akin to his own sensibility. The tensions between these influences correspond to tensions within Larkin himself. Yeats and Auden were models for what he terms 'the management of lines, the formal distancing of emotion', and for his skill in combining concrete and abstract language ('fulfilment's desolate attic'). In turn, Larkin makes the Yeatsian stanza absorb, in a compressed form, features deriving from his original wish to be a novelist: social observation, stories, colloquial idioms. Larkin was seen as a key figure in the so-called 'Movement' linked with Robert Conquest's anthology *New Lines* (1956). Conquest stressed 'a rational structure and comprehensible language'. Yet this does not cover the intensity of Larkin's poetry, its symbolic dimension or his flirtations with freer verse – all illustrated by 'Going'.

Larkin's relation to England is as complex as that of another poet he admired, Edward Thomas. Society, symbolised and sustained by marriage, was problematic for him since he linked his poetic vocation with solitude. His social portraiture can imply distaste. Yet in 'MCMXIV' and 'The Whitsun Weddings', Larkin orchestrates collective national experiences. Other poems recall Hardy's mourning note. At the points where Larkin's sensibility connects with his postwar contexts, he often speaks for loss, alteration, the absence of 'home'.

Going

There is an evening coming in
Across the fields, one never seen before,
That lights no lamps.

Silken it seems at a distance, yet
When it is drawn up over the knees and breast
It brings no comfort.

Where has the tree gone, that locked
Earth to the sky? What is under my hands,
That I cannot feel?

What loads my hands down?

Wedding-Wind

The wind blew all my wedding-day,
And my wedding-night was the night of the high wind;
And a stable door was banging, again and again,
That he must go and shut it, leaving me
Stupid in candlelight, hearing rain,
Seeing my face in the twisted candlestick,
Yet seeing nothing. When he came back
He said the horses were restless, and I was sad
That any man or beast that night should lack
The happiness I had.

                    Now in the day
All's ravelled under the sun by the wind's blowing.
He has gone to look at the floods, and I
Carry a chipped pail to the chicken-run,
Set it down, and stare. All is the wind
Hunting through clouds and forests, thrashing
My apron and the hanging cloths on the line.
Can it be borne, this bodying-forth by wind
Of joy my actions turn on, like a thread
Carrying beads? Shall I be let to sleep
Now this perpetual morning shares my bed?
Can even death dry up
These new delighted lakes, conclude
Our kneeling as cattle by all-generous waters?

Deceptions

Of course I was drugged, and so heavily I did not regain my consciousness till the next morning. I was horrified to discover that I had been ruined, and for some days I was inconsolable, and cried like a child to be killed or sent back to my aunt.

MAYHEW, London Labour and the London Poor

Even so distant, I can taste the grief,
Bitter and sharp with stalks, he made you gulp.
The sun's occasional print, the brisk brief
Worry of wheels along the street outside
Where bridal London bows the other way,
And light, unanswerable and tall and wide,
Forbids the scar to heal, and drives
Shame out of hiding. All the unhurried day
Your mind lay open like a drawer of knives.

Slums, years, have buried you. I would not dare
Console you if I could. What can be said,
Except that suffering is exact, but where
Desire takes charge, readings will grow erratic?
For you would hardly care
That you were less deceived, out on that bed,
Than he was, stumbling up the breathless stair
To burst into fulfilment's desolate attic.

I Remember, I Remember

Coming up England by a different line
For once, early in the cold new year,
We stopped, and, watching men with number-plates
Sprint down the platform to familiar gates,
'Why, Coventry!' I exclaimed. 'I was born here.'

I leant far out, and squinnied for a sign
That this was still the town that had been 'mine'
So long, but found I wasn't even clear
Which side was which. From where those cycle-crates
Were standing, had we annually departed

For all those family hols?...A whistle went:
Things moved. I sat back, staring at my boots.
'Was that,' my friend smiled, 'where you "have your roots"?'
No, only where my childhood was unspent,
I wanted to retort, just where I started:

By now I've got the whole place clearly charted.
Our garden, first: where I did not invent
Blinding theologies of flowers and fruits,
And wasn't spoken to by an old hat.
And here we have that splendid family

I never ran to when I got depressed,
The boys all biceps and the girls all chest,
Their comic Ford, their farm where I could be
'Really myself'. I'll show you, come to that,
The bracken where I never trembling sat,

Determined to go through with it; where she
Lay back, and 'all became a burning mist'.
And, in those offices, my doggerel
Was not set up in blunt ten-point, nor read
By a distinguished cousin of the mayor,

Who didn't call and tell my father *There*
Before us, had we the gift to see ahead –
'You look as if you wished the place in Hell,'
My friend said, 'judging from your face.' 'Oh well,
I suppose it's not the place's fault,' I said.

'Nothing, like something, happens anywhere.'

Mr Bleaney

'This was Mr Bleaney's room. He stayed
The whole time he was at the Bodies, till
They moved him.' Flowered curtains, thin and frayed,
Fall to within five inches of the sill,

Whose window shows a strip of building land,
Tussocky, littered. 'Mr Bleaney took
My bit of garden properly in hand.'
Bed, upright chair, sixty-watt bulb, no hook

Behind the door, no room for books or bags –
'I'll take it.' So it happens that I lie
Where Mr Bleaney lay, and stub my fags
On the same saucer-souvenir, and try

Stuffing my ears with cotton-wool, to drown
The jabbering set he egged her on to buy.
I know his habits – what time he came down,
His preference for sauce to gravy, why

He kept on plugging at the four aways –
Likewise their yearly frame: the Frinton folk
Who put him up for summer holidays,
And Christmas at his sister's house in Stoke.

But if he stood and watched the frigid wind
Tousling the clouds, lay on the fusty bed
Telling himself that this was home, and grinned,
And shivered, without shaking off the dread

That how we live measures our own nature,
And at his age having no more to show
Than one hired box should make him pretty sure
He warranted no better, I don't know.

An Arundel Tomb

Side by side, their faces blurred,
The earl and countess lie in stone,
Their proper habits vaguely shown
As jointed armour, stiffened pleat,
And that faint hint of the absurd –
The little dogs under their feet.

Such plainness of the pre-baroque
Hardly involves the eye, until
It meets his left-hand gauntlet, still
Clasped empty in the other; and
One sees, with a sharp tender shock,
His hand withdrawn, holding her hand.

They would not think to lie so long.
Such faithfulness in effigy
Was just a detail friends would see:
A sculptor's sweet commissioned grace
Thrown off in helping to prolong
The Latin names around the base.

They would not guess how early in
Their supine stationary voyage
The air would change to soundless damage,
Turn the old tenantry away;
How soon succeeding eyes begin
To look, not read. Rigidly they

Persisted, linked, through lengths and breadths
Of time. Snow fell, undated. Light
Each summer thronged the glass. A bright
Litter of birdcalls strewed the same
Bone-riddled ground. And up the paths
The endless altered people came,

Washing at their identity.
Now, helpless in the hollow of
An unarmorial age, a trough
Of smoke in slow suspended skeins
Above their scrap of history,
Only an attitude remains:

Time has transfigured them into
Untruth. The stone fidelity
They hardly meant has come to be
Their final blazon, and to prove
Our almost-instinct almost true:
What will survive of us is love.

The Whitsun Weddings

That Whitsun, I was late getting away:
    Not till about
One-twenty on the sunlit Saturday
Did my three-quarters-empty train pull out,
All windows down, all cushions hot, all sense
Of being in a hurry gone. We ran
Behind the backs of houses, crossed a street
Of blinding windscreens, smelt the fish-dock; thence
The river's level drifting breadth began,
Where sky and Lincolnshire and water meet.

All afternoon, through the tall heat that slept
    For miles inland,
A slow and stopping curve southwards we kept.
Wide farms went by, short-shadowed cattle, and
Canals with floatings of industrial froth;
A hothouse flashed uniquely: hedges dipped
And rose: and now and then a smell of grass
Displaced the reek of buttoned carriage-cloth
Until the next town, new and nondescript,
Approached with acres of dismantled cars.

At first, I didn't notice what a noise
    The weddings made
Each station that we stopped at: sun destroys
The interest of what's happening in the shade,
And down the long cool platforms whoops and skirls
I took for porters larking with the mails,
And went on reading. Once we started, though,
We passed them, grinning and pomaded, girls
In parodies of fashion, heels and veils,
All posed irresolutely, watching us go,

As if out on the end of an event
    Waving goodbye
To something that survived it. Struck, I leant
More promptly out next time, more curiously,
And saw it all again in different terms:
The fathers with broad belts under their suits
And seamy foreheads; mothers loud and fat;

An uncle shouting smut; and then the perms,
The nylon gloves and jewellery-substitutes,
The lemons, mauves, and olive-ochres that

Marked off the girls unreally from the rest.
    Yes, from cafés
And banquet-halls up yards, and bunting-dressed
Coach-party annexes, the wedding-days
Were coming to an end. All down the line
Fresh couples climbed aboard: the rest stood round;
The last confetti and advice were thrown,
And, as we moved, each face seemed to define
Just what it saw departing: children frowned
At something dull; fathers had never known

Success so huge and wholly farcical;
    The women shared
The secret like a happy funeral;
While girls, gripping their handbags tighter, stared
At a religious wounding. Free at last,
And loaded with the sum of all they saw,
We hurried towards London, shuffling gouts of steam.
Now fields were building-plots, and poplars cast
Long shadows over major roads, and for
Some fifty minutes, that in time would seem

Just long enough to settle hats and say
    I nearly died,
A dozen marriages got under way.
They watched the landscape, sitting side by side
– An Odeon went past, a cooling tower,
And someone running up to bowl – and none
Thought of the others they would never meet
Or how their lives would all contain this hour.
I thought of London spread out in the sun,
Its postal districts packed like squares of wheat:

There we were aimed. And as we raced across
    Bright knots of rail
Past standing Pullmans, walls of blackened moss
Came close, and it was nearly done, this frail
Travelling coincidence; and what it held
Stood ready to be loosed with all the power
That being changed can give. We slowed again,

And as the tightened brakes took hold, there swelled
A sense of falling, like an arrow-shower
Sent out of sight, somewhere becoming rain.

MCMXIV

Those long uneven lines
Standing as patiently
As if they were stretched outside
The Oval or Villa Park,
The crowns of hats, the sun
On moustached archaic faces
Grinning as if it were all
An August Bank Holiday lark;

And the shut shops, the bleached
Established names on the sunblinds,
The farthings and sovereigns,
And dark-clothed children at play
Called after kings and queens,
The tin advertisements
For cocoa and twist, and the pubs
Wide open all day;

And the countryside not caring:
The place-names all hazed over
With flowering grasses, and fields
Shadowing Domesday lines
Under wheat's restless silence;
The differently-dressed servants
With tiny rooms in huge houses,
The dust behind limousines;

Never such innocence,
Never before or since,
As changed itself to past
Without a word – the men
Leaving the gardens tidy,
The thousands of marriages
Lasting a little while longer:
Never such innocence again.

Friday Night in the Royal Station Hotel

Light spreads darkly downwards from the high
Clusters of lights over empty chairs
That face each other, coloured differently.
Through open doors, the dining-room declares
A larger loneliness of knives and glass
And silence laid like carpet. A porter reads
An unsold evening paper. Hours pass,
And all the salesmen have gone back to Leeds,
Leaving full ashtrays in the Conference Room.

In shoeless corridors, the lights burn. How
Isolated, like a fort, it is –
The headed paper, made for writing home
(If home existed) letters of exile: *Now
Night comes on. Waves fold behind villages.*

Cut Grass

Cut grass lies frail:
Brief is the breath
Mown stalks exhale.
Long, long the death

It dies in the white hours
Of young-leafed June
With chestnut flowers,
With hedges snowlike strewn,

White lilac bowed,
Lost lanes of Queen Anne's lace,
And that high-builded cloud
Moving at summer's pace.

IAN HAMILTON FINLAY

(*born* 1925)

Ian Hamilton Finlay was born in the Bahamas. His family returned to Scotland, where he has lived ever since. Finlay's work as poet, artist and creator of a famous garden – 'Little Sparta' – is all of a piece, and challenges the way in which we categorise art-forms. The garden contains poems and texts carved in stone, ceramic and wood. This is one way of making "concrete poetry" or making poetry concrete. Like Edwin Morgan, Finlay found in concrete poetry and American poets (such as Louis Zukofsky and Robert Creeley) potential liberation from the expected categories of Scottish literature. Yet his early lyrics, such as 'Orkney Interior', had already obliquely rebelled against the epic scale which Hugh MacDiarmid was then holding out as a goal for Scottish poets. 'Orkney Interior' combines surrealism with Scottish "feyness" in a manner that resists (obvious) social and political purpose. In fact, Finlay's experimental poems have something in common with early MacDiarmid, but he distils Scottish landscape and its spiritual horizons into a greater purity. As with Little Sparta, the impulse here seems visionary and utopian. Unlike Morgan, Finlay moved away from syntax and any pronounced appeal to the ear so that word and image could come as close together as possible. Yet, as in the boat-litany of 'Green Waters', his rhythms retain a subtle music. We are compelled both to see and hear his briefest poems, with their aural and visual puns, and they become haunting mantras. Morgan refers to Finlay's 'not-quite-innocent eye asking us humorously and gently to look at simple things'.

Green Waters

Green Waters
Blue Spray
Grayfish

Anna T
Karen B
Netta Croan

Constant Star
Daystar
Starwood

Starlit Waters
Moonlit Waters
Drift

Orkney Interior

Doing what the moon says, he shifts his chair
Closer to the stove and stokes it up
With the very best fuel, a mixture of dried fish
And tobacco he keeps in a bucket with crabs

Too small to eat. One raises its pincer
As if to seize hold of the crescent moon
On the calendar which is almost like a zodiac
With inexplicable and pallid blanks. Meanwhile

A lobster is crawling towards the clever
Bait that is set inside the clock
On the shelf by the wireless – an inherited dried fish
Soaked in whiskey and carefully trimmed

With potato flowers from the Golden Wonders
The old man grows inside his ears.
Click! goes the clock-lid, and the unfortunate lobster
Finds itself a prisoner inside the clock,

An adapted cuckoo-clock. It shows no hours, only
Tides and moons and is fitted out
With two little saucers, one of salt and one of water
For the lobster to live on while, each quarter-tide,

It must stick its head through the tiny trapdoor
Meant for the cuckoo. It will be trained to read
The broken barometer and wave its whiskers
To Scottish Dance Music, till it grows too old.

Then the old man will have to catch himself another lobster.
Meanwhile he is happy and takes the clock
Down to the sea. He stands and oils it
In a little rock pool that reflects the moon.

from One Word Poems

A Grey Shore Between Day and Night
dusk

The Stones of the Field are the Birds of the Air
peewits

The Cloud's Anchor
swallow

Curfew
curlew

Deep-Vee Hull
geese

The Boat's Blueprint
water

A Patch for a Rip-tide
sail

Dove

Dove, dead in its snows

Late Night Shipping Forecast

A shoal
of names
in nets
of rain

JOHN MONTAGUE

(*born* 1929)

John Montague was born in Brooklyn and grew up as a Catholic in Co. Tyrone. Montague's sequence, *The Rough Field* (1972) represents his home place, Garvaghey (literally, 'rough field'), as a microcosm of the Northern Irish "Troubles": their historical origins in repression and bigotry, their contemporary horror. (The Garvaghey Road later became a focus for Catholic resistance to Orange parades.) As his *Collected Poems* (1995) indicates, Montague also brings perspectives and structures to bear from outside Ireland. After leaving University College Dublin, he lived in France and in America. Influenced by the Black Mountain poets Charles Olson and Robert Creeley, he describes himself as attracted both to their 'open-form' and to 'rooted poets' like Hugh MacDiarmid. In miniature, 'Windharp' connects the two poles. Seamus Heaney, who has learned from Montague's landscapes, sees them as 'suffusing' the present with the past, and his poetic demeanour as that of 'a survivor, a repository, a bearer and keeper of what had almost been lost'. This is so even in an early lyric such as 'The Water Carrier'. The poem suggests more than its own source in 'memoried life'. Its 'pure' and 'rust-tinged' water, the sensations concentrated into 'heavy greenness', symbolise poetic and human sources more generally. Montague does, in fact, 'stylise' this scene, and other poems below also show his capacity to hold out images for our inspection and make them emblematic. In 'The Trout' slow-moving lines mimic slow motion and 'photographic calm'. His celebrated love poem 'All Legendary Obstacles' also moves from anticipation to an intense climax, partly by switching the perspective to make us look through the old lady's 'neat circle'.

The Water Carrier

Twice daily I carried water from the spring,
Morning before leaving for school, and evening;
Balanced as a fulcrum between two buckets.

A bramble-rough path ran to the river
Where you stepped carefully across slime-topped stones,
With corners abraded as bleakly white as bones.

At the widening pool (for washing and cattle)
Minute fish flickered as you dipped,
Circling to fill, with rust-tinged water.

The second or enamel bucket was for spring water
Which, after racing through a rushy meadow,
Came bubbling in a broken drain-pipe,

Corroded wafer thin with rust.
It ran so pure and cold, it fell
Like manacles of ice on the wrists.

You stood until the bucket brimmed
Inhaling the musty smell of unpicked berries,
That heavy greenness fostered by water.

Recovering the scene, I had hoped to stylise it,
Like the portrait of an Egyptian water carrier:
But pause, entranced by slight but memoried life.

I sometimes come to take the water there,
Not as return or refuge, but some pure thing,
Some living source, half-imagined and half-real,

Pulses in the fictive water that I feel.

The Trout
(for Barrie Cooke)

Flat on the bank I parted
Rushes to ease my hands
In the water without a ripple
And tilt them slowly downstream
To where he lay, tendril-light,
In his fluid sensual dream.

Bodiless lord of creation,
I hung briefly above him
Savouring my own absence,
Senses expanding in the slow
Motion, the photographic calm
That grows before action.

As the curve of my hands
Swung under his body
He surged, with visible pleasure.
I was so preternaturally close
I could count every stipple
But still cast no shadow, until

The two palms crossed in a cage
Under the lightly pulsing gills.
Then (entering my own enlarged
Shape, which rode on the water)
I gripped. To this day I can
Taste his terror on my hands.

All Legendary Obstacles

All legendary obstacles lay between
Us, the long imaginary plain,
The monstrous ruck of mountains
And, swinging across the night,
Flooding the Sacramento, San Joaquin,
The hissing drift of winter rain.

All day I waited, shifting
Nervously from station to bar
As I saw another train sail
By, the San Francisco Chief or
Golden Gate, water dripping
From great flanged wheels.

At midnight you came, pale
Above the negro porter's lamp.
I was too blind with rain
And doubt to speak, but
Reached from the platform
Until our chilled hands met.

You had been travelling for days
With an old lady, who marked
A neat circle on the glass
With her glove, to watch us
Move into the wet darkness
Kissing, still unable to speak.

Windharp
(for Patrick Collins)

The sounds of Ireland,
that restless whispering
you never get away
from, seeping out of
low bushes and grass,
heatherbells and fern,
wrinkling bog pools,
scraping tree branches,
light hunting cloud,
sound hounding sight,
a hand ceaselessly
combing and stroking
the landscape, till
the valley gleams
like the pile upon
a mountain pony's coat.

THOM GUNN

(*born* 1929)

In the 1980s Thom Gunn 'came across a reference to myself as an Anglo-American poet and I thought, "Yes, that's what I am. I'm an Anglo-American poet".' Gunn grew up in Hampstead. His mother committed suicide when he was 15: the unbearable tragedy evoked by 'The Gas-poker'. In 1950, after two years of National Service, Gunn entered Cambridge University to study English. He was stimulated by F.R. Leavis's advocacy of concrete realisation through form; and, like other poets of his generation, by Elizabethan drama and the Jacobean lyric. Also, for Gunn, Yeats's *Collected Poems* (1950) ended the idea that 'Eliot was *the* modern poet...suddenly here was somebody as good or better...someone with a lot more vigour, a bigger range, and more exciting'. The two early sonnets below suggest these influences together with that of Auden. 'From the Highest Camp', a concealed comment on Gunn's need (at that time) to conceal his homosexuality, sustains its allegory with a passionate wit that recalls Donne. In 1954 Gunn went to Stanford University, San Francisco, and he eventually settled in California. His third collection *My Sad Captains* (1961) showed that his initial grouping with Larkin and the English 'Movement' poets had been thrown into question by his interest in William Carlos Williams and younger American Modernists. Syllabic poems like 'Considering the Snail', held together by a strict syllable count rather than iambic rhythm, were Gunn's bridge to free verse: they 'allowed me to enter something much more relaxed, much less tense, something more colloquial'. Some critics think that Gunn's Californian poetry became a little too relaxed, but *The Man with Night Sweats* (1992), and *Boss Cupid* (2000) vindicate his (Anglo-American) aesthetic of moving, as he says, between 'the open and the closed – spontaneity and finish'. These collections, which mourn friends who have died from AIDS, are also shaped by the values that 'for humanist atheists like myself...arise in confrontation with death'.

Lerici

Shelley was drowned near here. Arms at his side
He fell submissive through the waves, and he
Was but a minor conquest of the sea:
The darkness that he met was nurse not bride.

Others make gestures with arms open wide,
Compressing in the minute before death
What great expense of muscle and of breath
They would have made if they had never died.

Byron was worth the sea's pursuit. His touch
Was masterful to water, audience
To which he could react until an end.
Strong swimmers, fishermen, explorers: such
Dignify death by thriftless violence –
Squandering with so little left to spend.

From the Highest Camp

Nothing in this bright region melts or shifts.
The local names are concepts: the Ravine,
Pemmican Ridge, North Col, Death Camp, they mean
The streetless rise, the dazzling abstract drifts,
To which particular names adhere by chance,
From custom lightly, not from character.
We stand on a white terrace and confer;
This is the last camp of experience.

What is that sudden yelp upon the air?
And whose are these cold droppings? whose malformed
Purposeless tracks about the slope? We know.
The abominable endures, existing where
Nothing else can: it is – unfed, unwarmed –
Born of rejection, of the boundless snow.

Considering the Snail

The snail pushes through a green
night, for the grass is heavy
with water and meets over
the bright path he makes, where rain
has darkened the earth's dark. He
moves in a wood of desire,

pale antlers barely stirring
as he hunts. I cannot tell
what power is at work, drenched there
with purpose, knowing nothing.
What is a snail's fury? All
I think is that if later

I parted the blades above
the tunnel and saw the thin
trail of broken white across
litter, I would never have
imagined the slow passion
to that deliberate progress.

To Isherwood Dying

It could be, Christopher, from your leafed-in house
In Santa Monica where you lie and wait
       You hear outside a sound resume
            Fitful, anonymous,
       Of Berlin fifty years ago
       As autumn days got late –
The whistling to their girls from young men who
       Stood in the deep dim street, below
Dingy façades which crumbled like a cliff,
       Behind which in a rented room
            You listened, wondering if
By chance one might be whistling up for you,
       Adding unsentimentally
            'It could not possibly be.'
Now it's a stricter vigil that you hold
And from the canyon's palms and crumbled gold
       It could be possibly
       You hear a single whistle call
            Come out
            Come out into the cold.
Courting insistent and impersonal.

[Christmas week, 1985]

Still Life

I shall not soon forget
The greyish-yellow skin
To which the face had set:
Lids tight: nothing of his,
No tremor from within,
Played on the surfaces.

He still found breath, and yet
It was an obscure knack.
I shall not soon forget
The angle of his head,
Arrested and reared back
On the crisp field of bed,

Back from what he could neither
Accept, as one opposed,
Nor, as a life-long breather,
Consentingly let go,
The tube his mouth enclosed
In an astonished O.

The Gas-poker

Forty-eight years ago
– Can it be forty-eight
Since then? – they forced the door
Which she had barricaded
With a full bureau's weight
Lest anyone find, as they did,
What she had blocked it for.

She had blocked the doorway so,
To keep the children out.
In her red dressing-gown
She wrote notes, all night busy
Pushing the things about,
Thinking till she was dizzy,
Before she had lain down.

The children went to and fro
On the harsh winter lawn
Repeating their lament,
A burden, to each other
In the December dawn,
Elder and younger brother,
Till they knew what it meant.

Knew all there was to know.
Coming back off the grass
To the room of her release,
They who had been her treasures
Knew to turn off the gas,
Take the appropriate measures,
Telephone the police.

One image from the flow
Sticks in the stubborn mind:
A sort of backwards flute.
The poker that she held up
Breathed from the holes aligned
Into her mouth till, filled up
By its music, she was mute.

Epitaph
carved in the AIDS Memorial Grove, Golden Gate Park

Walker within this circle, pause.
Although they all died of one cause,
Remember how their lives were dense
With fine, compacted difference.

TED HUGHES

(1930–1998)

Ted Hughes spent his first seven years in the Calder Valley which he mythologises in *Remains of Elmet* (1979) as 'the last British Celtic kingdom to fall to the Angles'. Despite moving from West to South Yorkshire, he remained haunted by a region that also seemed 'in mourning for the first world war'. His father was one of the few survivors from a locally recruited regiment. 'Wilfred Owen's Photographs', by means of a historical parable, insists on the Great War's continuing significance. Like Thom Gunn, Hughes went to Cambridge (in 1951) after two years of National Service. Unlike Gunn, he felt that the academic study of English was 'killing' his Muse, and switched to archaeology and anthropology. Hughes defined his poetry against the 'Movement' principles which then seemed to fit Larkin and Gunn: 'One of the things those poets had in common I think was the post-war mood of having had enough...enough rhetoric, enough overweening push of any kind, enough of the dark gods, enough of the id.' Hughes, in contrast, was 'all for opening negotiations with whatever happened to be out there'. All his poetic models were Romantic: Yeats's mysticism, Graves's White Goddess, Dylan Thomas. And Hughes's own rejection of narrow nonconformism made him receptive to Lawrence's insistence, in his animal poems, on sensory and unconscious life. A Romantic view of monarchy as symbolising 'an essential centre' in a community lay behind his acceptance of the Poet Laureateship in 1984.

Hughes's early poetry, at its best in *Lupercal* (1960), is powered by strongly stressed mimetic rhythms. Echoes of Anglo-Saxon alliterative metre enrich the texture, and help his rhythms to resist containment by stanzaic pattern: 'Blood is the belly of logic; he will lick...' Similarly, Hughes implies that the human animal should be less contained by logic, society and religion. 'The Otter' (which recalls Edward Thomas's 'The Combe') obliquely mourns human self-estrangement and 'the old shape' of England. For Hughes, writing poetry parallels the way in which a Native American shaman communes with spirit-animals on behalf of his people. His relationship with his wife Sylvia Plath, who committed suicide in 1963, led him to take this mystical or Freudian perspective possibly too far. In *Crow* (1970) and in *Birthday Letters* (1998), which reflects on his life with Plath, Hughes's language of the id and the dark gods can be repetitious. Also, his verse tends to become looser rather than freer. However, *Moortown* (1979), grounded in a Devon farm, renewed (as in 'Ravens') Hughes's true 'magic'. This, for Simon Armitage, was to make marks on a page 'that somehow detailed the absolute matter and manner of a bird or an eel or a foal or a wolf or a bear'.

The Thought-Fox

I imagine this midnight moment's forest:
Something else is alive
Beside the clock's loneliness
And this blank page where my fingers move.

Through the window I see no star:
Something more near
Though deeper within darkness
Is entering the loneliness:

Cold, delicately as the dark snow
A fox's nose touches twig, leaf;
Two eyes serve a movement, that now
And again now, and now, and now

Sets neat prints into the snow
Between trees, and warily a lame
Shadow lags by stump and in hollow
Of a body that is bold to come

Across clearings, an eye,
A widening deepening greenness,
Brilliantly, concentratedly,
Coming about its own business

Till, with a sudden sharp hot stink of fox
It enters the dark hole of the head.
The window is starless still; the clock ticks,
The page is printed.

Wind

This house has been far out at sea all night,
The woods crashing through darkness, the booming hills,
Winds stampeding the fields under the window
Floundering black astride and blinding wet

Till day rose; then under an orange sky
The hills had new places, and wind wielded
Blade-light, luminous black and emerald,
Flexing like the lens of a mad eye.

At noon I scaled along the house-side as far as
The coal-house door. Once I looked up –
Through the brunt wind that dented the balls of my eyes
The tent of the hills drummed and strained its guyrope,

The fields quivering, the skyline a grimace,
At any second to bang and vanish with a flap:
The wind flung a magpie away and a black-
Back gull bent like an iron bar slowly. The house

Rang like some fine green goblet in the note
That any second would shatter it. Now deep
In chairs, in front of the great fire, we grip
Our hearts and cannot entertain book, thought,

Or each other. We watch the fire blazing,
And feel the roots of the house move, but sit on,
Seeing the window tremble to come in,
Hearing the stones cry out under the horizons.

Wilfred Owen's Photographs

When Parnell's Irish in the House
Pressed that the British Navy's cat-
O-nine-tails be abolished, what
Shut against them? It was
Neither Irish nor English nor of that
Decade, but of the species.

Predictably, Parliament
Squared against the motion. As soon
Let the old school tie be rent
Off their necks, and give thanks, as see gone
No shame but a monument –
Trafalgar not better known.

'To discontinue it were as much
As ship not powder and cannonballs
But brandy and women' (Laughter). Hearing which
A witty profound Irishman calls
For a 'cat' into the House, and sits to watch
The gentry fingering its stained tails.

Whereupon...
                    quietly, unopposed,
The motion was passed.

Relic

I found this jawbone at the sea's edge:
There, crabs, dogfish, broken by the breakers or tossed
To flap for half an hour and turn to a crust
Continue the beginning. The deeps are cold:
In that darkness camaraderie does not hold:
Nothing touches but, clutching, devours. And the jaws,
Before they are satisfied or their stretched purpose
Slacken, go down jaws; go gnawn bare. Jaws
Eat and are finished and the jawbone comes to the beach:
This is the sea's achievement; with shells,
Vertebrae, claws, carapaces, skulls.

Time in the sea eats its tail, thrives, casts these
Indigestibles, the spars of purposes
That failed far from the surface. None grow rich
In the sea. This curved jawbone did not laugh
But gripped, gripped and is now a cenotaph.

The Bull Moses

A hoist up and I could lean over
The upper edge of the high half-door,
My left foot ledged on the hinge, and look in at the byre's
Blaze of darkness: a sudden shut-eyed look
Backward into the head.

Blackness is depth
Beyond star. But the warm weight of his breathing,
The ammoniac reek of his litter, the hotly-tongued
Mash of his cud, steamed against me.
Then, slowly, as onto the mind's eye –
The brow like masonry, the deep-keeled neck:
Something come up there onto the brink of the gulf,
Hadn't heard of the world, too deep in itself to be called to,
Stood in sleep. He would swing his muzzle at a fly
But the square of sky where I hung, shouting, waving,
Was nothing to him; nothing of our light
Found any reflection in him.
                              Each dusk the farmer led him
Down to the pond to drink and smell the air,
And he took no pace but the farmer
Led him to take it, as if he knew nothing
Of the ages and continents of his fathers,
Shut, while he wombed, to a dark shed
And steps between his door and the duckpond;
The weight of the sun and the moon and the world hammered
To a ring of brass through his nostrils. He would raise
His streaming muzzle and look out over the meadows,
But the grasses whispered nothing awake, the fetch
Of the distance drew nothing to momentum
In the locked black of his powers. He came strolling gently back,
Paused neither toward the pig-pens on his right,
Nor toward the cow-byres on his left: something
Deliberate in his leisure, some beheld future
Founding in his quiet.
                              I kept the door wide,
Closed it after him and pushed the bolt.

An Otter

I

Underwater eyes, an eel's
Oil of water body, neither fish nor beast is the otter:
    Four-legged yet water-gifted, to outfish fish;
        With webbed feet and long ruddering tail
        And a round head like an old tomcat.

Brings the legend of himself
From before wars or burials, in spite of hounds and vermin-poles;
   Does not take root like the badger. Wanders, cries;
     Gallops along land he no longer belongs to;
     Re-enters the water by melting.

     Of neither water nor land. Seeking
Some world lost when first he dived, that he cannot come at since,
   Takes his changed body into the holes of lakes;
     As if blind, cleaves the stream's push till he licks
     The pebbles of the source; from sea

     To sea crosses in three nights
Like a king in hiding. Crying to the old shape of the starlit land,
   Over sunken farms where the bats go round,
     Without answer. Till light and birdsong come
     Walloping up roads with the milk wagon.

   II

The hunt's lost him. Pads on mud,
Among sedges, nostrils a surface bead,
The otter remains, hours. The air,
Circling the globe, tainted and necessary,

Mingling tobacco-smoke, hounds and parsley,
Comes carefully to the sunk lungs.
So the self under the eye lies,
Attendant and withdrawn. The otter belongs

In double robbery and concealment –
From water that nourishes and drowns, and from land
That gave him his length and the mouth of the hound.
He keeps fat in the limpid integument

Reflections live on. The heart beats thick,
Big trout muscle out of the dead cold;
Blood is the belly of logic; he will lick
The fishbone bare. And can take stolen hold

On a bitch otter in a field full
Of nervous horses, but linger nowhere.
Yanked above hounds, reverts to nothing at all,
To this long pelt over the back of a chair.

Full Moon and Little Frieda

A cool small evening shrunk to a dog bark and the clank of a
        bucket –

And you listening.
A spider's web, tense for the dew's touch.
A pail lifted, still and brimming – mirror
To tempt a first star to a tremor.

Cows are going home in the lane there, looping the hedges with
        their warm wreaths of breath –
A dark river of blood, many boulders,
Balancing unspilled milk.

'Moon!' you cry suddenly, 'Moon! Moon!'

The moon has stepped back like an artist gazing amazed at a work

That points at him amazed.

Ravens

As we came through the gate to look at the few new lambs
On the skyline of lawn smoothness,
A raven bundled itself into air from midfield
And slid away under hard glistenings, low and guilty.
Sheep nibbling, kneeling to nibble the reluctant nibbled grass.
Sheep staring, their jaws pausing to think, then chewing again,
Then pausing. Over there a new lamb
Just getting up, bumping its mother's nose
As she nibbles the sugar coating off it
While the tattered banners of her triumph swing and drip from
        her rear-end.
She sneezes and a glim of water flashes from her rear-end.
She sneezes again and again, till she's emptied.
She carries on investigating her new present and seeing how it works.

Over here is something else. But you are still interested
In that new one, and its new spark of voice,
And its tininess.
Now over here, where the raven was,
Is what interests you next. Born dead,
Twisted like a scarf, a lamb of an hour or two,
Its insides, the various jellies and crimsons and transparencies
And threads and tissues pulled out
In straight lines, like tent ropes
From its upward belly opened like a lamb-wool slipper,
The fine anatomy of silvery ribs on display and the cavity,
The head also emptied through the eye-sockets,
The woolly limbs swathed in birth-yolk and impossible
To tell now which in all this field of quietly nibbling sheep
Was its mother. I explain
That it died being born. We should have been here, to help it.
So it died being born. 'And did it cry?' you cry.
I pick up the dangling greasy weight by the hooves soft as dogs' pads
That had trodden only womb-water
And its raven-drawn strings dangle and trail,
Its loose head joggles, and 'Did it cry?' you cry again.
Its two-fingered feet splay in their skin between the pressures
Of my fingers and thumb. And there is another,
Just born, all black, splaying its tripod, inching its new points
Towards its mother, and testing the note
It finds in its mouth. But you have eyes now
Only for the tattered bundle of throwaway lamb.
'Did it cry?' you keep asking, in a three-year-old field-wide
Piercing persistence. 'Oh yes' I say 'it cried.'

Though this one was lucky insofar
As it made the attempt into a warm wind
And its first day of death was blue and warm
The magpies gone quiet with domestic happiness
And skylarks not worrying about anything
And the blackthorn budding confidently
And the skyline of hills, after millions of hard years,
Sitting soft.

GEOFFREY HILL

(*born* 1932)

Geoffrey Hill grew up in Worcestershire. An only child, he took to composing poetry during walks in the countryside. In 1950 he entered Oxford University to study English. A Professor of English, now attached to Boston University, Hill is perhaps the most complex poet-critic since William Empson. His criticism (as in *The Lords of Limit*, 1984) centres on the relation between language and moral responsibility, poetry and truth. He sees the poet's craft as the means whereby 'the inertia of language, which is also the coercive force of language' might be overcome. Preoccupied with the Great War and the Holocaust, he admires the linguistic scrupulousness with which Sorley and Douglas counter 'inertia' and 'coercion'. When Hill discusses his own poetry as 'religious' poetry, related scruples appear: 'one is trying to make lyrical poetry out of... the sense of not being able to grasp true religious experience'.

Hill's first collection *For the Unfallen* (1959), along with Larkin's *The Less Deceived* and Hughes's *Lupercal*, formed a trinity of widely influential collections at the end of the 1950s. Hill was radical in returning humanity to a cosmic stage between heaven and hell. In 'Genesis' he aligns God creating the world with the poet creating words. This brings home the significance of Christ's incarnation: 'There is no bloodless myth will hold.' The poem's vigorous rhythms suggest the spirit breathing upon matter. Similarly, 'God's Little Mountain' conveys 'a region of pure force'. In 'Lachrimae' Hill reinvents Donne's drama (in his 'Holy Sonnets') of man struggling to admit God. The epigraph comes from the Catholic martyr, St Robert Southwell, whose combination of 'discipline' and 'wildness' Hill admires. 'Atonement' in the first sonnet signals Hill's desire for its root meaning 'at-one-ment'. This desire is cultural as well as religious; directed at Englishness as well as Anglicanism. Besides his acute historical sense of the English language and English poetry, Hill makes other approaches to 'Platonic England'. He layers several Englands in the prose poems of *Mercian Hymns* (1971) and in 'An Apology for the Revival of Christian Architecture' (the title alludes to a 19th century debate about building-styles for churches). In *Mercian Hymns* boyhood memories of wartime England mingle, often amusingly, with the career of Offa, the 8th century King of Mercia. In 'An Apology' symbolic houses suggest that the condition of England is a state of deadlock. A corrupt yet nostalgically drawn English past faces 'the half-built ruins' of the present.

Genesis

I

Against the burly air I strode
Crying the miracles of God.

And first I brought the sea to bear
Upon the dead weight of the land;
And the waves flourished at my prayer,
The rivers spawned their sand.

And where the streams were salt and full
The tough pig-headed salmon strove,
Ramming the ebb, in the tide's pull,
To reach the steady hills above.

II

The second day I stood and saw
The osprey plunge with triggered claw,
Feathering blood along the shore,
To lay the living sinew bare.

And the third day I cried: 'Beware
The soft-voiced owl, the ferret's smile,
The hawk's deliberate stoop in air,
Cold eyes, and bodies hooped in steel,
Forever bent upon the kill.'

III

And I renounced, on the fourth day,
This fierce and unregenerate clay,

Building as a huge myth for man
The watery Leviathan,

And made the long-winged albatross
Scour the ashes of the sea
Where Capricorn and Zero cross,
A brooding immortality –
Such as the charmed phoenix has
In the unwithering tree.

IV

The phoenix burns as cold as frost;
And, like a legendary ghost,
The phantom-bird goes wild and lost,
Upon a pointless ocean tossed.

So, the fifth day, I turned again
To flesh and blood and the blood's pain.

V

On the sixth day, as I rode
In haste about the works of God,
With spurs I plucked the horse's blood.

By blood we live, the hot, the cold,
To ravage and redeem the world:
There is no bloodless myth will hold.

And by Christ's blood are men made free
Though in close shrouds their bodies lie
Under the rough pelt of the sea;

Though Earth has rolled beneath her weight
The bones that cannot bear the light.

God's Little Mountain

Below, the river scrambled like a goat
Dislodging stones. The mountain stamped its foot,
Shaking, as from a trance. And I was shut
With wads of sound into a sudden quiet.

I thought the thunder had unsettled heaven,
All was so still. And yet the sky was riven
By flame that left the air cold and engraven.
I waited for the word that was not given,

Pent up into a region of pure force,
Made subject to the pressure of the stars;
I saw the angels lifted like pale straws;
I could not stand before those winnowing eyes

And fell, until I found the world again.
Now I lack grace to tell what I have seen;
For though the head frames words the tongue has none.
And who will prove the surgeon to this stone?

Merlin

I will consider the outnumbering dead:
For they are the husks of what was rich seed.
Now, should they come together to be fed,
They would outstrip the locusts' covering tide.

Arthur, Elaine, Mordred; they are all gone
Among the raftered galleries of bone.
By the long barrows of Logres they are made one,
And over their city stands the pinnacled corn.

In Memory of Jane Fraser

When snow like sheep lay in the fold
And winds went begging at each door,
And the far hills were blue with cold,
And a cold shroud lay on the moor,

She kept the siege. And every day
We watched her brooding over death
Like a strong bird above its prey.
The room filled with the kettle's breath.

Damp curtains glued against the pane
Sealed time away. Her body froze
As if to freeze us all, and chain
Creation to a stunned repose.

She died before the world could stir.
In March the ice unloosed the brook
And water ruffled the sun's hair.
Dead cones upon the alder shook.

Ovid in the Third Reich

non peccat, quaecumque potest peccasse negare,
solaque famosam culpa professa facit.

AMORES, III, XIV

I love my work and my children. God
Is distant, difficult. Things happen.
Too near the ancient troughs of blood
Innocence is no earthly weapon.

I have learned one thing: not to look down
So much upon the damned. They, in their sphere,
Harmonise strangely with the divine
Love. I, in mine, celebrate the love-choir.

from Mercian Hymns

I

King of the perennial holly-groves, the riven sandstone: overlord of
the M5: architect of the historic rampart and ditch, the citadel
at Tamworth, the summer hermitage in Holy Cross: guardian of
the Welsh Bridge and the Iron Bridge: contractor to the desirable
new estates: saltmaster: money-changer: commissioner for oaths:
martyrologist: the friend of Charlemagne.

'I liked that,' said Offa, 'sing it again.'

VI

The princes of Mercia were badger and raven. Thrall to their free-
dom, I dug and hoarded. Orchards fruited above clefts. I drank
from honeycombs of chill sandstone.

'A boy at odds in the house, lonely among brothers.' But I, who had
none, fostered a strangeness; gave myself to unattainable toys.

Candles of gnarled resin, apple-branches, the tacky mistletoe. 'Look'
they said and again 'look.' But I ran slowly; the landscape flowed
away, back to its source.

In the schoolyard, in the cloakrooms, the children boasted their
scars of dried snot; wrists and knees garnished with impetigo.

XIV

Dismissing reports and men, he put pressure on the wax, blistered it to a crest. He threatened malefactors with ash from his noon cigar.

When the sky cleared above Malvern, he lingered in his orchard; by the quiet hammer-pond. Trout-fry simmered there, translucent, as though forming the water's underskin. He had a care for natural minutiae. What his gaze touched was his tenderness. Woodlice sat pellet-like in the cracked bark and a snail sugared its new stone.

At dinner, he relished the mockery of drinking his family's health. He did this whenever it suited him, which was not often.

XXII

We ran across the meadow scabbed with cow-dung, past the crab-apple trees and camouflaged nissen hut. It was curfew-time for our war-band.

At home the curtains were drawn. The wireless boomed its commands. I loved the battle-anthems and the gregarious news.

Then, in the earthy shelter, warmed by a blue-glassed storm-lantern, I huddled with stories of dragon-tailed airships and warriors who took wing immortal as phantoms.

from Lachrimae
OR
Seven tears figured in seven passionate Pavans

> *Passions I allow, and loves I approve, onely*
> *I would wishe that men would alter their*
> *object and better their intent.*
>
> ST ROBERT SOUTHWELL,
> Marie Magdalens Funeral Teares, 1591.

1 *Lachrimae Verae*

Crucified Lord, you swim upon your cross
and never move. Sometimes in dreams of hell
the body moves but moves to no avail
and is at one with that eternal loss.

You are the castaway of drowned remorse,
you are the world's atonement on the hill.
This is your body twisted by our skill
into a patience proper for redress.

I cannot turn aside from what I do;
you cannot turn away from what I am.
You do not dwell in me nor I in you

however much I pander to your name
or answer to your lords of revenue,
surrendering the joys that they condemn.

7 *Lachrimae Amantis*

What is there in my heart that you should sue
so fiercely for its love? What kind of care
brings you as though a stranger to my door
through the long night and in the icy dew

seeking the heart that will not harbour you,
that keeps itself religiously secure?
At this dark solstice filled with frost and fire
your passion's ancient wounds must bleed anew.

So many nights the angel of my house
has fed such urgent comfort through a dream,
whispered 'your lord is coming, he is close'

that I have drowsed half-faithful for a time
bathed in pure tones of promise and remorse:
'tomorrow I shall wake to welcome him.'

from An Apology for the Revival of Christian Architecture in England

9 *The Laurel Axe*

Autumn resumes the land, ruffles the woods
with smoky wings, entangles them. Trees shine
out from their leaves, rocks mildew to moss-green;
the avenues are spread with brittle floods.

Platonic England, house of solitudes,
rests in its laurels and its injured stone,
replete with complex fortunes that are gone,
beset by dynasties of moods and clouds.

It stands, as though at ease with its own world,
the mannerly extortions, languid praise,
all that devotion long since bought and sold,

the rooms of cedar and soft-thudding baize,
tremulous boudoirs where the crystals kissed
in cabinets of amethyst and frost.

11 *Idylls of the King*

The pigeon purrs in the wood; the wood has gone;
dark leaves that flick to silver in the gust,
and the marsh-orchids and the heron's nest,
goldgrimy shafts and pillars of the sun.

Weightless magnificence upholds the past.
Cement recesses smell of fur and bone
and berries wrinkle in the badger-run
and wiry heath-fern scatters its fresh rust.

'O clap your hands' so that the dove takes flight,
bursts through the leaves with an untidy sound,
plunges its wings into the green twilight

above this long-sought and forsaken ground,
the half-built ruins of the new estate,
warheads of mushrooms round the filter-pond.

SYLVIA PLATH
(1932–1963)

Sylvia Plath grew up in New England. Her father died when she was eight. His absence contributes to a poetic drama of insecurity in which the female persona at once desires and resists traditional roles. In 1950 Plath entered Smith College. Pressures to conform to both a feminine and academic ideal, together with her intense literary ambition, created further conflicts. Obsessive over-achievement led to her breakdown and attempted suicide in 1953: these events figure in Plath's novel *The Bell Jar* (1963). In 1955 Plath went to Cambridge on a Fulbright scholarship, and met Ted Hughes. They married in 1956. It was also a marriage of literary influences (Yeats, Dylan Thomas, Marianne Moore...). Plath learned from Hughes's concreteness, but the dialogue between their poems exposes significant differences. Plath speaks for the interior workings of the unconscious forces which Hughes (to some extent) distances by embodying them in animal life. Plath separated from Hughes in 1962. In February 1963 she committed suicide. The selection here mostly represents the powerful poems that Plath wrote during the last three years of her life, first collected in *Ariel* (1965).

The legend of Sylvia Plath's life and death – revived by Hughes's *Birthday Letters* (1998) and the publication of her full *Journals* (2000) – can get in the way of her poetry. This is so, even though her poetry, like her journal, mythologises her life. In 1959 she noted: 'My main thing now is to start with real things: real emotions, and leave out the baby gods...the moon-mothers, the mad maudlins...and get into me, Ted, friends, mother and brother and father and family. The real world. Real situations, behind which the great gods play the drama of blood, lust and death.' Here Plath resolves to stop imposing minor myths on her material. But she correctly anticipates that her poetry of 'real things' will have a grander mythic backdrop rather than none at all. For example, when she speaks as a mother, she conveys the elemental rather than domestic meaning of that state. Further, maternity and poetry are entangled in her work. Sometimes this suggests creative fertility ('Metaphors'), sometimes the reverse ('Stillborn'), sometimes a chilling sense that motherhood and bodily life must be sacrificed for the sake of artistic 'perfection' ('Edge'). Yet Plath's poetry is also 'accomplished' in a positive way. Hughes refers to her 'mosaic kind of patterning of almost separate, distinctive units of meaning'. Her verse-patterns, however, are extremely various. They range from compressed catalogues to copious stanzas – as in 'The Bee Meeting'. This dramatic monologue transforms a 'real' event into a nightmare which delivers the dissociated speaker to 'the great gods': 'They are leading me to the shorn grove'. Plath often seems to represent life from somewhere outside it. Hence both the darkness and the vividness of her vision.

Metaphors

I'm a riddle in nine syllables,
An elephant, a ponderous house,
A melon strolling on two tendrils.
O red fruit, ivory, fine timbers!
This loaf's big with its yeasty rising.
Money's new-minted in this fat purse.
I'm a means, a stage, a cow in calf.
I've eaten a bag of green apples,
Boarded the train there's no getting off.

You're

Clownlike, happiest on your hands,
Feet to the stars, and moon-skulled,
Gilled like a fish. A common-sense
Thumbs-down on the dodo's mode.
Wrapped up in yourself like a spool,
Trawling your dark as owls do.
Mute as a turnip from the Fourth
Of July to All Fools' Day,
O high-riser, my little loaf.

Vague as fog and looked for like mail.
Farther off than Australia.
Bent-backed Atlas, our travelled prawn.
Snug as a bud and at home
Like a sprat in a pickle jug.
A creel of eels, all ripples.
Jumpy as a Mexican bean.
Right, like a well-done sum.
A clean slate, with your own face on.

Stillborn

These poems do not live: it's a sad diagnosis.
They grew their toes and fingers well enough,
Their little foreheads bulged with concentration.
If they missed out on walking about like people
It wasn't for any lack of mother-love.

O I cannot understand what happened to them!
They are proper in shape and number and every part.
They sit so nicely in the pickling fluid!
They smile and smile and smile and smile at me.
And still the lungs won't fill and the heart won't start.

They are not pigs, they are not even fish,
Though they have a piggy and a fishy air –
It would be better if they were alive, and that's what they were.
But they are dead, and their mother near dead with distraction,
And they stupidly stare, and do not speak of her.

Morning Song

Love set you going like a fat gold watch.
The midwife slapped your footsoles, and your bald cry
Took its place among the elements.

Our voices echo, magnifying your arrival. New statue.
In a drafty museum, your nakedness
Shadows our safety. We stand round blankly as walls.

I'm no more your mother
Than the cloud that distils a mirror to reflect its own slow
Effacement at the wind's hand.

All night your moth-breath
Flickers among the flat pink roses. I wake to listen:
A far sea moves in my ear.

One cry, and I stumble from bed, cow-heavy and floral
In my Victorian nightgown.
Your mouth opens clean as a cat's. The window square

Whitens and swallows its dull stars. And now you try
Your handful of notes;
The clear vowels rise like balloons.

Among the Narcissi

Spry, wry, and gray as these March sticks,
Percy bows, in his blue peajacket, among the narcissi.
He is recuperating from something on the lung.

The narcissi, too, are bowing to some big thing:
It rattles their stars on the green hill where Percy
Nurses the hardship of his stitches, and walks and walks.

There is a dignity to this; there is a formality –
The flowers vivid as bandages, and the man mending.
They bow and stand: they suffer such attacks!

And the octogenarian loves the little flocks.
He is quite blue; the terrible wind tries his breathing.
The narcissi look up like children, quickly and whitely.

The Bee Meeting

Who are these people at the bridge to meet me? They are the
         villagers —
The rector, the midwife, the sexton, the agent for bees.
In my sleeveless summery dress I have no protection,
And they are all gloved and covered, why did nobody tell me?
They are smiling and taking out veils tacked to ancient hats.

I am nude as a chicken neck, does nobody love me?
Yes, here is the secretary of bees with her white shop smock,
Buttoning the cuffs at my wrists and the slit from my neck to my
       knees.
Now I am milkweed silk, the bees will not notice.
They will not smell my fear, my fear, my fear.

Which is the rector now, is it that man in black?
Which is the midwife, is that her blue coat?
Everybody is nodding a square black head, they are knights in visors,
Breastplates of cheesecloth knotted under the armpits.
Their smiles and their voices are changing. I am led through a
       beanfield.

Strips of tinfoil winking like people,
Feather dusters fanning their hands in a sea of bean flowers,
Creamy bean flowers with black eyes and leaves like bored hearts.
Is it blood clots the tendrils are dragging up that string?
No, no, it is scarlet flowers that will one day be edible.

Now they are giving me a fashionable white straw Italian hat
And a black veil that moulds to my face, they are making me one
       of them.
They are leading me to the shorn grove, the circle of hives.
Is it the hawthorn that smells so sick?
The barren body of hawthorn, etherising its children.

Is it some operation that is taking place?
It is the surgeon my neighbours are waiting for,
This apparition in a green helmet,
Shining gloves and white suit.
Is it the butcher, the grocer, the postman, someone I know?

I cannot run, I am rooted, and the gorse hurts me
With its yellow purses, its spiky armoury.
I could not run without having to run forever.
The white hive is snug as a virgin,
Sealing off her brood cells, her honey, and quietly humming.

Smoke rolls and scarves in the grove.
The mind of the hive thinks this is the end of everything.
Here they come, the outriders, on their hysterical elastics.
If I stand very still, they will think I am cow-parsley,
A gullible head untouched by their animosity,

Not even nodding, a personage in a hedgerow.
The villagers open the chambers, they are hunting the queen.
Is she hiding, is she eating honey? She is very clever.
She is old, old, old, she must live another year, and she knows it.
While in their fingerjoint cells the new virgins

Dream of a duel they will win inevitably,
A curtain of wax dividing them from the bride flight,
The upflight of the murderess into a heaven that loves her.
The villagers are moving the virgins, there will be no killing.
The old queen does not show herself, is she so ungrateful?

I am exhausted, I am exhausted —
Pillar of white in a blackout of knives.
I am the magician's girl who does not flinch.
The villagers are untying their disguises, they are shaking hands.
Whose is that long white box in the grove, what have they
        accomplished, why am I cold.

Poppies in October

Even the sun-clouds this morning cannot manage such skirts.
Nor the woman in the ambulance
Whose red heart blooms through her coat so astoundingly —

A gift, a love gift
Utterly unasked for
By a sky

Palely and flamily
Igniting its carbon monoxides, by eyes
Dulled to a halt under bowlers.

O my God, what am I
That these late mouths should cry open
In a forest of frost, in a dawn of cornflowers.

Edge

The woman is perfected.
Her dead

Body wears the smile of accomplishment,
The illusion of a Greek necessity

Flows in the scrolls of her toga,
Her bare

Feet seem to be saying:
We have come so far, it is over.

Each dead child coiled, a white serpent,
One at each little

Pitcher of milk, now empty.
She has folded

Them back into her body as petals
Of a rose close when the garden

Stiffens and odours bleed
From the sweet, deep throats of the night flower.

The moon has nothing to be sad about,
Staring from her hood of bone.

She is used to this sort of thing.
Her blacks crackle and drag.

FLEUR ADCOCK

(*born* 1934)

Fleur Adcock was born in Auckland. She spent the Second World War in England, but returned to New Zealand at the age of 13, later studying Classics at Victoria University, Wellington. In 1963 she decided to leave New Zealand's social constrictions and unchanging weather, and settled in London. Adcock writes of these moves: 'I learned to live with an almost permanent sense of free-floating, unfocused nostalgia, and with the combination of crushed humility and confident arrogance that comes from not quite belonging. It is no bad thing to be an outsider, if one wants to see places and events clearly enough to write about them.' Her poem 'Foreigner' exemplifies that principle. However, Adcock's sense of being 'outside', her knowledge of Classical poetry and wide-ranging alertness to other poetic traditions have too often caused her work to be labelled 'cool' or 'detached'. It is true that her *Poems 1960-2000* (2000) displays a pervasive shaping intelligence which depends on lithe syntax lightly anchored by rhyme or assonance. Again, there is Adcock's attitude to Sylvia Plath. She respects Plath's craft but says: 'I shy away from cults. She's too extreme. She's a bad influence.' 'The Pangolin', indeed, may rebuke Hughes and Plath. However, the speaker does not deny the power of 'hot-blooded beasts', just as 'Things' and 'Excavations' do not deny bad experiences even if they present them as satirical parables. In 'The Ex-Queen Among the Astronomers' the astronomers' detachment is condemned (the ex-queen, Adcock says, 'represents what happens to a certain type of person who is brought up to please men'). When Adcock mentions "Classical" influences like Catullus and Propertius, she highlights 'the way they talked about their love affairs and their agonies and frustrations'. Similarly, she has called form 'a way of just putting a straitjacket around the mad, wailing, hysterical self inside'.

The Pangolin

There have been all those tigers, of course,
and a leopard, and a six-legged giraffe,
and a young deer that ran up to my window
before it was killed, and once a blue horse,
and somewhere an impression of massive dogs.
Why do I dream of such large, hot-blooded beasts
covered with sweating fur and full of passions
when there could be dry lizards and cool frogs,
or slow, modest creatures, as a rest
from all those panting, people-sized animals?

Hedgehogs or perhaps tortoises would do,
but I think the pangolin would suit me best:
a vegetable animal, who goes
disguised as an artichoke or asparagus-tip
in a green coat of close-fitting leaves,
with his flat shovel-tail and his pencil-nose:
the scaly anteater. Yes, he would fit
more aptly into a dream than into his cage
in the Small Mammal House; so I invite him
to be dreamt about, if he would care for it.

Things

There are worse things than having behaved foolishly in public.
There are worse things than these miniature betrayals,
committed or endured or suspected; there are worse things
than not being able to sleep for thinking about them.
It is 5 a.m. All the worse things come stalking in
and stand icily about the bed looking worse and worse and worse.

The Ex-Queen Among the Astronomers

They serve revolving saucer eyes,
dishes of stars; they wait upon
huge lenses hung aloft to frame
the slow procession of the skies.

They calculate, adjust, record,
watch transits, measure distances.
They carry pocket telescopes
to spy through when they walk abroad.

Spectra possess their eyes; they face
upwards, alert for meteorites,
cherishing little glassy worlds:
receptacles for outer space.

But she, exile, expelled, ex-queen,
swishes among the men of science
waiting for cloudy skies, for nights
when constellations can't be seen.

She wears the rings he let her keep;
she walks as she was taught to walk
for his approval, years ago.
His bitter features taunt her sleep.

And so when these have laid aside
their telescopes, when lids are closed
between machine and sky, she seeks
terrestrial bodies to bestride.

She plucks this one or that among
the astronomers, and is become
his canopy, his occultation;
she sucks at earlobe, penis, tongue

mouthing the tubes of flesh; her hair
crackles, her eyes are comet-sparks.
She brings the distant briefly close
above his dreamy abstract stare.

Foreigner

These winds bully me:

I am to lie down in a ditch
quiet under the thrashing nettles
and pull the mud up to my chin.

Not that I would submit so
to one voice only;
but by the voices of these several winds
merged into a flowing fringe of tones
that swirl and comb over the hills
I am compelled.

I shall lie sound-proofed in the mud,
a huge caddis-fly larva,
a face floating upon Egyptian unguents
in a runnel at the bottom of England.

Excavations

Here is a hole full of men shouting
'I don't love you. I loved you once
but I don't now. I went off you,
or I was frightened, or my wife was pregnant,
or I found I preferred men instead.'

What can I say to that kind of talk?
'Thank you for being honest, you
who were so shifty when it happened,
pretending you were suddenly busy
with your new job or your new conscience.'

I chuck them a shovelful of earth
to make them blink for a bit, to smirch
their green eyes and their long lashes
or their brown eyes... Pretty bastards:
the rain will wash their bawling faces

and I bear them little enough ill will.
Now on to the next hole,
covered and fairly well stamped down,
full of the men whom I stopped loving
and didn't always tell at the time –

being, I found, rather busy
with my new man or my new freedom.
These are quiet and unaccusing,
cuddled up with their subsequent ladies,
hardly unsettling the bumpy ground.

Swings and Roundabouts

My ancestors are creeping down from the north –
from Lancashire and the West Riding,
from sites all over Leicestershire,

down through the Midlands; from their solid outpost
in Lincolnshire, and their halts in Rutland,
down through Northants and Beds and Bucks.

They're doing it backwards, through the centuries:
from the Industrial Revolution
they're heading south, past the Enclosures

and the Civil War, through Elizabethan times
to the dissolution of the monasteries,
the Wars of the Roses, and beyond.

From back-to-backs in Manchester they glide
in reverse to stocking-frames in Syston,
from there back to their little farms,

then further back to grander premises,
acquiring coats of arms and schooling
in their regression to higher things.

They're using the motorways; they're driving south
in their armour or their ruffs and doublets
along the M1 and the A1.

They've got as far as the South Mimms roundabout.
A little group in merchants' robes
is filtering through London, aiming

for a manor-house and lands in Chislehurst
across the road from a school I went to;
and somewhere round about Footscray

they'll meet me riding my bike with Lizzie Wood
when I was twelve; they'll rush right through me
and blow the lot of us back to Domesday.

TONY HARRISON

(*born* 1937)

Tony Harrison was born into a working-class family in Leeds. He was educated
at Leeds Grammar School and Leeds University, where he studied Classics.
Harrison formed, he says, a 'grim determination that I would like the whole
venture of my life to be poetry – including earning my living'. He has written
verse plays, film and opera libretti, creating versions of Aeschylus, Racine,
Molière and the English Mystery plays for the National Theatre. This edu-
cational and literary upward mobility became a key theme in his poetry. The
two 16-line 'Meredithian' sonnets below belong to his continuing sequence *The
School of Eloquence*, which defines and fulfils what he terms his 'obsessive
commitment to all forms of articulation', interweaving the lives and deaths of
his parents, their exploitation by the class system, the effects of class on liter-
ature and language, parables of stammering and dumbness. By playing off Leeds
dialect against standard English, Harrison lays claim to 'your lousy leasehold
Poetry'. 'Long Distance' presents a moving counterpoint between his own and
his father's ways of expressing grief, while 'Loving Memory' (from 'Art &
Extinction') registers the need for 'art' to rescue something from 'extinction'
together with the difficulties that it encounters. Harrison has also been effective
as a 'public poet'. For instance, two poems attacking the Gulf War made a stir
when they were published in the *Guardian*. Yet 'A Kumquat for John Keats',
set in Florida, may be his richest work. It distils the positive spirit of his poetic
enterprise and represents his most vital handling of a favourite form, the couplet.
In his early poem 'Them & [uz]' Harrison recalls being rebuked for reading
Keats's 'Ode to a Nightingale' in a Yorkshire accent. Now he addresses Keats
familiarly, as poet to poet. Yet the pulse of celebration, sensory delight and
fulfilled love that impels 'A Kumquat' is countered by autobiographical and
historical images that correspond to the fruit's ambiguously located 'sourness'.

A Kumquat for John Keats

Today I found the right fruit for my prime,
not orange, not tangelo, and not lime,
nor moon-like globes of grapefruit that now hang
outside our bedroom, nor tart lemon's tang
(though last year full of bile and self-defeat
I wanted to believe no life was sweet)
not the tangible sunshine of the tangerine,
and no incongruous citrus ever seen
at greengrocers' in Newcastle or Leeds
mis-spelt by the spuds and mud-caked swedes
a fruit an older poet might substitute
for the grape John Keats thought fit to be Joy's fruit,

when, two years before he died, he tried to write
how Melancholy dwelled inside Delight,
and if he'd known the citrus that I mean
that's not orange, lemon, lime or tangerine,
I'm pretty sure that Keats, though he had heard
'of candied apple, quince and plum and gourd'
instead of 'grape against the palate fine'
would have, if he'd known it, plumped for mine,
this Eastern citrus scarcely cherry size
he'd bite just once and then apostrophise
and pen one stanza how the fruit had all
the qualities of fruit before the Fall,
but in the next few lines be forced to write
how Eve's apple tasted at the second bite,
and if John Keats had only lived to be,
because of extra years, in need like me,
at 42 he'd help me celebrate
that Micanopy kumquat that I ate
whole, straight off the tree, sweet pulp and sour skin –
or was it sweet outside, and sour within?
For however many kumquats that I eat
I'm not sure if it's flesh or rind that's sweet,
and being a man of doubt at life's mid-way
I'd offer Keats some kumquats and I'd say:
You'll find that one part's sweet and one part's tart:
say where the sweetness or the sourness start.
I find I can't, as if one couldn't say
exactly where the night became the day,
which makes for me the kumquat taken whole
best fruit, and metaphor, to fit the soul
of one in Florida at 42 with Keats
crunching kumquats, thinking, as he eats
the flesh, the juice, the pith, the pips, the peel,
that this is how a full life ought to feel,
its perishable relish prick the tongue,
when the man who savours life 's no longer young,
the fruits that were his futures far behind.
Then it's the kumquat fruit expresses best
how days have darkness round them like a rind,
life has a skin of death that keeps its zest.

History, a life, the heart, the brain
flow to the taste buds and flow back again.

That decade or more past Keats's span
makes me an older, not a wiser man,
who knows that it's too late for dying young,
but since youth leaves some sweetnesses unsung,
he's granted days and kumquats to express
Man's Being ripened by his Nothingness.
And it isn't just the gap of sixteen years,
a bigger crop of terrors, hopes and fears,
but a century of history on this earth
between John Keats's death and my own birth –
years like an open crater, gory, grim,
with bloody bubbles leering at the rim;
a thing no bigger than an urn explodes
and ravishes all silence, and all odes,
Flora asphyxiated by foul air
unknown to either Keats or Lemprière,
dehydrated Naiads, Dryad amputees
dragging themselves through slagscapes with no trees,
a shirt of Nessus fire that gnaws and eats
children half the age of dying Keats...

Now were you twenty five or six years old
when that fevered brow at last grew cold?
I've got no books to hand to check the dates.
My grudging but glad spirit celebrates
that all I've got to hand 's the kumquats, John,
the fruit I'd love to have your verdict on,
but dead men don't eat kumquats, or drink wine,
they shiver in the arms of Proserpine,
not warm in bed beside their Fanny Brawne,
nor watch her pick ripe grapefruit in the dawn
as I did, waking, when I saw her twist,
with one deft movement of a sunburnt wrist,
the moon, that feebly lit our last night's walk
past alligator swampland, off its stalk.
I thought of moon-juice juleps when I saw,
as if I'd never seen the moon before,
the planet glow among the fruit, and its pale light
make each citrus on the tree its satellite.

Each evening when I reach to draw the blind
stars seem the light zest squeezed through night's black rind;
the night's peeled fruit the sun, juiced of its rays,

first stains, then streaks, then floods the world with days,
days, when the very sunlight made me weep,
days, spent like the nights in deep, drugged sleep,
days in Newcastle by my daughter's bed,
wondering if she, or I, weren't better dead,
days in Leeds, grey days, my first dark suit,
my mother's wreaths stacked next to Christmas fruit,
and days, like this in Micanopy. Days!

As strong sun burns away the dawn's grey haze
I pick a kumquat and the branches spray
cold dew in my face to start the day.
The dawn's molasses make the citrus gleam
still in the orchards of the groves of dream.
The limes, like Galway after weeks of rain,
glow with a greenness that is close to pain,
the dew-cooled surfaces of fruit that spent
all last night flaming in the firmament.
The new day dawns. O days! My spirit greets
the kumquat with the spirit of John Keats.
O kumquat, comfort for not dying young,
both sweet and bitter, bless the poet's tongue!
I burst the whole fruit chilled by morning dew
against my palate. Fine, for 42!

I search for buzzards as the air grows clear
and see them ride fresh thermals overhead.
Their bleak cries were the first sound I could hear
when I stepped at the start of sunrise out of doors,
and a noise like last night's bedsprings on our bed
from Mr Fowler sharpening farmers' saws.

from Long Distance

Though my mother was already two years dead
Dad kept her slippers warming by the gas,
put hot water bottles her side of the bed
and still went to renew her transport pass.

You couldn't just drop in. You had to phone.
He'd put you off an hour to give him time
to clear away her things and look alone
as though his still raw love were such a crime.

He couldn't risk my blight of disbelief
though sure that very soon he'd hear her key
scrape in the rusted lock and end his grief.
He *knew* she'd just popped out to get the tea.

I believe life ends with death, and that is all.
You haven't both gone shopping; just the same,
in my new black leather phone book there's your name
and the disconnected number I still call.

Loving Memory
(for Teresa Stratas)

The fosses where Caractacus fought Rome
blend with grey bracken and become a blur
above the Swedish Nightingale's last home.

Somehow my need for you makes me seek her.

The Malverns darken as the dusk soaks in.
The rowan berries' dark red glaze grows dull.
The harvest moon's scraped silver and bruised tin
is only one night off from being full.

Death keeps all hours, but graveyards close at nights.
I hurry past the Malvern Hospital
where a nurse goes round small wards and puts on lights
and someone there's last night begins to fall.

'The oldest rocks this earth can boast', these hills,
packed with extinction, make me burn for you.

I ask two women leaving with dead daffodils:
Where's Jenny Lind's grave, please? They both say: *Who?*

SEAMUS HEANEY

(*born* 1939)

Seamus Heaney is one of the few modern poets to reach a wide audience. What 'The Harvest Bow' calls his 'original townland' is Mossbawn, Co. Derry, where his father was a farmer and cattle-dealer. Heaney received a Catholic education at St Columb's College, Derry, and (from 1957) studied English at Queen's University, Belfast. In the early 1960s the Belfast writers' 'Group', run by Philip Hobsbaum, fostered Heaney's talents. In 1972 Heaney left Belfast and a lectureship at Queen's to live in rural Wicklow; he then moved to Dublin. In 1984 he was appointed to a professorship at Harvard. He became Professor of Poetry at Oxford (1989-94). In 1995 he won the Nobel Prize.

Death of a Naturalist (1966) made an extraordinary impact. Heaney's early poetry is aware of various "pastoral" predecessors, including Kavanagh and Hughes. Yet these are absorbed into a wholly distinctive poetic landscape, 'a clean new music'. Unlike Kavanagh, Heaney begins at a point where his 'parish', his 'townland', is not the daily context of adult life. It is a childhood source that becomes fundamental to his poetry: a 'helicon'. Hence, perhaps, the appeal of Hughes, with his emphasis on the senses and the unconscious. Yet if Heaney learned from Hughes's sound-effects, he held more strictly to concentrated stanza-form. When the Northern Irish "Troubles" began in 1969, Heaney looked, he says, for 'images and symbols adequate to our predicament'. For instance, his structures became more archaelogical, more alert to the history carried by language, place-names and images – a history he saw as potentially reconciling. In 'Bogland' memory, as a poetic source, had already become collective.

'Bogland' heralds a series of poems (mainly in *North*, 1975) based on the mummified bodies found in Danish peat bogs: victims of Iron Age ritual or justice. 'The Tollund Man' expresses the profoundly religious spirit in which Heaney seeks to make this symbolism 'adequate' or redemptive (the last section refers to atrocities by Protestant paramilitaries in the 1920s). Perhaps the deepest level of Heaney's Troubles poetry is its quest for healing. His 'Mossbawn' poems and 'The Harvest Bow' offer models of peace that include Heaney's practice and image of his own craft. His poetry works like the 'love-knot of straw' that 'brightens as it tightens twist by twist'. The different texture of 'The Mud Vision' (from *The Haw Lantern*, 1987) is influenced by Edwin Muir's parables. Another source is a Richard Long artwork ('Mud Hand Circles' in the shape of a rose window). At one level, the poem evokes 'the moment of energy, revelation and danger' – Heaney's phrase for 1969. Since the late 1980s Heaney has continued to explore visionary possibilities: 'the marvellous'.

Death of a Naturalist

All year the flax-dam festered in the heart
Of the townland; green and heavy-headed
Flax had rotted there, weighted down by huge sods.

Daily it sweltered in the punishing sun.
Bubbles gargled delicately, bluebottles
Wove a strong gauze of sound around the smell.
There were dragonflies, spotted butterflies,
But best of all was the warm thick slobber
Of frogspawn that grew like clotted water
In the shade of the banks. Here, every spring
I would fill jampotfuls of the jellied
Specks to range on window-sills at home,
On shelves at school, and wait and watch until
The fattening dots burst into nimble-
Swimming tadpoles. Miss Walls would tell us how
The daddy frog was called a bullfrog
And how he croaked and how the mammy frog
Laid hundreds of little eggs and this was
Frogspawn. You could tell the weather by frogs too
For they were yellow in the sun and brown
In rain.

    Then one hot day when fields were rank
With cowdung in the grass the angry frogs
Invaded the flax-dam; I ducked through hedges
To a coarse croaking that I had not heard
Before. The air was thick with a bass chorus.
Right down the dam gross-bellied frogs were cocked
On sods; their loose necks pulsed like sails. Some hopped:
The slap and plop were obscene threats. Some sat
Poised like mud grenades, their blunt heads farting.
I sickened, turned, and ran. The great slime kings
Were gathered there for vengeance and I knew
That if I dipped my hand the spawn would clutch it.

Personal Helicon
(for Michael Longley)

As a child, they could not keep me from wells
And old pumps with buckets and windlasses.
I loved the dark drop, the trapped sky, the smells
Of waterweed, fungus and dank moss.

One, in a brickyard, with a rotted board top.
I savoured the rich crash when a bucket
Plummeted down at the end of a rope.
So deep you saw no reflection in it.

A shallow one under a dry stone ditch
Fructified like any aquarium.
When you dragged out long roots from the soft mulch
A white face hovered over the bottom.

Others had echoes, gave back your own call
With a clean new music in it. And one
Was scaresome, for there, out of ferns and tall
Foxgloves, a rat slapped across my reflection.

Now, to pry into roots, to finger slime,
To stare, big-eyed Narcissus, into some spring
Is beneath all adult dignity. I rhyme
To see myself, to set the darkness echoing.

Bogland
(for T.P. Flanagan)

We have no prairies
To slice a big sun at evening –
Everywhere the eye concedes to
Encroaching horizon,

Is wooed into the cyclops' eye
Of a tarn. Our unfenced country
Is bog that keeps crusting
Between the sights of the sun.

They've taken the skeleton
Of the Great Irish Elk
Out of the peat, set it up,
An astounding crate full of air.

Butter sunk under
More than a hundred years
Was recovered salty and white.
The ground itself is kind, black butter

Melting and opening underfoot,
Missing its last definition
By millions of years.
They'll never dig coal here,

Only the waterlogged trunks
Of great firs, soft as pulp.
Our pioneers keep striking
Inwards and downwards,

Every layer they strip
Seems camped on before.
The bogholes might be Atlantic seepage.
The wet centre is bottomless.

The Tollund Man

I

Some day I will go to Aarhus
To see his peat-brown head,
The mild pods of his eyelids,
His pointed skin cap.

In the flat country nearby
Where they dug him out,
His last gruel of winter seeds
Caked in his stomach,

Naked except for
The cap, noose and girdle,
I will stand a long time.
Bridegroom to the goddess,

She tightened her torc on him
And opened her fen,
Those dark juices working
Him to a saint's kept body,

Trove of the turfcutters'
Honeycombed workings.
Now his stained face
Reposes at Aarhus.

II

I could risk blasphemy,
Consecrate the cauldron bog
Our holy ground and pray
Him to make germinate

The scattered, ambushed
Flesh of labourers,
Stockinged corpses
Laid out in the farmyards,

Tell-tale skin and teeth
Flecking the sleepers
Of four young brothers, trailed
For miles along the lines.

III

Something of his sad freedom
As he rode the tumbril
Should come to me, driving,
Saying the names

Tollund, Grauballe, Nebelgard,
Watching the pointing hands
Of country people,
Not knowing their tongue.

Out there in Jutland
In the old man-killing parishes
I will feel lost,
Unhappy and at home.

Mossbawn: Two Poems in Dedication

(for Mary Heaney)

1 *Sunlight*

There was a sunlit absence.
The helmeted pump in the yard
heated its iron,
water honeyed

in the slung bucket
and the sun stood
like a griddle cooling
against the wall

of each long afternoon.
So, her hands scuffled
over the bakeboard,
the reddening stove

sent its plaque of heat
against her where she stood
in a floury apron
by the window.

Now she dusts the board
with a goose's wing,
now sits, broad-lapped,
with whitened nails

and measling shins:
here is a space
again, the scone rising
to the tick of two clocks.

And here is love
like a tinsmith's scoop
sunk past its gleam
in the meal-bin.

2 *The Seed Cutters*

They seem hundreds of years away. Brueghel,
You'll know them if I can get them true.
They kneel under the hedge in a half-circle
Behind a windbreak wind is breaking through.
They are the seed cutters. The tuck and frill
Of leaf-sprout is on the seed potatoes
Buried under that straw. With time to kill,
They are taking their time. Each sharp knife goes
Lazily halving each root that falls apart
In the palm of the hand: a milky gleam,
And, at the centre, a dark watermark.
Oh, calendar customs! Under the broom
Yellowing over them, compose the frieze
With all of us there, our anonymities.

The Harvest Bow

As you plaited the harvest bow
You implicated the mellowed silence in you
In wheat that does not rust
But brightens as it tightens twist by twist
Into a knowable corona,
A throwaway love-knot of straw.

Hands that aged round ashplants and cane sticks
And lapped the spurs on a lifetime of gamecocks
Harked to their gift and worked with fine intent
Until your fingers moved somnambulant:
I tell and finger it like braille,
Gleaning the unsaid off the palpable.

And if I spy into its golden loops
I see us walk between the railway slopes
Into an evening of long grass and midges,
Blue smoke straight up, old beds and ploughs in hedges,
An auction notice on an outhouse wall –
You with a harvest bow in your lapel,

Me with the fishing rod, already homesick
For the big lift of these evenings, as your stick
Whacking the tips off weeds and bushes
Beats out of time, and beats, but flushes
Nothing: that original townland
Still tongue-tied in the straw tied by your hand.

The end of art is peace
Could be the motto of this frail device
That I have pinned up on our deal dresser –
Like a drawn snare
Slipped lately by the spirit of the corn
Yet burnished by its passage, and still warm.

The Mud Vision

Statues with exposed hearts and barbed-wire crowns
Still stood in alcoves, hares flitted beneath
The dozing bellies of jets, our menu-writers
And punks with aerosol sprays held their own
With the best of them. Satellite link-ups
Wafted over us the blessings of popes, heliports
Maintained a charmed circle for idols on tour
And casualties on their stretchers. We sleepwalked
The line between panic and formulae, screentested
Our first native models and the last of the mummers,
Watching ourselves at a distance, advantaged
And airy as a man on a springboard
Who keeps limbering up because the man cannot dive.

And then in the foggy midlands it appeared,
Our mud vision, as if a rose window of mud
Had invented itself out of the glittery damp,
A gossamer wheel, concentric with its own hub
Of nebulous dirt, sullied yet lucent.
We had heard of the sun standing still and the sun
That changed colour, but we were vouchsafed
Original clay, transfigured and spinning.

And then the sunsets ran murky, the wiper
Could never entirely clean off the windscreen,
Reservoirs tasted of silt, a light fuzz
Accrued in the hair and the eyebrows, and some
Took to wearing a smudge on their foreheads
To be prepared for whatever. Vigils
Began to be kept around puddled gaps,
On altars bulrushes ousted the lilies
And a rota of invalids came and went
On beds they could lease placed in range of the shower.

A generation who had seen a sign!
Those nights when we stood in an umber dew and smelled
Mould in the verbena, or woke to a light
Furrow-breath on the pillow, when the talk
Was all about who had seen it and our fear
Was touched with a secret pride, only ourselves
Could be adequate then to our lives. When the rainbow
Curved flood-brown and ran like a water-rat's back
So that drivers on the hard shoulder switched off to watch,
We wished it away, and yet we presumed it a test
That would prove us beyond expectation.

We lived, of course, to learn the folly of that.
One day it was gone and the east gable
Where its trembling corolla had balanced
Was starkly a ruin again, with dandelions
Blowing high up on the ledges, and moss
That slumbered on through its increase. As cameras raked
The site from every angle, experts
Began their *post factum* jabber and all of us
Crowded in tight for the big explanations.
Just like that, we forgot that the vision was ours,
Our one chance to know the incomparable
And dive to a future. What might have been origin
We dissipated in news. The clarified place
Had retrieved neither us nor itself – except
You could say we survived. So say that, and watch us
Who had our chance to be mud-men, convinced and estranged,
Figure in our own eyes for the eyes of the world.

An August Night

His hands were warm and small and knowledgeable.
When I saw them again last night, they were two ferrets,
Playing all by themselves in a moonlit field.

from Lightenings

The annals say: when the monks of Clonmacnoise
Were all at prayers inside the oratory
A ship appeared above them in the air.

The anchor dragged along behind so deep
It hooked itself into the altar rails
And then, as the big hull rocked to a standstill,

A crewman shinned and grappled down the rope
And struggled to release it. But in vain.
'This man can't bear our life here and will drown,'

The abbot said, 'unless we help him.' So
They did, the freed ship sailed, and the man climbed back
Out of the marvellous as he had known it.

MICHAEL LONGLEY

(*born* 1939)

Michael Longley was born in Belfast, the son of English parents who had moved there from London. In 1958 he went to Trinity College Dublin to study Classics. Derek Mahon, a product of the same state (effectively, Protestant) school, entered Trinity in 1960. The poets served their literary apprenticeships in Dublin – not, as is sometimes assumed, at Philip Hobsbaum's Belfast 'Group'. But Longley attended the Group later on and first met Seamus Heaney there. From 1970 to 1991, Longley worked for the Arts Council of Northern Ireland.

Since *No Continuing City* (1969) Longley, whose early influences include Robert Graves, has been interested in formal economy and formal variety. The "Troubles" tested all poetry's structures, however. Longley first approached the minefield through his father's involvement in the Great War and the achievement of war poets such as Rosenberg and Douglas. Yet his work does not divide war poetry (or elegy), Nature poetry and love poetry into totally separate genres. 'Bog Cotton' juxtaposes war zones and the west of Ireland. Also, war zones may cast mutual light on one another. In *Gorse Fires* (1991) and *The Ghost Orchid* (1995) Longley 'freeze-frames' passages from the *Odyssey* and the *Iliad*. This lets him see ancient Greece in terms of Ireland and vice versa. 'The Butchers' links Odysseus's slaughter of Penelope's suitors with the notorious Shankill Butchers. The sonnet 'Ceasefire' appeared in the *Irish Times* in the week of the 1994 IRA ceasefire. A structural template that Longley shares with MacNeice, whose *Selected Poems* he edited (1988), is a sense of how syntax operates in Classical poetry. 'The Butchers' (like 'The Beech Tree') consists of a single sentence: 'a formal substitute for the rhyme-schemes and stanzaic shapes which I used in my earlier work'.

Wounds

Here are two pictures from my father's head –
I have kept them like secrets until now:
First, the Ulster Division at the Somme
Going over the top with 'Fuck the Pope!'
'No Surrender!': a boy about to die,
Screaming 'Give 'em one for the Shankill!'
'Wilder than Gurkhas' were my father's words
Of admiration and bewilderment.
Next comes the London-Scottish padre
Resettling kilts with his swagger-stick,
With a stylish backhand and a prayer.
Over a landscape of dead buttocks
My father followed him for fifty years.

At last, a belated casualty,
He said – lead traces flaring till they hurt –
'I am dying for King and Country, slowly.'
I touched his hand, his thin head I touched.

Now, with military honours of a kind,
With his badges, his medals like rainbows,
His spinning compass, I bury beside him
Three teenage soldiers, bellies full of
Bullets and Irish beer, their flies undone.
A packet of Woodbines I throw in,
A lucifer, the Sacred Heart of Jesus
Paralysed as heavy guns put out
The night-light in a nursery for ever;
Also a bus-conductor's uniform –
He collapsed beside his carpet-slippers
Without a murmur, shot through the head
By a shivering boy who wandered in
Before they could turn the television down
Or tidy away the supper dishes.
To the children, to a bewildered wife,
I think 'Sorry Missus' was what he said.

Bog Cotton

Let me make room for bog cotton, a desert flower –
Keith Douglas, I nearly repeat what you were saying
When you apostrophised the poppies of Flanders
And the death of poetry there: that was in Egypt
Among the sandy soldiers of another war.

(It hangs on by a thread, denser than thistledown,
Reluctant to fly, a weather vane that traces
The flow of cloud shadow over monotonous bog –
And useless too, though it might well bring to mind
The plumpness of pillows, the staunching of wounds,

Rags torn from a petticoat and soaked in water
And tied to the bushes around some holy well
As though to make a hospital of the landscape –

Cures and medicines as far as the horizon
Which nobody harvests except with the eye.)

You saw that beyond the thirstier desert flowers
There fell hundreds of thousands of poppy petals
Magnified to blood stains by the middle distance
Or through the still unfocused sights of a rifle –
And Isaac Rosenberg wore one behind his ear.

The Linen Industry

Pulling up flax after the blue flowers have fallen
And laying our handfuls in the peaty water
To rot those grasses to the bone, or building stooks
That recall the skirts of an invisible dancer,

We become a part of the linen industry
And follow its processes to the grubby town
Where fields are compacted into window-boxes
And there is little room among the big machines.

But even in our attic under the skylight
We make love on a bleach green, the whole meadow
Draped with material turning white in the sun
As though snow reluctant to melt were our attire.

What's passion but a battering of stubborn stalks,
Then a gentle combing out of fibres like hair
And a weaving of these into christening robes,
Into garments for a marriage or funeral?

Since it's like a bereavement once the labour's done
To find ourselves last workers in a dying trade,
Let flax be our matchmaker, our undertaker,
The provider of sheets for whatever the bed –

And be shy of your breasts in the presence of death,
Say that you look more beautiful in linen
Wearing white petticoats, the bow on your bodice
A butterfly attending the embroidered flowers.

Ghetto

I

Because you will suffer soon and die, your choices
Are neither right nor wrong: a spoon will feed you,
A flannel keep you clean, a toothbrush bring you back
To your bathroom's view of chimney-pots and gardens.
With so little time for inventory or leavetaking,
You are packing now for the rest of your life
Photographs, medicines, a change of underwear, a book,
A candlestick, a loaf, sardines, needle and thread.
These are your heirlooms, perishables, wordly goods.
What you bring is the same as what you leave behind,
Your last belonging a list of your belongings.

II

As though it were against the law to sleep on pillows
They have filled a cathedral with confiscated feathers:
Silence irrefrangible, no room for angels' wings,
Tons of feathers suffocating cherubim and seraphim.

III

The little girl without a mother behaves like a mother
With her rag doll to whom she explains fear and anguish,
The meagreness of the bread ration, how to make it last,
How to get back to the doll's house and lift up the roof
And, before the flame-throwers and dynamiters destroy it,
How to rescue from their separate rooms love and sorrow,
Masterpieces the size of a postage stamp, small fortunes.

IV

From among the hundreds of thousands I can imagine one
Behind the barbed-wire fences as my train crosses Poland.
I see him for long enough to catch the sprinkle of snowflakes
On his hair and schoolbag, and then I am transported
Away from that world of broken hobby-horses and silent toys.
He turns into a little snowman and refuses to melt.

V

For street-singers in the marketplace, weavers, warp-makers,
Those who suffer in sewing-machine repair shops, excrement-
Removal workers, there are not enough root vegetables,

Beetroots, turnips, swedes, nor for the leather-stitchers
Who are boiling leather so that their children may eat;
Who are turning like a thick slice of potato-bread
This page, which is everything I know about potatoes,
My delivery of Irish Peace, Beauty of Hebron, Home
Guard, Arran Banners, Kerr's Pinks, resistant to eelworm,
Resignation, common scab, terror, frost, potato-blight.

VI

There will be performances in the waiting room, and time
To jump over a skipping rope, and time to adjust
As though for a dancing class the ribbons in your hair.
This string quartet is the most natural thing in the world.

VII

Fingers leave shadows on a violin, harmonics,
A blackbird fluttering between electrified fences.

VIII

Lessons were forbidden in that terrible school.
Punishable by death were reading and writing
And arithmetic, so that even the junior infants
Grew old and wise in lofts studying these subjects.
There were drawing lessons, and drawings of kitchens
And farms, farm animals, butterflies, mothers, fathers
Who survived in crayon until in pen and ink
They turned into guards at executions and funerals
Torturing and hanging even these stick figures.
There were drawings of barracks and latrines as well
And the only windows were the windows they drew.

The Butchers

When he had made sure there were no survivors in his house
And that all the suitors were dead, heaped in blood and dust
Like fish that fishermen with fine-meshed nets have hauled
Up gasping for salt water, evaporating in the sunshine,
Odysseus, spattered with muck and like a lion dripping blood

From his chest and cheeks after devouring a farmer's bullock,
Ordered the disloyal housemaids to sponge down the armchairs
And tables, while Telemachos, the oxherd and the swineherd
Scraped the floor with shovels, and then between the portico
And the roundhouse stretched a hawser and hanged the women
So none touched the ground with her toes, like long-winged thrushes
Or doves trapped in a mist-net across the thicket where they roost,
Their heads bobbing in a row, their feet twitching but not for long,
And when they had dragged Melanthios's corpse into the haggard
And cut off his nose and ears and cock and balls, a dog's dinner,
Odysseus, seeing the need for whitewash and disinfectant,
Fumigated the house and the outhouses, so that Hermes
Like a clergyman might wave the supernatural baton
With which he resurrects or hypnotises those he chooses,
And waken and round up the suitors' souls, and the housemaids',
Like bats gibbering in the nooks of their mysterious cave
When out of the clusters that dangle from the rocky ceiling
One of them drops and squeaks, so their souls were bat-squeaks
As they flittered after Hermes, their deliverer, who led them
Along the clammy sheughs, then past the oceanic streams
And the white rock, the sun's gatepost in that dreamy region,
Until they came to a bog-meadow full of bog-asphodels
Where the residents are ghosts or images of the dead.

Ceasefire

I

Put in mind of his own father and moved to tears
Achilles took him by the hand and pushed the old king
Gently away, but Priam curled up at his feet and
Wept with him until their sadness filled the building.

II

Taking Hector's corpse into his own hands Achilles
Made sure it was washed and, for the old king's sake,
Laid out in uniform, ready for Priam to carry
Wrapped like a present home to Troy at daybreak.

III

When they had eaten together, it pleased them both
To stare at each other's beauty as lovers might,
Achilles built like a god, Priam good-looking still
And full of conversation, who earlier had sighed:

IV

'I get down on my knees and do what must be done
And kiss Achilles' hand, the killer of my son.'

The White Garden

So white are the white flowers in the white garden that I
Disappear in no time at all among lace and veils.
For whom do I scribble the few words that come to me
From beyond the arch of white roses as from nowhere,
My memorandum to posterity? Listen. 'The saw
Is under the garden bench and the gate is unlatched.'

The Beech Tree

Leaning back like a lover against this beech tree's
Two-hundred-year-old pewter trunk, I look up
Through skylights into the leafy cumulus, and join
Everybody who has teetered where these huge roots
Spread far and wide our motionless mossy dance,
As though I'd begun my eclogues with a beech
As Virgil does, the brown envelopes unfolding
Like fans their transparent downy leaves, tassels
And prickly cups, mast, a fall of vermilion
And copper and gold, then room in the branches
For the full moon and her dusty lakes, winter
And the poet who recollects his younger self
And improvises a last line for the georgics
About snoozing under this beech tree's canopy.

DEREK MAHON
(*born* 1941)

Derek Mahon grew up in Belfast where his father was a shipyard worker. Belfast and the Antrim coast shaped his imaginative landscape. In 1960, he entered Trinity College Dublin to study French and English. Like Michael Longley, he found Trinity (where Alec Reid, a friend of Samuel Beckett, presided over the literary scene) 'a very fertile environment'. In the later 1960s Mahon travelled in France and North America, a sign of his literary horizons. He has translated French symbolist poetry and Philippe Jaccottet (1988); and *Night-Crossing* (1968) owes something to Hart Crane and Robert Lowell. Mahon, a freelance writer, now lives in Dublin. His *Collected Poems* appeared in 1999.

For Mahon, there is conflict between poetry and the ethos of Protestant Ulster where, as in Scotland, Calvinism has been unfriendly to the arts. 'Courtyards in Delft' portrays his youthful self ('A strange child with a taste for verse') as resisting a Protestant 'trim composure' which represses turbulent life, and may incubate violence. Yet tension between 'chaste / Perfection' and turbulence marks Mahon's own work. His attraction to Yeats's stanza-forms reflects his belief in poetry as 'The hissing chemicals inside the well-wrought urn'. Mahon's stanzas are beautifully wrought. Clause and line interact more flexibly than in Yeats. Tone and sound are finely adjusted to 'wild flowers', 'bathtubs' or the 'firmament'. Yet 'Jail Journal' signals a poetry of pain. This can be sensed, too, from Mahon's elegy for MacNeice which discloses differences as well as affinities between the poets. Mahon interprets MacNeice's 'Snow' as perhaps a less robust poem than it is. This points to his affinity with a bleaker influence, Beckett. Like MacNeice and Beckett, Mahon retains traces of the (Anglican) Protestantism he has rejected. Humanity, he implies, needs spiritual redemption more than political solutions. Also, as 'Rage for Order' seems to accept, poetry cannot influence events. It is merely 'An eddy of semantic scruple'. Thus Mahon enfolds the Northern Irish "Troubles" into poems that take a long view of European history with its many burnings of 'witches and heretics'. In his celebrated poem 'A Disused Shed in Co. Wexford the symbolic mushrooms, placed amid cumulative historical disasters, beg to be 'saved'. Mahon applies the word 'faith' to poetry, and what he requires is: 'Soul, Song and Formal Necessity'.

In Carrowdore Churchyard
(at the grave of Louis MacNeice)

Your ashes will not stir, even on this high ground,
However the wind tugs, the headstones shake.
This plot is consecrated, for your sake,
To what lies in the future tense. You lie
Past tension now, and spring is coming round
Igniting flowers on the peninsula.

Your ashes will not fly, however the rough winds burst
Through the wild brambles and the reticent trees.
All we may ask of you we have; the rest
Is not for publication, will not be heard.
Maguire, I believe, suggested a blackbird
And over your grave a phrase from Euripides.

Which suits you down to the ground, like this churchyard
With its play of shadow, its humane perspective.
Locked in the winter's fist, these hills are hard
As nails, yet soft and feminine in their turn
When fingers open and the hedges burn.
This, you implied, is how we ought to live –

The ironical, loving crush of roses against snow,
Each fragile, solving ambiguity. So
From the pneumonia of the ditch, from the ague
Of the blind poet and the bombed-out town you bring
The all-clear to the empty holes of spring,
Rinsing the choked mud, keeping the colours new.

First Love

    This is a circling of itself and you –
A form of words, compact and compromise,
    Prepared in the false dawn of the half-true
Beyond which the shapes of truth materialise.
    This is a blind with sunlight filtering through.

    This is a stirring in the silent hours,
As lovers do with thoughts they cannot frame
    Or leave, but bring to darkness like night-flowers,
Words never choosing but the words choose them –
    Birds crowing, wind whistling off pale stars.

    This is a night-cry, neither here nor there,
A ghostly echo from the clamorous dead
    Who cried aloud in anger and despair
Outlasting stone and bronze, but took instead
    Their lost grins underground with them for ever.

This is at one remove, a substitute
For final answers; but the wise man knows
    To cleave to the one living absolute
Beyond paraphrase, and shun a shrewd repose.
    The words are aching in their own pursuit

    To say 'I love you' out of indolence
As one might speak at sea without forethought,
    Drifting inconsequently among islands.
This is a way of airing my distraught
    Love of your silence; you are the soul of silence.

Jail Journal

For several days I have been under
House arrest. My table has become
A sundial to its empty bottle.
With wise abandon
Lover and friend have gone.

In the window opposite
An old lady sits each afternoon
Talking to no one. I shout.
Either she is deaf or
She has reason.

I have books, provisions, running water
And a little stove. It wouldn't matter
If cars moved silently at night
And no light or laughter
Came from the houses down the street.

It's taking longer than almost anything –
But I know, when it's over
And back come friend and lover,
I shall forget it like a childhood illness
Or a sleepless night-crossing.

Rage for Order

Somewhere beyond
The scorched gable end
And the burnt-out
Buses there is a poet indulging his
Wretched rage for order –

Or not as the case
May be, for his
Is a dying art,
An eddy of semantic scruple
In an unstructurable sea.

He is far
From his people,
And the fitful glare
Of his high window is as
Nothing to our scattered glass.

His posture is
Grandiloquent and
Deprecating, like this,
His diet ashes,
His talk of justice and his mother

The rhetorical
Device of a Claudian emperor –
Nero if you prefer,
No mother there;
And this in the face of love, death and the wages of the poor.

If he is silent
It is the silence
Of enforced humility,
If anxious to be heard
It is the anxiety of a last word

When the drums start –
For his is a dying art.
Now watch me
As I make history,
Watch as I tear down

To build up
With a desperate love,
Knowing it cannot be
Long now till I have need of his
Terminal ironies.

The Snow Party
(for Louis Asekoff)

Bashō, coming
To the city of Nagoya,
Is asked to a snow party.

There is a tinkling of china
And tea into china;
There are introductions.

Then everyone
Crowds to the window
To watch the falling snow.

Snow is falling on Nagoya
And farther south
On the tiles of Kyōto;

Eastward, beyond Irago,
It is falling
Like leaves on the cold sea.

Elsewhere they are burning
Witches and heretics
In the boiling squares,

Thousands have died since dawn
In the service
Of barbarous kings;

But there is silence
In the houses of Nagoya
And the hills of Ise.

Nostalgias

The chair squeaks in a high wind,
Rain falls from its branches;
The kettle yearns for the mountain,
The soap for the sea.
In a tiny stone church
On a desolate headland
A lost tribe is singing 'Abide with Me'.

A Disused Shed in Co. Wexford

Let them not forget us, the weak souls among the asphodels.
SEFERIS, Mythistorema

(for J.G. Farrell)

Even now there are places where a thought might grow –
Peruvian mines, worked out and abandoned
To a slow clock of condensation,
An echo trapped for ever, and a flutter
Of wild flowers in the lift-shaft,
Indian compounds where the wind dances
And a door bangs with diminished confidence,
Lime crevices behind rippling rain-barrels,
Dog corners for bone burials;
And in a disused shed in Co. Wexford,

Deep in the grounds of a burnt-out hotel,
Among the bathtubs and the washbasins
A thousand mushrooms crowd to a keyhole.
This is the one star in their firmament
Or frames a star within a star.
What should they do there but desire?
So many days beyond the rhododendrons
With the world waltzing in its bowl of cloud,
They have learnt patience and silence
Listening to the rooks querulous in the high wood.

They have been waiting for us in a foetor
Of vegetable sweat since civil war days,
Since the gravel-crunching, interminable departure
Of the expropriated mycologist.
He never came back, and light since then
Is a keyhole rusting gently after rain.
Spiders have spun, flies dusted to mildew
And once a day, perhaps, they have heard something –
A trickle of masonry, a shout from the blue
Or a lorry changing gear at the end of the lane.

There have been deaths, the pale flesh flaking
Into the earth that nourished it;
And nightmares, born of these and the grim
Dominion of stale air and rank moisture.
Those nearest the door grow strong –
'Elbow room! Elbow room!'
The rest, dim in a twilight of crumbling
Utensils and broken pitchers, groaning
For their deliverance, have been so long
Expectant that there is left only the posture.

A half century, without visitors, in the dark –
Poor preparation for the cracking lock
And creak of hinges; magi, moonmen,
Powdery prisoners of the old regime,
Web-throated, stalked like triffids, racked by drought
And insomnia, only the ghost of a scream
At the flash-bulb firing-squad we wake them with
Shows there is life yet in their feverish forms.
Grown beyond nature now, soft food for worms,
They lift frail heads in gravity and good faith.

They are begging us, you see, in their wordless way,
To do something, to speak on their behalf
Or at least not to close the door again.
Lost people of Treblinka and Pompeii!
'Save us, save us,' they seem to say,
'Let the god not abandon us
Who have come so far in darkness and in pain.
We too had our lives to live.
You with your light meter and relaxed itinerary,
Let not our naive labours have been in vain!'

Courtyards in Delft
– Pieter de Hooch, 1659

(for Gordon Woods)

Oblique light on the trite, on brick and tile –
Immaculate masonry, and everywhere that
Water tap, that broom and wooden pail
To keep it so. House-proud, the wives
Of artisans pursue their thrifty lives
Among scrubbed yards, modest but adequate.
Foliage is sparse, and clings; no breeze
Ruffles the trim composure of those trees.

No spinet-playing emblematic of
The harmonies and disharmonies of love,
No lewd fish, no fruit, no wide-eyed bird
About to fly its cage while a virgin
Listens to her seducer, mars the chaste
Perfection of the thing and the thing made.
Nothing is random, nothing goes to waste.
We miss the dirty dog, the fiery gin.

That girl with her back to us who waits
For her man to come home for his tea
Will wait till the paint disintegrates
And ruined dikes admit the esurient sea;
Yet this is life too, and the cracked
Outhouse door a verifiable fact
As vividly mnemonic as the sunlit
Railings that front the houses opposite.

I lived there as a boy and know the coal
Glittering in its shed, late-afternoon
Lambency informing the deal table,
The ceiling cradled in a radiant spoon.
I must be lying low in a room there,
A strange child with a taste for verse,
While my hard-nosed companions dream of fire
And sword upon parched veldt and fields of rain-swept gorse.

Heraclitus on Rivers

Nobody steps into the same river twice.
The same river is never the same
Because that is the nature of water.
Similarly your changing metabolism
Means that you are no longer you.
The cells die, and the precise
Configuration of the heavenly bodies
When she told you she loved you
Will not come again in this lifetime.

You will tell me that you have executed
A monument more lasting than bronze;
But even bronze is perishable.
Your best poem, you know the one I mean,
The very language in which the poem
Was written, and the idea of language,
All these things will pass away in time.

Ghosts

We live the lives our parents never knew
when they sang 'Come Back to Sorrento':
driving west in the evening from Pompeii,
its little houses sealed up in a tomb
of ash and pumice centuries ago
and now exposed to the clear light of day,
we found an old hotel with a sea view
and Naples' lights reflected in the bay
where, with a squeal of seagulls far below,
white curtains blew like ghosts into the room.

DOUGLAS DUNN
(*born* 1942)

Douglas Dunn grew up in Renfrewshire. Educated at Hull University, he later became a librarian there. *Terry Street* (1969) suggested that Dunn's proximity to Philip Larkin was literary as well as literal. Yet Dunn presents a different urban landscape from Larkin's Hull: one viewed in close-up and more compassionately, as in the concluding grace-note 'I wish him grass'. Now a Professor of English at St Andrews University, Dunn has remained on the 'Anglo' wing of Scottish poetry. When he explores questions like the politics of language, as in *Barbarians* (1979), he is closer to the class-concerns of Tony Harrison than to poets interested in cultural and national identity. In his *Faber Book of Twentieth-Century Scottish Poetry* (1992) Dunn rejoices that 'the liberty of three languages' is now 'established', but remembers when 'a Scottish poet writing in English could be bullied into believing that his or her language was not a native tongue'. Dunn writes much discursive and narrative poetry, including his recent epic *The Donkey's Ears* (2000). The selection below, which includes two sonnets, features his lyrics. Their cadences are often 'haunted' by absence – actual, potential, or perpetual. 'The Friendship of Young Poets' is a wonderful sigh of nostalgia for something that never happened. Dunn also writes fine love poetry. 'France' is one of the intensely moving poems in *Elegies* (1985), dedicated to the memory of his first wife who died of cancer. The book has been compared to Hardy's elegies.

A Removal from Terry Street

On a squeaking cart, they push the usual stuff,
A mattress, bed ends, cups, carpets, chairs,
Four paperback westerns. Two whistling youths
In surplus US Army battle-jackets
Remove their sister's goods. Her husband
Follows, carrying on his shoulders the son
Whose mischief we are glad to see removed,
And pushing, of all things, a lawnmower.
There is no grass in Terry Street. The worms
Come up cracks in concrete yards in moonlight.
That man, I wish him well. I wish him grass.

Love Poem

I live in you, you live in me;
We are two gardens haunted by each other.
Sometimes I cannot find you there,
There is only the swing creaking, that you have just left,
Or your favourite book beside the sundial.

The Friendship of Young Poets

There must have been more than just one of us,
But we never met. Each kept in his world of loss
The promise of literary days, the friendship
Of poets, mysterious, that sharing of books
And talking in whispers in crowded bars
Suspicious enough to be taken for love.

We never met. My youth was as private
As the bank at midnight, and in its safety
No talking behind backs, no one alike enough
To be pretentious with and quote lines at.

There is a boat on the river now, and
Two young men, one rowing, one reading aloud.
Their shirt sleeves fill with wind, and from the oars
Drop scales of perfect river like melting glass.

Port Logan and a Vision of Live Maps

Cartographical morass
And the dissolve of speculation;
Strabo in the poop
Studying the periplum...

Infinity of routes where steel wanders,
Clydeside machinery...
And here is my gift from the sea,
A bobbing grapefruit that comes in on a wave.

France

A dozen sparrows scuttled on the frost.
We watched them play. We stood at the window,
And, if you saw us, then you saw a ghost
In duplicate. I tied her nightgown's bow.
She watched and recognised the passers-by.
Had they looked up, they'd know that she was ill –
'Please, do not draw the curtains when I die' –
From all the flowers on the windowsill.

'It's such a shame,' she said. 'Too ill, too quick.'
'I would have liked us to have gone away.'
We closed our eyes together, dreaming France,
Its meadows, rivers, woods and *jouissance.*
I counted summers, our love's arithmetic.
'Some other day, my love. Some other day.'

Long Ago

In a house I visited when I was young
I looked in through a partly opened door.
An old man sang 'Long Ago and Far Away'
To a rocking-horse, a friend's grandfather
Whose first-born son was lost at sea
Half-a-century before
In a ship whose name I have forgotten.

Whenever that sad song is played or sung
I'm in that house again, by that same door.
A woman tugs my sleeve. 'Come away,'
She says. 'Leave him alone.'
He sings, but he's no longer there.
The rocking-horse is rocking like the sea.
Ocean is everywhere
And the room is wind and rain.

EILÉAN NÍ CHUILLEANÁIN

(*born* 1942)

Eiléan Ní Chuilleanáin grew up in Cork. Her family was academic, literary and connected – like Paul Durcan's – with the Irish Republican movement earlier in the century. For instance, her mother the novelist Eilís Dillon was the niece of Joseph Mary Plunkett, an executed leader of the Easter Rising (to whom Paul Muldoon's poem 'Anseo' alludes). Ní Chuilleanáin was educated at University College Cork and at Oxford. She lectures in Medieval and Renaissance English at Trinity College Dublin. Her publications (as editor) include *Irish Women: Image and Achievement* (1985).

Since her first collection *Acts and Monuments* (1972) Ní Chuilleanáin has shown an ability to objectify her most intense concerns which – as the sonnet 'Studying the Language' might suggest – seem ultimately religious in tendency. On one level, 'The Second Voyage' is a vivid rendering of a motif in the *Odyssey*. On another, it is a parable of human affiliations, choices, destinies. This also applies to 'J'ai Mal à nos Dents' whose nun-heroine moves between the collective of the Irish family and the collective of her order. The poem is simultaneously crossed by differing languages and histories: her brother tries, from neutral Ireland, to imagine the nun's situation in occupied France where her memories render her 'half drunk' on strengthening wine and eating 'dandelions for the sake of their roots'. The delicately orchestrated 'voices' of 'J'ai Mal à nos Dents' suggest, too, how women's histories lie 'under the surface'.

The Second Voyage

Odysseus rested on his oar and saw
The ruffled foreheads of the waves
Crocodiling and mincing past: he rammed
The oar between their jaws and looked down
In the simmering sea where scribbles of weed defined
Uncertain depth, and the slim fishes progressed
In fatal formation, and thought
                  If there was a single
Streak of decency in these waves now, they'd be ridged
Pocked and dented with the battering they've had,
And we could name them as Adam named the beasts,
Saluting a new one with dismay, or a notorious one
With admiration; they'd notice us passing
And rejoice at our shipwreck, but these
Have less character than sheep and need more patience.

I know what I'll do he said;
I'll park my ship in the crook of a long pier
(And I'll take you with me he said to the oar)
I'll face the rising ground and walk away
From tidal waters, up riverbeds
Where herons parcel out the miles of stream,
Over gaps in the hills, through warm
Silent valleys, and when I meet a farmer
Bold enough to look me in the eye
With 'where are you off to with that long
Winnowing fan over your shoulder?'
There I will stand still
And I'll plant you for a gatepost or a hitching-post
And leave you as a tidemark. I can go back
And organise my house then.
                                            But the profound
Unfenced valleys of the ocean still held him;
He had only the oar to make them keep their distance;
The sea was still frying under the ship's side.
He considered the water-lilies, and thought about fountains
Spraying as wide as willows in empty squares,
The sugarstick of water clattering into the kettle,
The flat lakes bisecting the rushes. He remembered spiders and frogs
Housekeeping at the roadside in brown trickles floored with mud,
Horsetroughs, the black canal, pale swans at dark:
His face grew damp with tears that tasted
Like his own sweat or the insults of the sea.

J'ai Mal à nos Dents
(in memory of Anna Cullinane [Sister Mary Antony])

The Holy Father gave her leave
To return to her father's house
At seventy-eight years of age.

When young in the Franciscan house at Calais
She complained to the dentist, *I have a pain in our teeth*
– Her body dissolving out of her first mother,
Her five sisters aching at home.

Her brother listened to news
Five times in a morning on Radio Éireann
In Cork, as the Germans entered Calais.
Her name lay under the surface, he could not see her
Working all day with the sisters,
Stripping the hospital, loading the sick on lorries.
While Reverend Mother walked the wards and nourished them
With jugs of wine to hold their strength.
J'étais à moitié saoûle. It was done,
They lifted the old sisters on to the pig-cart
And the young walked out on the road to Desvres,
The wine still buzzing and the planes over their heads.

Je mangerai les pissenlits par les racines.
A year before she died she lost her French accent
Going home in her habit to care for her sister Nora
(Une malade à soigner une malade).
They handed her back her body,
Its voices and its death.

Studying the Language

On Sundays I watch the hermits coming out of their holes
Into the light. Their cliff is as full as a hive.
They crowd together on warm shoulders of rock
Where the sun has been shining, their joints crackle.
They begin to talk after a while.
I listen to their accents, they are not all
From this island, not all old,
Not even, I think, all masculine.

They are so wise, they do not pretend to see me.
They drink from the scattered pools of melted snow:
I walk right by them and drink when they have done.
I can see the marks of chains around their feet.

I call this my work, these decades and stations –
Because, without these, I would be a stranger here.

PAUL DURCAN

(*born* 1944)

Paul Durcan grew up in Dublin, but Co. Mayo became his utopian dream-place. His family history is intertwined with the history of the Irish state. His grandfather's brother was John MacBride, an executed leader of the Easter Rising. In 1964 Durcan rebelled against his father, a judge, and the Irish establishment. He dropped out of University College Dublin and went to London where he (and hence Irish poetry) experienced the swinging 60s. Bob Dylan joined Patrick Kavanagh as an artistic role-model. Durcan's compelling public readings indicate how the structure of his poems is geared to dramatic performance (the selection below is from his more lyrical work).

Derek Mahon has said that Durcan, based in Ireland since 1971, 'takes the madness of public life personally'. The strange world of his poetry is a form of therapy. In collections such as *Sam's Cross* (1978) and *Going Home to Russia* (1987) he tries to write an alternative Ireland into existence. Part satirical, part religious in its moral intensity, this can be seen as a poetry of preparation for Mary Robinson (who quoted Durcan when she was elected President in 1990). Yet Durcan's visionary impulse goes deeper into language and structure: the panoramic sentence of 'Birth of a Coachman' embraces Ireland and the reader; 'The Kilfenora Teaboy', 'The Hay-Carrier' and 'The Riding School' imply various kinds of mystery by their tones of address and styles of refrain. One of Durcan's refrains in 'The Riding School', 'Delight in art whose end is peace', was taken by Yeats from Coventry Patmore, then by Heaney (in 'The Harvest Bow') from Yeats. That refrain-chain suggests how Durcan's poetry makes Ireland itself his poetic parish. As 'Ireland 1977' implies, he is a "national poet" in a special sense. When his poems rearrange family relations, they rearrange social relations. 'The Kilfenora Teaboy' subverts patriarchal, patriotic role-models. Similarly, Durcan's poetry takes the "Troubles" personally. His protest-poems can be controversial because of how they phrase his opposition to violence (as in his elegy for the victims of the Omagh bombing in *Greetings to Our Friends in Brazil*, 1999). Durcan's poems are often variations on themes suggested 'after' paintings – part of his utopian drive to make life resemble art. Mahon calls his poetry 'a politics of the soul'.

The Kilfenora Teaboy

I'm the Kilfenora teaboy
And I'm not so very young,
But though the land is going to pieces
I will not take up the gun;
I am happy making tea,

I make lots of it when I can,
And when I can't – I just make do;
And I do a small bit of sheepfarming on the side.

Oh but it's the small bit of furze between two towns
Is what makes the Kilfenora teaboy really run.

I have nine healthy daughters
And please God I will have more,
Sometimes my dear wife beats me
But on the whole she's a gentle soul;
When I'm not making her some tea
I sit out and watch them all
Ring-a-rosying in the street;
And I do a small bit of sheepfarming on the side.

Oh but it's the small bit of furze between two towns
Is what makes the Kilfenora teaboy really run.

Oh indeed my wife is handsome,
She has a fire lighting in each eye,
You can pluck laughter from her elbows
And from her knees pour money's tears;
I make all my tea for her,
I'm her teaboy on the hill,
And I also thatch her roof;
And I do a small bit of sheepfarming on the side.

Oh but it's the small bit of furze between two towns
Is what makes the Kilfenora teaboy really run.

And I'm not only a famous teaboy,
I'm a famous caveman too;
I paint pictures by the hundred
But you can't sell walls;
Although the people praise my pictures
As well as my turf-perfumèd blend
They rarely fling a fiver in my face;
Oh don't we do an awful lot of dying on the side?

But oh it's the small bit of furze between two towns
Is what makes the Kilfenora teaboy really run.

Birth of a Coachman

His father and grandfather before him were coachmen:
How strange, then, to think that this small, bloody, lump of flesh,
This tiny moneybags of brains, veins, and intestines,
This zipped-up purse of most peculiar coin,
Will one day be coachman of the Cork to Dublin route,
In a great black greatcoat and white gauntlets,
In full command of one of our famous coaches
– *Wonder, Perseverance, Diligence,* or *Lightning* –
In charge of all our lives on foul winter nights,
Crackling his whip, whirling it, lashing it,
Driving on the hapless horses across the moors
Of the Kilworth hills, beating them on
Across rivers in spate, rounding sharp bends
On only two wheels, shriekings of axle-trees,
Rock-scrapes, rut-squeals, quagmire-squelches,
For ever in dread of the pitiless highwayman
Lurking in ambush with a brace of pistols;
Then cantering carefully in the lee of the Galtees,
Bowing his head to the stone gods of Cashel;
Then again thrusting through Urlingford;
Doing his bit, and his nut, past the Devilsbit;
Praising the breasts of the hills round Port Laoise;
Sailing full furrow through the Curragh of Kildare,
Through the thousand sea-daisies of a thousand white sheep;
Thrashing gaily the air at first glimpse of the Liffey;
Until stepping down from his high perch in Dublin
Into the sanctuary of a cobbled courtyard,
Into the arms of a crowd like a triumphant toreador
All sweat and tears: the man of the moment
Who now is but a small body of but some fleeting seconds old.

Ireland 1977

'I've become so lonely, I could die' – he writes,
The native who is an exile in his native land:
'Do you hear me whispering to you across the Golden Vale?
Do you hear me bawling to you across the hearthrug?'

Wives May Be Coveted but not by Their Husbands

We lived in a remote dower house in Cork
Leaving the doors and windows always unlocked.
When herds of deer came streaming through the kitchen
At first we laughed, but then we quarrelled –
As the years went by, we quarrelled more than laughed:
'You seem to care more about deer than about me' –
'I am weary of subsisting in an eyrie of antlers' –
'Be a man and erect a fence' –
'Be a woman and put venison in the pot'.
When an old gold stag dawdled by her rocking chair
And she caressed his warm hide with smiling hands,
I locked myself in the attic and sulked for weeks.
Stags, does, and fauns, grew thick around her bed
As in her bloom of life she evolved, alone.

The Hay-Carrier
(after Veronica Bolay)

Have you ever saved hay in Mayo in the rain?
Have you ever made hay in Mayo in the sun?
Have you ever carried above your head a haycock on a pitchfork?
Have you ever slept in a haybarn on the road from Mayo into Egypt?
I am a hay-carrier.
My father was a hay-carrier.
My mother was a hay-carrier.
My brothers were hay-carriers.
My sisters were hay-carriers.
My wife is a hay-carrier.
My son is a hay-carrier.
His sons are hay-carriers.
His daughters are hay-carriers.
We were always all hay-carriers.
We will always be hay-carriers.
For the great gate of night stands painted red –
And all of heaven lies waiting to be fed.

The One-Armed Crucifixion
(after Giacomo Manzù)

How many thousands of hours on the shore at Galway,
In the drizzle off the back of the sea,
On the sodden sands,
Did we spend hurling together, father and son?
Pucking the *sliotar*, one to the other,
Hour in, hour out, year in, year out.
How many thousands of times, old man,
Did you strike a high ball for your young son
To crouch, to dart, to leap,
To pluck the ball one-handed out of the climbing air?

The Riding School
(after Karel Dujardin)

Dung, cobble, wall, cypress;
Delight in art whose end is peace;
No cold-eyed horseman of the Irish skies
Can compare with me
Leading out the Grey of the Blues.

I in my red blanket
Under the Cave Hill Mountain
Leading out the Grey of the Blues:
The blindness of history in my eyes;
The blindness of history in my hands.

To get up at four every morning
And to lead out the Grey of the Blues;
Delight in art whose end is peace;
Hold his reins with my eyes open;
His dappled hindquarters;
His summer coat;
His knotted mane;
His combed-out tail;
His swanface;
His bullneck;

His spineline;
His tiny, prancing grace-notes.

And I in my red blanket
Under the Cave Hill Mountain
Leading out the Grey of the Blues:
The blindness of history in my eyes;
The blindness of history in my hands.

I take pride in my work;
Delight in art whose end is peace;
The way I lead out a song;
The way I hold the reins of a song in my hands
Between my stubby fingers.
I talk to my song;
My song talks to me.
In the blackest weathers
We have our sunniest hours.
How many early mornings
In black rain I have talked my song
Round and round the pink paddock!

I in my red blanket
Under the Cave Hill Mountain
Leading out the Grey of the Blues:
The blindness of history in my eyes;
The blindness of history in my hands.

My song is nearing the end of its tether;
Lament in art whose end is war;
Opera glasses, helicopters, TV crews;
Our slayings are what's news.
We are taking our curtain call,
Our last encore.
True to our natures
We do not look into the camera lenses
But at one another.
In a gap of oblivion, gone.

I in my red blanket
Under the Cave Hill Mountain
Leading out the Grey of the Blues:
The blindness of history in my eyes;
The blindness of history in my hands.

TOM LEONARD

(*born* 1944)

Tom Leonard grew up in Glasgow where he still lives. He studied at Glasgow University: it may or may not please him that he is now studied there. Both his selections *Intimate Voices* (1984) and *Reports from the Present* (1995) contain prose and poetry. Leonard has also edited *Radical Renfrew* (1990), an anthology of West of Scotland poetry 'from The French Revolution to The First World War'. Leonard's phonetic use of Glasgow dialect is politically as well as poetically radical. It points to social, educational and literary exclusion. Wounded or violent Glasgow voices nail the class-assumptions we may bring to poetry. Yet they also express the vision that (in 'The Good Thief') relocates the Crucifixion near a football match, possibly one between Celtic and Rangers. The 'Paroakial', 'reclaiming the local', matters profoundly to Leonard. (His ironical gloss on 'bunnit husslin' is: 'you mean deliberately purveying a cloth-cap image?') Leonard's 'translation' of William Carlos Williams's 'This Is Just to Say' (the original concerns plums rather than 'speshlz') salutes a poet whose rhythmic freedoms have influenced him. He has argued that 'the largely American-initiated breakdown in prescriptive grammar has facilitated the release of new – and multiple – voices in British poetry, from a variety of class/cultural backgrounds'. Similarly, he has attacked Hugh MacDiarmid's fans for stressing his "contribution to Modern Scottish Literature", rather than his revolutionary attitude to language. Like most satirists, Leonard is obsessed with what he opposes: 'Poughit. rih'.

The Good Thief

heh jimmy
yawright ih
stull wayiz urryi
ih

heh jimmy
ma right insane yirra pape
ma right insane yirwanny us jimmy
see it nyir eyes
wanny uz

heh

heh jimmy
lookslik wirgonny miss thi gemm

gonny miss thi GEMM jimmy
nearly three a cloke thinoo

dork init
good jobe theyve gote thi lights

Poetry

the pee as in pulchritude,
oh pronounced ough
as in bough

the ee rather poised
(pronounced ih as in wit)
then a languid high tea...

pause: then the coda –
ray pronounced rih
with the left eyebrow raised
– what a gracious bouquet!

Poetry.
Poughit. rih.

That was my education
– and nothing to do with me.

Paroakial

thahts no whurrits aht
thahts no cool man
jiss paroakial

aw theez sporran heads
tahty scoan vibes
thi haggis trip

bad buzz man
dead seen

goahty learna new langwij
sumhm ihnturnashnl
Noah Glasgow hangup
bunnit husslin

gitinty elektroniks man
really blow yir mine
real good blast
no whuhta mean

mawn
turn yirself awn

Jist ti Let Yi No
(from the American of Carlos Williams)

ahv drank
thi speshlz
that wurrin
thi frij

n thit
yiwurr probbli
hodn back
furthi pahrti

awright
they wur great
thaht stroang
thaht cawld

CAROL RUMENS

(*born* 1944)

Carol Rumens grew up in London. She is a freelance writer and teacher of creative writing. In recent years she has divided her time between Belfast and London. Rumens's poetry (like her utopian house in 'Stanzas for a New Start') is generously open to new possibilities of design and content. And it does not segregate private from public experience, home from abroad. Her first-person voice sometimes dramatises her dual consciousness of speaking as a woman and speaking as English. Disturbingly close to home, Northern Ireland functions as a catalyst to expose the cultural and metaphysical instability of any 'home'. Rumens wrote in 1993: ' "My" Belfast is a muse-city, a city of weather and uncertainty…I want to show a city where, in spite of everything, peace, love, friends and poems are sometimes made, and where a female imagination can find mirrors'. 'Stealing the Genre' is a powerful two-way mirror: on England and Ireland, on gender and nation. It 'steals' and subverts the Irish Jacobite *aisling*, or dream-vision, in which a male poet personifies Ireland as a woman.

The Impenitent

The wife of the poet can't be innocent
Her eyes must be narrow
The wife of the poet can't be humble
She must lift her chin high
The wife of the poet won't be flattered
If he writes a poem in her blood
The wife of the poet knows the missing word
But she'll never tell him.

The husband of the poet can't be light-hearted
He must watch the pennies
The husband of the poet can't be clean
He must live in his dust
The husband of the poet can't be original
He must be, or obey, her muse
The husband of the poet knows the missing word
And that it's *'wife'*.

Stealing the Genre

It was the shortest night of the year. I'd been drinking
But I was quite lucid and calm. So, having seen her
The other side of the bar, shedding her light
On no one who specially deserved it, I got to my feet
And simply went over and asked her, in a low voice,
If she'd come to my bed. She raised her eyebrows strangely
But didn't say 'no'. I went out. I felt her follow.

My mind was a storm as we silently crossed the courtyard
In the moist white chill of the dawn. Dear God, I loved her.
I'd loved her in books, I'd adored her at the first sighting.
But no, I'm a woman, English, not young. How could I?
She'd vanished for years. And now she was walking beside me.
Oh what am I going to do, what are *we* going to do?
Perhaps she'll know. She's probably an old hand –
But this sudden thought was the most disturbing of all.

As soon as we reached my room, though, it was plain
She hadn't a clue. We stood like window-displays
In our dawn-damp suits with the short, straight, hip-hugging skirts
(Our styles are strangely alike, I suppose it's because
Even she has to fight her corner in a man's world)
And discussed the rain, which was coming down, and the view,
Which was nothing much, a fuchsia hedge and some trees,
And we watched each other, as women do watch each other,
And tried not to yawn. Why don't you lie down for a bit?
I whispered, inspired. She gratefully kicked off her shoes.

She was onto the bed in no time, and lay as if dumped
On the furthest edge, her face – dear God – to the wall.
I watched for a while, and, thinking she might be in tears,
Caressed the foam-padded viscose that passed for her shoulder,
And begged her not to feel guilty. Then I discovered
That all she was doing was breathing, dead to the world.

It wasn't an insult, exactly, but it was a let-down –
And yet I admired her. Sleep. If only I could.
I rested my hand at an uncontroversial location
South of her breasts, maybe north, I don't remember,
And ached with desire and regret and rationalisation.

I'd asked her to bed. And she'd come to bed. End of story.
Only it wasn't the story I'd wanted to tell.
Roll on, tomorrow, I urged, but tomorrow retorted:
I'm here already, and nothing ever gets better.

But then, unexpectedly, I began to feel pleased.
To think she was here, at my side, so condensed, so weighty!
In my humble position (a woman, English, not young,
Et cetera) what more could I ask of an Irish dawn
Than this vision, alive, though dead to the world, on my duvet?
What have I done to deserve her? Oh, never mind,
Don't think about words like 'deserve'. So we lay in grace.
The light. Her hair. My hand. Her breath. And the fuchsias.
I thought of the poem I'd write, and fell asleep, smiling.

I woke in a daze of sublime self-congratulation
And saw she was gone. My meadow, my cloud, my aisling!
I could hardly believe my own memory. I wanted to scream
All over the courtyard, come back, come to bed, but how could I?
She might be anywhere, people were thick in the day
Already, and things were normal. Why are things normal?

I keened her name to the walls, I swam bitterest rivers,
I buried my face in the cloth where her blushes had slipped
And left a miraculous print that would baffle the laundry:
Oh let me die now. And the dark was all flame as I drank
The heart-breaking odour of Muguets des Bois and red wine –
Hers, though I have to admit, it could have been mine.

Prayer for Northern Ireland

Night, be starry-sensed for her,
Your bitter frost be fleece to her.
Comb the vale, slow mist, for her.
Lough, be a muscle, tensed for her.

And coals, the only fire in her,
And rain, the only news of her.
Small hills, keep sisters' eyes on her.
Be reticent, desire for her.

Go, stories, leave the breath in her,
The last word to be said by her,
And leave no heart for dead in her.
Steer this ship of dread from her.

No husband lift a hand to her,
No daughter shut the blind on her.
May sails be sewn, seeds grown, for her.
May every kiss be kind to her.

Stanzas for a New Start

Home for a long time fought with me for air,
And I pronounced it uninhabitable.
Then, in an old tradition of reversal,
I understood I'd left my future there.

I chased across the badlands of recession:
I'd make a bid for any cuckoo's nest
That sang the joys of owner-occupation.
No loan shark lacked the details of my quest.

Now it's acquired refinement. It's a passion
Long-pursued, a serious late career.
I've shelved my dreams of contract and completion.
Haste doesn't suit the eternal first-time buyer.

Home, after all, is not a simple thing.
Even indoors there should be garden voices,
Earth-breaking rootage, brilliant mirroring,
A constant foliation of loved faces.

Doors are a must, but let them make a palace,
Let each room smile another, on and on –
The glittering, the plain, the small, the spacious,
The sacred and the haunted and the one

Hope rests her case in – windswept, cornerless.

SELIMA HILL

(*born* 1945)

Selima Hill has spent most of her life working with children. She has lived
on the Dorset coast in recent years. Her collections of poetry include *The
Accumulation of Small Acts of Kindness* (1989), a long poem in the form of a
journal kept by a schizophrenic, and *A Little Book of Meat* (1993), a sequence
spoken by a farm woman (a version of Flannery O'Connor) who falls in love
with a travelling slaughterman. Hill's lyrics share the concerns that shape her
long poems into monologues by obsessed female speakers. These concerns are
primarily psychological: the forces that drive, or mutually complicate, erotic
and familial emotion. Her psychic landscapes have points of contact with Sylvia
Plath's; but their structure is more narrative, their focus more social. Hill uses
ancient cultures to set contemporary women's lives in archetypal contexts, and
she exposes "domestic" interiors to the wild. Her sonnet 'The Hare', like so
many of her poems, blurs the boundary between humans and animals. Hill
insists on our fleshly, creaturely existence. Animals also figure in another densely
woven sonnet, 'Three Sisters'. This disquieting elegy blends preparations for
a funeral, sibling tensions, the Fates at work.

The Fowlers of the Marshes

Three thousand years ago
they were fowling in the marshes
around Thebes – men in knotted skirts
and tiered faïence collars,
who avoided the brown crocodile,
and loved the ibis, which they stalked
with long striped cats on strings,
under the eye of Nut, the goddess of the sky.

My mother's hushed peculiar world's the same:
she haunts it like the fowlers of the marshes,
tiptoeing gaily into history, sustained by gods
as strange to me as Lady Nut, and Anubis,
the oracular, the jackal-masked.
When I meet her at the station, I say
Hello, Mum! and think *Hello, Thoth,*
This is the Weighing of the Heart.

The Diving Archaeologists

Led to the Sacred Well of Sacrifice
by the ancient peculiar map
of Diego de Landa, the archbishop,
here in the hot jungle,
where temples sink in mud,
he decides to send for Paterson,
the diver, who is gathering sponges
off the Bahama Islands.

Bound virgins, carrying jade
and chipped obsidian to appease
the glittering serpents,
were thrown into the well
by singing priests at daybreak –
fair female appellants
sent to talk to the goddess
and reason with her under water.

The divers, weighted by their new
iron shoes and necklaces of lead,
are let down into the well
by native boys, who are crying.
The air-valves go pht! pht!
as the waters close
and the light rays
change to purple.

Sunk on ledges, in soft
gruel-thick mud, they find
drowned women's bones, and nodules
of yellow perfumed resin,
and the presents of jade
and obsidian, carefully
broken by the priests
to release their sacred spirits.

When the divers surface,
trailing slimy loops of weed
like hair, their helmets
bump against the bottom of the raft.

The native boys throw down
their wide bleached hats
in fear, and call out
on the swaying pontoon:

El Amo! The Master!
In her anger, the goddess
has swallowed him,
and now she comes knocking,
as a warning – we must not
go down where the women hold
their secret meetings,
in the Well of Chichén Itzá.

The Flowers

After lunch my daughter picked
handfuls of the wild flowers
she knew her grandfather liked best
and piled them in the basket of her bicycle,
beside an empty jam-jar and a trowel;
then, swaying like a candle-bearer,
she rode off to the church
and, like a little dog, I followed her.

She cleared the grave of nettles
and wild parsley, and dug a shallow hole
to put the jam-jar in. She arranged
the flowers to look their best
and scraped the moss from the stone,
so you could see whose grave
she had been caring for.
It didn't take her long – no longer
than making his bed in the morning
when he had got too old to help her.

Not knowing how to leave him,
how to say goodbye, I hesitated
by the rounded grave. *Come on,*
my daughter said, *It's finished now.*
And so we got our bicycles and rode home

down the lane, moving apart
and coming together again,
in and out of the ruts.

Three Sisters

Three sisters, like three hens, eye one another;
six hands, like sparrows, flutter up and down
making wreaths for you, the sisters' brother,
from winter flowers whose petals have turned brown,
from rosemary and basil's grey and blue,
from lavender, and ivy from the apple;
from snowdrops tied in ribbon, berried yew –
six hands like hymns; the kitchen like a chapel
where hens and rabbits wander in and out,
and flowers and fruit trees grow between the stones:
three lemons for the mousse; a lily; trout,
ten tickling fingers checking it for bones.
Chop, chop. That's it. There's nothing we can do.
A fly. A knife. The sickly smell of rue.

The Hare

Beside the river in the dead of night,
a cry, and then another, like a spell,
turns the darkened beeches into light,
the silence of the woods into a bell;
and in the cottage on the moonlit hill
a woman shivers in her narrow bed
to hear the hare; and then the hare is still;
she feels its dusty fur against her head,
its ginger paws, that panic like trapped flies,
or tiny fish that see, or sense, dry land;
she feels it move; she hears its wild cries
glittering inside her ear like sand:
he's lost inside the forest of her hair,
and finds, and steals, his mother's kisses there.

CIARAN CARSON

(*born* 1948)

Ciaran Carson grew up in Belfast. It might also be said that Belfast grows up in his poetry. He spent his childhood in the Catholic Falls Road area, and Irish was his first tongue. His father, a postman and storyteller, figures in his writings as a Muse of memory, narrative and language. Carson studied English at Queen's University, Belfast. From 1975 to 1998 he worked for the Arts Council of Northern Ireland. Part of his role was to promote Irish traditional music. The aesthetics and culture of the music have inspired two prose-works: *The Pocket Guide to Irish Traditional Music* (1986) and *Last Night's Fun* (1996). Irish music and the strategies of the traditional story-teller, John Campbell, influenced Carson's move from the more conventional verse-structures of *The New Estate* (1976) to the long lines of *The Irish for No* (1987) and *Belfast Confetti* (1989).

Two literary influences were the long-lined stanzas of the American poet C.K. Williams and the approach to language in the work of Carson's Belfast contemporary, Paul Muldoon. As compared with Muldoon, and despite the stress on words and alphabets in recent collections such as *Opera Et Cetera* (1996), Carson is more centrally a narrative poet. His distinctive rhythms come from the boundary between poetry and prose, a boundary where poetry renews itself. Most of his poems speak in the voice of someone trying to 'piece together the exploded fragments'. This does not simply place Carson's poetry as "Troubles" poetry (he has said that his poems are not 'about' the Troubles, but may be 'of' them). "Belfast" is not only an arena where individual identity is defined or invaded by the conflicting histories inscribed in street-names or advertised on walls. It also represents wider problems of how we locate ourselves in time and space. As the hapless 'Exiles' Club' has learned, Belfast – both its material fabric and its shape in memory – is not solid but fluid. Here Carson's urban poetry gives a new twist to the rural parochial microcosm as developed by Seamus Heaney. The title of 'Hamlet' signifies 'village' as well as Shakespeare's play. Carson brilliantly makes the parish of Belfast pub-talk – 'time / Is conversation' – take in, and take on, tragic patterns. The dialogues between Carson's poems and other poems (such as MacNeice's 'Snow') have led to him being called a "postmodernist". But his 'exploded fragments' of literature and language belong to a more positive creative flow than that term often implies.

Belfast Confetti

Suddenly as the riot squad moved in, it was raining exclamation
    marks,
Nuts, bolts, nails, car-keys. A fount of broken type. And the explosion
Itself – an asterisk on the map. This hyphenated line, a burst of
    rapid fire...
I was trying to complete a sentence in my head, but it kept stuttering,
All the alleyways and side-streets blocked with stops and colons.

I know this labyrinth so well – Balaclava, Raglan, Inkerman, Odessa
    Street –
Why can't I escape? Every move is punctuated. Crimea Street.
    Dead end again.
A Saracen, Kremlin-2 mesh. Makrolon face-shields. Walkie-talkies.
    What is
My name? Where am I coming from? Where am I going? A
    fusillade of question-marks.

The Exiles' Club

Every Thursday in the upstairs lounge of the Wollongong Bar, they
    make
Themselves at home with Red Heart Stout, Park Drive cigarettes
    and Dunville's whiskey,
A slightly-mouldy batch of soda farls. Eventually, they get down
    to business.
After years they have reconstructed the whole of the Falls Road,
    and now
Are working on the back streets: Lemon, Peel and Omar, Balaclava,
    Alma.

They just about keep up with the news of bombings and demolition,
    and are
Struggling with the finer details: the names and dates carved out
On the back bench of the Leavers' Class in Slate Street School;
    the Nemo Café menu;
The effects of the 1941 Blitz, the entire contents of Paddy Lavery's
    pawnshop.

Turn Again

There is a map of the city which shows the bridge that was never
    built.
A map which shows the bridge that collapsed; the streets that never
    existed.

Ireland's Entry, Elbow Lane, Weigh-House Lane, Back Lane,
    Stone-Cutter's Entry –
Today's plan is already yesterday's – the streets that were there are
    gone.
And the shape of the jails cannot be shown for security reasons.

The linen backing is falling apart – the Falls Road hangs by a thread.
When someone asks me where I live, I remember where I used to
    live.
Someone asks me for directions, and I think again. I turn into
A side-street to try to throw off my shadow, and history is changed.

Snow

A white dot flicked back and forth across the bay window: not
A table-tennis ball, but 'ping-pong', since this is happening in
    another era,
The extended leaves of the dining-table – scratched mahogany
    veneer –
Suggesting many such encounters, or time passing: the celluloid
    diminuendo
As it bounces off into a corner and ticks to an incorrigible stop.
I pick it up days later, trying to get that pallor right: it's neither ivory
Nor milk. Chalk is better; and there's a hint of pearl, translucent
Lurking just behind opaque. I broke open the husk so many times
And always found it empty; the pith was a wordless bubble.

Though there's nothing in the thing itself, bits of it come back
    unbidden,
Playing in the archaic dusk till the white blip became invisible.
Just as, the other day, I felt the tacky pimples of a ping-pong bat
When the bank-clerk counted out my money with her rubber
    thimble, and knew
The black was bleeding into red. Her face was snow and roses just
    behind
The bullet-proof glass: I couldn't touch her if I tried. I crumpled up
    the chit –
No use in keeping what you haven't got – and took a stroll to
    Ross's auction.

There was this Thirties scuffed leather sofa I wanted to make a bid
    for.
Gestures, prices: soundlessly collateral in the murmuring room.

I won't say what I paid for it: anything's too much when you have
    nothing.
But in the dark recesses underneath the cushions I found myself
    kneeling
As decades of the Rosary dragged by, the slack of years ago hauled up
Bead by bead; and with them, all the haberdashery of loss – cuff
            buttons,
Broken ball-point pens and fluff, old pennies, pins and needles,
            and yes,
A ping-pong ball. I cupped it in my hands like a crystal, seeing not
The future, but a shadowed parlour just before the blinds are drawn.
    Someone
Has put up two trestles. Handshakes all round, nods and whispers.
Roses are brought in, and suddenly, white confetti seethes against
    the window.

Hamlet

As usual, the clock in The Clock Bar was a good few minutes fast:
A fiction no one really bothered to maintain, unlike the story
The comrade on my left was telling, which no one knew for certain
    truth:
Back in 1922, a sergeant, I forget his name, was shot outside the
National Bank...
Ah yes, what year was it that they knocked it down? Yet, its
    memory's as fresh
As the inky smell of new pound notes – which interferes with the
    beer-and-whiskey
Tang of now, like two dogs meeting in the revolutionary 69 of a
    long sniff,
Or cattle jostling shit-stained flanks in the Pound. For *pound,* as
    some wag
Interrupted, was an off-shoot of the Falls, from the Irish, *fál,* a hedge;
Hence, *any kind of enclosed thing*, its twigs and branches
    commemorated

By the soldiers' drab and olive camouflage, as they try to melt
Into a brick wall; red coats might be better, after all. *At any rate,*
This sergeant's number came up; not a winning one. The bullet had his
    name on it.
Though Sergeant X, as we'll call him, doesn't really feature in the
    story:
The nub of it is, *This tin can which was heard that night, trundling*
    down
From the bank, down Balaclava Street. Which thousands heard, and
    no one ever
Saw. Which was heard for years, any night that trouble might be
Round the corner...and when it skittered to a halt, you knew
That someone else had snuffed it: a name drifting like an afterthought,
A scribbled wisp of smoke you try and grasp, as it becomes
    diminuendo, then
Vanishes. For *fál*, is also *frontier, boundary*, as in *the undiscovered*
    country
From whose bourne no traveller returns, the illegible, thorny hedge of
    time itself –
Heartstopping mornents, measured not by the pulse of a wristwatch,
    nor
The archaic anarchists' alarm-clock, but a mercury tilt device
Which 'only connects' on any given bump on the road. So, by this
    wingèd messenger
The promise 'to pay the bearer' is fulfilled:

As someone buys another round, an Allied Irish Banks £10 note
    drowns in
The slops of the counter; a Guinness stain blooms on the artist's
    impression
Of the sinking of *The Girona*; a tiny foam hisses round the
    salamander brooch
Dredged up to show how love and money endure, beyond death
    and the Armada,
Like the bomb-disposal expert in his suit of salamander-cloth.
Shielded against the blast of time by a strangely-medieval visor,
He's been outmoded by this jerky robot whose various attachments
    include
A large hook for turning over corpses that may be booby-trapped;
But I still have this picture of his hands held up to avert the future
In a final act of *No surrender*, as, twisting through the murky fathoms
Of what might have been, he is washed ashore as pearl and coral.

This *strange eruption to our state* is seen in other versions of the
    Falls:
A no-go area, a ghetto, a demolition zone. For the ghost, as it turns
    out –
All this according to your man, and I can well believe it – this tin
    ghost,
Since the streets it haunted were abolished, was never heard again.
The sleeve of Raglan Street has been unravelled; the helmet of
    Balaclava
Is torn away from the mouth. The dim glow of Garnet has gone out,
And with it, all but the memory of where I lived. I, too, heard the
    ghost:
A roulette trickle, or the hesitant annunciation of a downpour,
    ricocheting
Off the window; a goods train shunting distantly into a siding,
Then groaning to a halt; the rainy cries of children after dusk.
For the voice from the grave reverberates in others' mouths, as the
    sails
Of the whitethorn hedge swell up in a little breeze, and tremble
Like the spiral blossom of Andromeda: so suddenly are shrouds and
    branches
Hung with street-lights, celebrating all that's lost, as fields are
    reclaimed
By the Starry Plough. So we name the constellations, to put a shape
On what was there; so, the storyteller picks his way between the
    isolated stars.

But, *Was it really like that?* And, *Is the story true?*
You might as well tear off the iron mask, and find that no one, after
    all,
Is there: nothing but a cry, a summons, clanking out from the smoke
Of demolition. Like some son looking for his father, or the father
    for his son,
We try to piece together the exploded fragments. Let these broken
    spars
Stand for the Armada and its proud full sails, for even if
The clock is put to rights, everyone will still believe it's fast:
The barman's shouts of *time* will be ignored in any case, since time
Is conversation; it is the hedge that flits incessantly into the present,
As words blossom from the drinkers' mouths, and the flotilla returns
    to harbour,
Long after hours.

JAMES FENTON

(*born* 1949)

James Fenton is often seen as the English poet who has most successfully built on those qualities of W.H. Auden's poetry that stem from his engagement with contemporary history. After studying philosophy, psychology and politics at Oxford, Fenton became a political journalist. He worked for the *New Statesman*, reported from Vietnam and Cambodia, spent a year as the *Guardian*'s German correspondent, and covered the collapse of the Marcos régime in the Philippines. Meanwhile, he published *Terminal Moraine* (1972) and *The Memory of War* (1982). *Out of Danger*, which includes political ballads in a rap idiom, appeared in 1993. Fenton is also a provocative critic and book reviewer. He believes in variety as the spice of poetry, and once wrote a 'Manifesto Against Manifestos'. From 1994 to 1999 Fenton was Professor of Poetry at Oxford.

In *All the Wrong Places: Adrift in the Politics of Asia* (1988), essays based on his career as a foreign correspondent, Fenton is aware of his questionable position as a 'western observer'. His poetry is equally conscious that its own perspective is part of any comment it might make. The title of 'In a Notebook' gives the poem an ambiguous status between a piece of reporting. and a provisional jotting. This allows Fenton to approach the collapse of South Vietnam through specific personal memories. The poem's form is also precisely judged. After an intricate series of refrains that suspend the action, it ends with the blunt facts of history. In keeping with his principle of variation, Fenton takes a very different approach in 'A German Requiem'. He uses freer verse and traumatised voices to represent the 'spaces' left by the Holocaust. 'Wind' is different again in its rhythmic and visionary sweep: a disturbing symbol of war as 'beautiful catastrophe'. Fenton recalls Keith Douglas's unflinching gaze. And, like Auden and Douglas, he brings war home. 'A Staffordshire Murderer' may be a "condition of England" poem, however fantastic its scenario. The poem assembles all the famous murders of the county to create a menacing allegorical landscape that exposes "heritage" to bloody history. Fenton is effective as a political poet because (like Auden) he fuses politics and psychology to suggest how power works: 'Every fear is a desire. Every desire is fear.' There is a unique Fenton atmosphere that blends wit with mystery, symbolist effects with the nonsense of Lear and Carroll.

In a Notebook

There was a river overhung with trees
With wooden houses built along its shallows
From which the morning sun drew up a haze
And the gyrations of the early swallows

Paid no attention to the gentle breeze
Which spoke discreetly from the weeping willows.
There was a jetty by the forest clearing
Where a small boat was tugging at its mooring.

And night still lingered underneath the eaves.
In the dark houseboats families were stirring
And Chinese soup was cooked on charcoal stoves.
Then one by one there came into the clearing
Mothers and daughters bowed beneath their sheaves.
The silent children gathered round me staring
And the shy soldiers setting out for battle
Asked for a cigarette and laughed a little.

From low canoes old men laid out their nets
While on the bank young boys with lines were fishing.
The wicker traps were drawn up by their floats.
The girls stood waist-deep in the river washing
Or tossed the day's rice on enamel plates
And I sat drinking bitter coffee wishing
The tide would turn to bring me to my senses
After the pleasant war and the evasive answers.

There was a river overhung with trees.
The girls stood waist-deep in the river washing,
And night still lingered underneath the eaves
While on the bank young boys with lines were fishing.
Mothers and daughters bowed beneath their sheaves
While I sat drinking bitter coffee wishing –
And the tide turned and brought me to my senses.
The pleasant war brought the unpleasant answers.

The villages are burnt, the cities void;
The morning light has left the river view;
The distant followers have been dismayed;
And I'm afraid, reading this passage now,
That everything I knew has been destroyed
By those whom I admired but never knew;
The laughing soldiers fought to their defeat
And I'm afraid most of my friends are dead.

Wind

This is the wind, the wind in a field of corn.
Great crowds are fleeing from a major disaster
Down the long valleys, the green swaying wadis,
Down through the beautiful catastrophe of wind.

Families, tribes, nations and their livestock
Have heard something, seen something. An expectation
Or a gigantic misunderstanding has swept over the hilltop
Bending the ear of the hedgerow with stories of fire and sword.

I saw a thousand years pass in two seconds.
Land was lost, languages rose and divided.
This lord went east and found safety.
His brother sought Africa and a dish of aloes.

Centuries, minutes later, one might ask
How the hilt of a sword wandered so far from the smithy.
And somewhere they will sing: 'Like chaff we were borne
In the wind.' This is the wind in a field of corn.

A German Requiem

It is not what they built. It is what they knocked down.
It is not the houses. It is the spaces between the houses.
It is not the streets that exist. It is the streets that no longer exist.
It is not your memories which haunt you.
It is not what you have written down.
It is what you have forgotten, what you must forget.
What you must go on forgetting all your life.
And with any luck oblivion should discover a ritual.
You will find out that you are not alone in the enterprise.
Yesterday the very furniture seemed to reproach you.
Today you take your place in the Widow's Shuttle.

*

The bus is waiting at the southern gate
To take you to the city of your ancestors

Which stands on the hill opposite, with gleaming pediments,
As vivid as this charming square, your home.
Are you shy? You should be. It is almost like a wedding,
The way you clasp your flowers and give a little tug at your veil. Oh,
The hideous bridesmaids, it is natural that you should resent them
Just a little, on this first day.
But that will pass, and the cemetery is not far.
Here comes the driver, flicking a toothpick into the gutter,
His tongue still searching between his teeth.
See, he has not noticed you. No one has noticed you.
It will pass, young lady, it will pass.

*

How comforting it is, once or twice a year,
To get together and forget the old times.
As on those special days, ladies and gentlemen,
When the boiled shirts gather at the graveside
And a leering waistcoat approaches the rostrum.
It is like a solemn pact between the survivors.
The mayor has signed it on behalf of the freemasonry.
The priest has sealed it on behalf of all the rest.
Nothing more need be said, and it is better that way –

*

The better for the widow, that she should not live in fear of surprise,
The better for the young man, that he should move at liberty
            between the armchairs,
The better that these bent figures who flutter among the graves
Tending the nightlights and replacing the chrysanthemums
Are not ghosts,
That they shall go home.
The bus is waiting, and on the upper terraces
The workmen are dismantling the houses of the dead.

*

But when so many had died, so many and at such speed,
There were no cities waiting for the victims.
They unscrewed the name-plates from the shattered doorways
And carried them away with the coffins.
So the squares and parks were filled with the eloquence of young
            cemeteries:
The smell of fresh earth, the improvised crosses
And all the impossible directions in brass and enamel.

*

'Doctor Gliedschirm, skin specialist, surgeries 14–16 hours or by
      appointment.'
Professor Sargnagel was buried with four degrees, two associate
      memberships
And instructions to tradesmen to use the back entrance.
Your uncle's grave informed you that he lived on the third floor, left.
You were asked please to ring, and he would come down in the lift
To which one needed a key...

*

Would come down, would ever come down
With a smile like thin gruel, and never too much to say.
How he shrank through the years.
How you towered over him in the narrow cage.
How he shrinks now...

*

But come. Grief must have its term? Guilt too, then.
And it seems there is no limit to the resourcefulness of recollection.
So that a man might say and think:
When the world was at its darkest,
When the black wings passed over the rooftops
(And who can divine His purposes?) even then
There was always, always a fire in this hearth.
You see this cupboard? A priest-hole!
And in that lumber-room whole generations have been housed and
      fed.
Oh, if I were to begin, if I were to begin to tell you
The half, the quarter, a mere smattering of what we went through!

*

His wife nods, and a secret smile,
Like a breeze with enough strength to carry one dry leaf
Over two pavingstones, passes from chair to chair.
Even the enquirer is charmed.
He forgets to pursue the point.
It is not what he wants to know.
It is what he wants not to know.
It is not what they say.
It is what they do not say.

A Staffordshire Murderer

Every fear is a desire. Every desire is fear.
The cigarettes are burning under the trees
Where the Staffordshire murderers wait for their accomplices
And victims. Every victim is an accomplice.

It takes a lifetime to stroll to the carpark
Stopping at the footbridge for reassurance,
Looking down at the stream, observing
(With one eye) the mallard's diagonal progress backwards.

You could cut and run, now. It is not too late.
But your fear is like a long-case clock
In the last whirring second before the hour,
The hammer drawn back, the heart ready to chime.

Fear turns the ignition. The van is unlocked.
You may learn now what you ought to know:
That every journey begins with a death,
That the suicide travels alone, that the murderer needs company.

And the Staffordshire murderers, nervous though they are,
Are masters of the conciliatory smile.
A cigarette? A tablet in a tin?
Would you care for a boiled sweet from the famous poisoner

Of Rugeley? These are his own brand.
He has never had any complaints.
He speaks of his victims as a sexual braggart
With a tradesman's emphasis on the word 'satisfaction'.

You are flattered as never before. He appreciates
So much, the little things – your willingness for instance
To bequeath your body at once to his experiments.
He sees the point of you as no one else does.

Large parts of Staffordshire have been undermined.
The trees are in it up to their necks. Fish
Nest in their branches. In one of the Five Towns
An ornamental pond disappeared overnight

Dragging the ducks down with it, down to the old seams
With a sound as of a gigantic bath running out,
Which is in turn the sound of ducks in distress.
Thus History murders mallards, while we hear nothing

Or what we hear we do not understand.
It is heard as the tramp's rage in the crowded precinct:
'Woe to the bloody city of Lichfield.'
It is lost in the enthusiasm of the windows

From which we are offered on the easiest terms
Five times over in colour and once in monochrome
The first reprisals after the drill-sergeant's coup.
How speedily the murder detail makes its way

Along the green beach, past the pink breakers,
And binds the whole cabinet to the oil-drums,
Where death is a preoccupied tossing of the head,
Where no decorative cloud lingers at the gun's mouth.

At the Dame's School dust gathers on the highwayman,
On Sankey and Moody, Wesley and Fox,
On the snoring churchwarden, on Palmer the Poisoner
And Palmer's house and Stanfield Hall.

The brilliant moss has been chipped from the Red Barn.
They say that Cromwell played ping-pong with the cathedral.
We train roses over the arches. In the Minster Pool
Crayfish live under carved stones. Every spring

The rats pick off the young mallards and
The good weather brings out the murderers
By the Floral Clock, by the footbridge,
The pottery murderers in jackets of prussian blue.

'Alack, George, where are thy shoes?'
He lifted up his head and espied the three
Steeple-house spires, and they struck at his life.
And he went by his eye over hedge and ditch

And no one laid hands on him, and he went
Thus crying through the streets, where there seemed
To be a channel of blood running through the streets,
And the market-place appeared like a pool of blood.

For this field of corpses was Lichfield
Where a thousand Christian Britons fell
In Diocletian's day, and 'much could I write
Of the sense that I had of the blood – '

That winter Friday. Today it is hot.
The cowparsley is so high that the van cannot be seen
From the road. The bubbles rise in the warm canal.
Below the lock-gates you can hear mallards.

A coot hurries along the tow-path, like a Queen's Messenger.
On the heli-pad, an arrival in blue livery
Sends the water-boatmen off on urgent business.
News of a defeat. Keep calm. The cathedral chimes.

The house by the bridge is the house in your dream.
It stares through new frames, unwonted spectacles,
And the paint, you can tell, has been weeping.
In the yard, five striped oildrums. Flowers in a tyre.

This is where the murderer works. But it is Sunday.
Tomorrow's bank holiday will allow the bricks to set.
You see? he has thought of everything. He shows you
The snug little cavity he calls 'your future home'.

And 'Do you know,' he remarks, 'I have been counting my victims.
Nine hundred and ninety nine, the Number of the Beast!
That makes you...' But he sees he has overstepped the mark:
'I'm sorry, but you cannot seriously have thought you were the first?'

A thousand preachers, a thousand poisoners,
A thousand martyrs, a thousand murderers –
Surely these preachers are poisoners, these martyrs murderers?
Surely this is all a gigantic mistake?

But there has been no mistake. God and the weather are glorious.
You have come as an anchorite to kneel at your funeral.
Kneel then and pray. The blade flashes a smile.
This is your new life. This murder is yours.

MEDBH McGUCKIAN

(*born* 1950)

Medbh McGuckian grew up in Belfast, and still lives there. She studied English at Queen's University, Belfast. She teaches creative writing and researches into Irish women's poetry. McGuckian began to publish poetry later than her Northern Irish contemporaries, Ciaran Carson and Paul Muldoon. *The Flower Master* (1982) and *Venus and the Rain* (1984) interpret their own belated appearance in print. 'The Flitting' (whose title literally means 'moving house') presents a woman speaker whose life has been defined by male 'structures': 'that fraternity of clothes'. She is also positioned between being an object of art (the portraits of 'these Dutch girls') and its creator ('If I painted'), and between motherhood and poetry. 'Mr McGregor's Garden', in which Beatrix Potter is a mask for McGuckian's art, more positively asserts her poetic powers. Potter's animals are obliged to serve as male muses, sometimes sexually. McGuckian's influences include Emily Dickinson and Sylvia Plath. Her poems subvert patriarchy as it has 'structurally' shaped both Northern Irish poetry and Northern Irish society. They refuse obvious "subject-matter" and an explicit logic of narrative or argument. They proceed, instead, by an interplay of images. Here, parts of the body, flowers, houses, gardens and colours have leading roles. McGuckian was annoyed at not being included in Frank Ormsby's anthology *A Rage for Order: Poetry of the Northern Ireland Troubles* (1992). She gave *Captain Lavender* (1994) a pointed epigraph: Picasso's remark in 1944: 'I have not painted the war...but I have no doubt that the war is in...these paintings I have done.'

Mr McGregor's Garden

Some women save their sanity with needles.
I complicate my life with studies
Of my favourite rabbit's head, his vulgar volatility,
Or a little ladylike sketching
Of my resident toad in his flannel box;
Or search for handsome fungi for my tropical
Herbarium, growing dry-rot in the garden,
And wishing that the climate were kinder,
Turning over the spiky purple heads among the moss
With my cheese-knife to view the slimy veil.

Unlike the cupboard-love of sleepers in the siding,
My hedgehog's sleep is under his control
And not the weather's; he can rouse himself
At half-an-hour's notice in the frost, or leave at will
On a wet day in August, by the hearth.

He goes by breathing slowly, after a large meal,
A lively evening, very cross if interrupted,
And returns with a hundred respirations
To the minute, weak and nervous when he wakens,
Busy with his laundry.

On sleepless nights while learning
Shakespeare off by heart,
I feel that Bunny's at my bedside
In a white cotton nightcap,
Tickling me with his whiskers.

The Orchid House

A flower's fragrance is a woman's virtue;
So I tell them underground in pairs,
Or in their fleshy white sleeves, how
Desirable their shapes, how one
Was lost for sixty years, with all
Its arching spikes, its honeyed tessellations,
And how in bloom they will resemble
Moths, the gloss of mirrors, Christmas
Stars, their helmets blushing
Red-brown when they marry.

The Flower Master

Like foxgloves in the school of the grass moon
We come to terms with shade, with the principle
Of enfolding space. Our scissors in brocade,
We learn the coolness of straight edges, how
To gently stroke the necks of daffodils
And make them throw their heads back to the sun.

We slip the thready stems of violets, delay
The loveliness of the hibiscus dawn with quiet ovals,
Spirals of feverfew like water splashing,
The papery legacies of bluebells. We do
Sea-fans with sea-lavender, moon-arrangements
Roughly for the festival of moon-viewing.

This black container calls for sloes, sweet
Sultan, dainty nipplewort, in honour
Of a special guest, who summoned to the
Tea ceremony, must stoop to our low doorway,
Our fontanelle, the trout's dimpled feet.

The Flitting

'You wouldn't believe all this house has cost me –
In body-language terms, it has turned me upside down.'
I've been carried from one structure to the other
On a chair of human arms, and liked the feel
Of being weightless, that fraternity of clothes...
Now my own life hits me in the throat, the bumps
And cuts of the walls as telling
As the poreholes in strawberries, tomato seeds.
I cover them for safety with these Dutch girls
Making lace, or leaning their almond faces
On their fingers with a mandolin, a dreamy
Chapelled ease abreast this other turquoise-turbanned,
Glancing over her shoulder with parted mouth.

She seems a garden escape in her unconscious
Solidarity with darkness, clove-scented
As an orchid taking fifteen years to bloom,
And turning clockwise as the honeysuckle.
Who knows what importance
She attaches to the hours?
Her narrative secretes its own values, as mine might
If I painted the half of me that welcomes death
In a faggotted dress, in a peacock chair,
No falser biography than our casual talk

Of losing a virginity, or taking a life, and
No less poignant if dying
Should consist in more than waiting.

I postpone my immortality for my children,
Little rock-roses, cushioned
In long-flowering sea-thrift and metrics,
Lacking elemental memories:
I am well-earthed here as the digital clock,
Its numbers flicking into place like overgrown farthings
On a bank where once a train
Ploughed like an emperor living out a myth
Through the cambered flesh of clover and wild carrot.

The Sitting

My half-sister comes to me to be painted:
She is posing furtively, like a letter being
Pushed under a door, making a tunnel with her
Hands over her dull-rose dress. Yet her coppery
Head is as bright as a net of lemons, I am
Painting it hair by hair as if she had not
Disowned it, or forsaken those unsparkling
Eyes as blue may be sifted from the surface
Of a cloud; and she questions my brisk
Brushwork, the note of positive red
In the kissed mouth I have given her,
As a woman's touch makes curtains blossom
Permanently in a house: she calls it
Wishfulness, the failure of the tampering rain
To go right into the mountain, she prefers
My sea-studies, and will not sit for me
Again, something half-opened, rarer
Than railroads, a soiled red-letter day.

PAUL MULDOON

(*born* 1951)

Paul Muldoon's innovative approach to poetic language has widely influenced poetry in these islands. Muldoon grew up near Moy, Co. Tyrone, an area which he transmutes into a wonderfully flexible poetic microcosm. He studied English at Queen's University, Belfast where (like Carson and McGuckian) he was taught by Seamus Heaney. Until 1986 he worked in Belfast as a radio producer for BBC Northern Ireland. He moved to the US, and is now Professor of Creative Writing at Princeton and (since 1999) Professor of Poetry at Oxford.

New Weather (1973) and *Mules* (1977) established Muldoon's range. In 'Dancers at the Moy', the Moy is already given mythic and historical significance. The poem is also a political parable which disturbingly mingles human and animal behaviour, as do other Muldoon poems. Later, the 'black and gold' river of horses becomes the 'self-renewing gold-black dragon' in 'Gathering Mushrooms'. (Here it connects with the 'dragon-ridden' days of Yeats's 'Nineteen Hundred and Nineteen'.) 'Duffy's Circus', another early parable, suggests that the world is wilder and stranger than various forms of authority allow. The "father" in Muldoon sometimes represents authority or a past order that his poetry questions. This applies to his poetic forebears: the structures of Heaney, Longley and Mahon, not to mention Yeats, are questioned by Muldoon's methods and emphases. Yet he preserves stanzas and (very subtly) rhyme, and develops the possibilities of sonnet-form. In fact, his work is intensely patterned, both within and across books, by repeated images, words, and even rhyme-schemes.

As most recently in *Hay* (1998), Muldoon's pattern-making co-exists with a sense that the play of language is infinite. However, his knack of raising our linguistic consciousness can have critical and political point. 'Anseo' illustrates how we are formed by the social codes that language exemplifies and transmits. (The boy destined to become a paramilitary has been named for an executed leader of the 1916 Rising.) And 'Gathering Mushrooms', which alludes to the 'dirty protest' by IRA prisoners in the late 1970s, implies that imprisonment is a state of mind induced by fixed ideas and words. Poetry ('song') cannot follow the script dictated by the voice of the last stanza. Muldoon has said: 'I want my own vision to be disturbed.' 'Quoof' suggests how poetry-as-language might disturb people's vision. 'The Frog' suggests how poetry-as-image might do so.

Dancers at the Moy

This Italian square
And circling plain
Black once with mares
And their stallions,
The flat Blackwater
Turning its stones

Over hour after hour
As their hooves shone
And lifted together
Under the black rain,
One or other Greek war
Now coloured the town

Blacker than ever before
With hungry stallions
And their hungry mares
Like hammocks of skin,
The flat Blackwater
Unable to contain

Itself as horses poured
Over acres of grain
In a black and gold river.
No band of Athenians
Arrived at the Moy fair
To buy for their campaign,

Peace having been declared
And a treaty signed.
The black and gold river
Ended as a trickle of brown
Where those horses tore
At briars and whins,

Ate the flesh of each other
Like people in famine.
The flat Blackwater
Hobbled on its stones
With a wild stagger
And sag in its backbone,

The local people gathered
Up the white skeletons.
Horses buried for years
Under the foundations
Give their earthen floors
The ease of trampolines.

Duffy's Circus

Once Duffy's Circus had shaken out its tent
In the big field near the Moy
God may as well have left Ireland
And gone up a tree. My father had said so.

There was no such thing as the five-legged calf,
The God of Creation
Was the God of Love.
My father chose to share such Nuts of Wisdom.

Yet across the Alps of each other the elephants
Trooped. Nor did it matter
When Wild Bill's Rain Dance
Fell flat. Some clown emptied a bucket of stars

Over the swankiest part of the crowd.
I had lost my father in the rush and slipped
Out the back. Now I heard
For the first time that long-drawn-out cry.

It came from somewhere beyond the corral.
A dwarf on stilts. Another dwarf.
I sidled past some trucks. From under a freighter
I watched a man sawing a woman in half.

Truce

It begins with one or two soldiers
And one or two following
With hampers over their shoulders.
They might be off wildfowling

As they would another Christmas Day,
So gingerly they pick their steps.
No one seems sure of what to do.
All stop when one stops.

A fire gets lit. Some spread
Their greatcoats on the frozen ground.
Polish vodka, fruit and bread
Are broken out and passed round.

The air of an old German song,
The rules of Patience, are the secrets
They'll share before long.
They draw on their last cigarettes

As Friday-night lovers, when it's over,
Might get up from their mattresses
To congratulate each other
And exchange names and addresses.

Ireland

The Volkswagen parked in the gap,
But gently ticking over.
You wonder if it's lovers
And not men hurrying back
Across two fields and a river.

Anseo

When the Master was calling the roll
At the primary school in Collegelands,
You were meant to call back *Anseo*
And raise your hand
As your name occurred.
Anseo, meaning here, here and now,
All present and correct,
Was the first word of Irish I spoke.

The last name on the ledger
Belonged to Joseph Mary Plunkett Ward
And was followed, as often as not,
By silence, knowing looks,
A nod and a wink, the Master's droll
'And where's our little Ward-of-court?'

I remember the first time he came back
The Master had sent him out
Along the hedges
To weigh up for himself and cut
A stick with which he would be beaten.
After a while, nothing was spoken;
He would arrive as a matter of course
With an ash-plant, a salley-rod.
Or, finally, the hazel-wand
He had whittled down to a whip-lash,
Its twist of red and yellow lacquers
Sanded and polished,
And altogether so delicately wrought
That he had engraved his initials on it.

I last met Joseph Mary Plunkett Ward
In a pub just over the Irish border.
He was living in the open,
In a secret camp
On the other side of the mountain.
He was fighting for Ireland,
Making things happen.
And he told me, Joe Ward,
Of how he had risen through the ranks
To Quartermaster, Commandant.
How every morning at parade
His volunteers would call back *Anseo*
And raise their hands
As their names occurred.

Gathering Mushrooms

The rain comes flapping through the yard
like a tablecloth that she hand-embroidered.
My mother has left it on the line.
It is sodden with rain.
The mushroom shed is windowless, wide,
its high-stacked wooden trays
hosed down with formaldehyde.
And my father has opened the Gates of Troy
to that first load of horse manure.
Barley straw. Gypsum. Dried blood. Ammonia.
Wagon after wagon
blusters in, a self-renewing gold-black dragon
we push to the back of the mind.
We have taken our pitchforks to the wind.

All brought back to me that September evening
fifteen years on. The pair of us
tripping through Barnett's fair demesne
like girls in long dresses
after a hail-storm.
We might have been thinking of the fire-bomb
that sent Malone House sky-high
and its priceless collection of linen
sky-high.
We might have wept with Elizabeth McCrum.
We were thinking only of psilocybin.
You sang of the maid you met on the dewy grass –
And she stooped so low gave me to know
it was mushrooms she was gathering O.

He'll be wearing that same old donkey-jacket
and the sawn-off waders.
He carries a knife, two punnets, a bucket.
He reaches far into his own shadow.
We'll have taken him unawares
and stand behind him, slightly to one side.
He is one of those ancient warriors
before the rising tide.
He'll glance back from under his peaked cap
without breaking rhythm:

his coaxing a mushroom – a flat or a cup –
the nick against his right thumb;
the bucket then, the punnet to left or right,
and so on and so forth till kingdom come.

We followed the overgrown towpath by the Lagan.
The sunset would deepen through cinnamon
to aubergine,
the wood-pigeon's concerto for oboe and strings,
allegro, blowing your mind.
And you were suddenly out of my ken, hurtling
towards the ever-receding ground,
into the maw
of a shimmering green-gold dragon.
You discovered yourself in some outbuilding
with your long-lost companion, me,
though my head had grown into the head of a horse
that shook its dirty-fair mane
and spoke this verse:

Come back to us. However cold and raw, your feet
were always meant
to negotiate terms with bare cement.
Beyond this concrete wall is a wall of concrete
and barbed wire. Your only hope
is to come back. If sing you must, let your song
tell of treading your own dung,
let straw and dung give a spring to your step.
If we never live to see the day we leap
into our true domain,
lie down with us now and wrap
yourself in the soiled grey blanket of Irish rain
that will, one day, bleach itself white.
Lie down with us and wait.

Plovers

The plovers come down hard, then clear again,
for they are the embodiment of rain.

Quoof

How often have I carried our family word
for the hot water bottle
to a strange bed,
as my father would juggle a red-hot half-brick
in an old sock
to his childhood settle.
I have taken it into so many lovely heads
or laid it between us like a sword.

An hotel room in New York City
with a girl who spoke hardly any English,
my hand on her breast
like the smouldering one-off spoor of the yeti
or some other shy beast
that has yet to enter the language.

The Frog

Comes to mind as another small upheaval
amongst the rubble.
His eye matches exactly the bubble
in my spirit-level.
I set aside hammer and chisel
and take him on the trowel.

The entire population of Ireland
springs from a pair left to stand
overnight in a pond
in the gardens of Trinity College,
two bottles of wine left there to chill
after the Act of Union.

There is, surely, in this story
a moral. A moral for our times.
What if I put him to my head
and squeezed it out of him,
like the juice of freshly squeezed limes,
or a lemon sorbet?

Lag

We were joined at the hip. We were joined at the hip
like some latter-day Chang and Eng,
though I lay in that dreadful kip
in North Carolina while you preferred to hang

loose in London, in that self-same
'room in Bayswater'. You wrapped yourself in a flag
(the red flag, with a white elephant, of Siam)
and contemplated the time lag.

It was Chang, I seem to recall, who tried to choke
Eng when he'd had one over the eight.
It was Chang whose breath was always so sickly-sour.

It was Chang who suffered a stroke.
Eng was forced to shoulder his weight.
It was Chang who died first. Eng lived on for five hours.

Horses

I

A sky. A field. A hedge flagrant with gorse.
I'm trying to remember, as best I can,
if I'm a man dreaming I'm a plowhorse
or a great plowhorse dreaming I'm a man.

II

Midsummer Eve. St John's wort. Spleenwort. Spurge.
I'm hard on the heels of the sage, Chuang Tzu,
when he slips into what was once a forge
through a door in the shape of a horseshoe.

JO SHAPCOTT

(*born* 1953)

Jo Shapcott was born in London, and educated at Trinity College Dublin, Oxford and Harvard. She has worked in education and arts administration. Shapcott's *Her Book: Poems 1988-1998* (2000) selects from three collections: *Electroplating the Baby* (1988), *Phrase Book* (1992) and *My Life Asleep* (1998). Shapcott is interested in the zone where poetry and science meet. Hence her way of approaching every poem as a new structural experiment, and her stress on creating an objective artefact. She resembles Norman Cameron in that some of her best poems take shape as witty conceits. This is true of the 'Divine' straining to hold his devout pose. This dramatic monologue plays with the more familiar genre of a poet contemplating a picture. Similarly, Shapcott's 'animal' poems, such as 'Life' and 'Rattlesnake', are beast-fables rather than (like Selima Hill's) psychic dramas. Yet most of her experiments, like the apparently more direct 'Lovebirds', seem designed to discover emotional truths.

I'm Contemplated by a Portrait of a Divine

I cannot speak to you. My lips are fused
where an archangel kissed them. I have never
made much of myself although I know,
sometimes, that space is touching me
because I have seen the crack in the universe
through which the galaxies stream. O God,
I will always know how to walk, no rest, until
it just ends in blackness when I fall down flat.
I have one arching eyebrow: my whole life
is in that eyebrow where an angel nestles
at the root of every hair, raising it up.
Dear Christ, I can hear vice rushing through
the grass. There is someone here.
If I could lick the glass
clean from this side, I might see her, though
I already know she would look the way
I want my soul to look. This pose
which I strain to keep, in which I lean
on the desk for dear life, is not a pose.
It's so important for keeping the drawer shut
in case my heart should slip out, fly up.

Life

My life as a bat
is for hearing
the world.

If I pitch it right
I can hear
just where you are.

If I pitch it right
I can hear inside your body:
the state of your health,

and more, I can hear
into your mind.
Bat death is not listening.

My life as a frog
is for touching
other things.

I'm very moist
so I don't get stuck
in the water.

I'm very moist
so I can cling
onto your back

for three days
and nights.
Frog death is separation.

My life as an iguana
is for tasting
everything.

My tongue is very fast
because the flavour
of the air is so subtle.

It's long enough
to surprise
the smallest piece of you

from extremely
far away.
Iguana death is a closed mouth.

Rattlesnake

My rattlesnake has warm skin.
He sleeps by my feet and rustles
through my dreams, his diamond
back glistening all night.

Better than a fat alarm clock
is his subtle rattle at seven,
his cool glide towards breakfast,
his little fangs clinking the tea cup.

Lovebirds

So she moved into the hospital the last nine days
to tend him with little strokes and murmurs
as he sank into the sheets. Nurse
set out a low bed for her, night-times, next to his.
He nuzzled up to her as she brushed
away the multiplying cells with a sigh,
was glad as she ignored the many
effluents and the tang of death. The second
last morning of his life he opened
his eyes, saying, 'I can't wake up'
but wouldn't close them for his nap
until he was sure she was there.
Later he moved quietly to deeper sleep,
as Doctor said he would, still listening
to her twittering on and on until the last.

IAN DUHIG

(*born* 1954)

Ian Duhig grew up in London in an Irish Catholic immigrant family. His status as second-generation 'Irish in Britain' has made him unusually aware of Irish and English poetic traditions. It has also made his poetry linguistically self-conscious and intricate. 'Nothing Pie', for instance, is a parable of adaptation to a new cultural environment. Significantly, the poet-speaker must find words to hold the balance between his father's Irish prickliness and his son's Leeds accent. Two of Duhig's poems here refer to poems by W.B. Yeats and Paul Muldoon (also in this anthology). Both references are irreverent, especially his rewriting of Yeats's 'Nineteen Hundred and Nineteen' as historical burlesque. Duhig begins with transvestism and ends by placing a peculiar slant on two of Yeats's invented personalities: Michael Robartes and Crazy Jane. Yet the poem's political, intellectual and sexual ingredients add up to more than 'mere anarchy' (to quote Yeats). In a different way from Yeats, Duhig suggests the volatile arrival of modernity. For all his allusiveness and comedy, he is no player of postmodernist games. As politically alert as James Fenton, Duhig is a serious questioner of authority. When his poems have fun with Irish texts, they are attacking what 'was expected' by Irish cultural or political nationalism, and doing so from a fresh angle. But, as 'Clare's Jig' and 'Straw School' indicate, Duhig does not spare England either.

From the Irish

According to Dineen, a Gael unsurpassed
in lexicographical enterprise, the Irish
for moon means 'the white circle in a slice
of half-boiled potato or turnip'. A star
is the mark on the forehead of a beast
and the sun is the bottom of a lake, or well.

Well, if I say to you your face
is like a slice of half-boiled turnip,
your hair is the colour of a lake's bottom
and at the centre of each of your eyes
is the mark of the beast, it is because
I want to love you properly, according to Dineen.

The Frog

(for Leon McAuley)

The ollamh faltered in his staves,
a gilly spilled his wine-cask:
the Ossory court circled a wonder;
'It is the living budget of The Morrígan!'
'It is the handsomest child of a Connachtman!'
'It is the ghost of a drunkard's stomach!'
'Without doubt, it's a Fomorian cat.'
'Without doubt, it's from Paddington.'
'Without doubt, it's an ugly bugger isn't it?'

The frog gulped, swivelled its headlamp eyes
and burped like an earl. The hall stilled,
its eyes fixed on Duvenold,
king and seer. He knew he must pronounce –
Warfare, Pestilence, the Gael in Chains –
that sort of thing. It was expected. 'Friends,'
he cried, 'this hare-fish means Death to Ireland;
Warfare, Pestilence, the Gael in Chains!
It also shags that poem of Muldoon's.'

Nineteen Hundred and Nineteen

Dismissed from Tlaltizapa for changing sex
Manuel Palafox sulked in Arenista. At markets
he bought chimoyas, limes and ink from Oaxtepec.
Some days he wore his twenty-ounce sombrero,
deerskin pants and "charro" boots. On others
gold-embroidered blouses and red kerseymere skirts.

He wrote to Magonistas: 'Zapata is finished.
He takes orders from Obregon. Rally the Peones!
Death to Carranza! Tierra y Libertad!'
He wrote to Lenin: 'Trotsky is finished.
Seek concord with the Ukraine Makhnovshchina.
Brest-Litovsk's a cock-up. Regards to the Missus.'

He wrote to Freud: 'Were you coked when you dreamt up this?
No Mexican has even heard of the sexual revolution.
All Eros last year now it's Thanatos, bloody Thanatos.
Jung was right – grow a beard, you think you're Moses.
I hope your jaw drops off. Regards to the Missus.'
At last he wrote to Yeats: 'Dear Willie, how's the Vision?

Mine's double, ha-ha. Shit. Willie, I'm finished
in Mexico – it's full of bigots. Ireland can't be worse.
I'll work. Your brother paints – I'll hold his ladders.
You can have my poems. The one about this year –
change it round – it'll do for Ireland. What happened
to my lift with Casement? Willie, GET ME OUT OF HERE!'

Shopping in Cashel for pulque, Michael Robartes –
'Research Assistant to a popular writer' –
itched in his Connemara Cloth. Himself well-known
for a Special Devotion to the Virgin of Guadaloupe,
he frowned on local talk of a drunken madwoman
in red skirts, publicly disputing with the bishop.

Nothing Pie

When I told my Dad that the locals called
a dandelion an 'Irish daisy',
I'd have to admit he looked disenthralled

and soon his farts were 'Yorkshire nightingales',
a dandelion a 'Yorkshire daisy',
a 'Yorkshire screwdriver' banged in his nails,

Tipperary invented the 'riding'
and 'Nothing pie' meant my Yorkshire pudding.
Abide with me, Daddy. Be abiding.

Now Owen's asking what our garden grows,
'bud' and 'good' full rhymes when he says 'budding'.
Mam will know. I call everything a rose.

Clare's Jig

I'd collected a good jig called 'The Self',
but lilting it last night for Dr Bottle
he chided me, opined it should be *Sylph*,
which is Greek, like much he says, meaning *beetle*.
He chokes the same and gibbets butterflies,
now all your rich men's fashionable rage.
My fellow inmates praise him to the skies,
and like a hawk he scans my every page,
the dumb morris of these poor whopstraw words.
When pressed, a melancholy Johnson said
'Why Sir, we are a nest of singing birds!'
Well I hear boughs breaking inside my head
so listen till the music has to stop,
for like a tree, I'm dying from the top.

Straw School

Her parents love her huge brown eyes and how hard she works at
          school,
a school which cannot teach the pupils who have forgotten straw.

Her podgy fingers can trim the chine to blanch and stiffen blades
and she can shave each brimstoned rod into sixteen equal spills.

Her lips can wet a spill to soften it for working but leave no ring
nor smudge the colours which have killed her once already.

She can plait Ivinghoe, Stanbride, Carrick bend, twist, narrow twist
Egginton twist, barley, double-barley, birdseye and whipcord.

Lists are old-fashioned poems but I catalogue the accomplishments
of Jenny Ibbens, dead by five a century ago who still keeps dying.

CAROL ANN DUFFY

(*born* 1955)

Carol Ann Duffy was born in Glasgow of Irish parents. She grew up in Stafford and was educated at Liverpool University. Duffy, whose poetry readings are extremely popular, writes lyrics on the verge of becoming drama or narrative. Her poems are full of voices telling stories, speaking in monologue or dialogue, formulating desires, prayers and utopias. As in 'The Virgin Punishing the Infant', 'Plainsong' and 'Prayer', she has an ability to open up religious experience from unexpected secular angles. Duffy's poems make their effect through an interplay between verse-form and the pulse of narration or dramatic speech. Duffy can combine emotional with formal intensity in a way that takes elements of Philip Larkin's aesthetic on to female ground.

The Virgin Punishing the Infant

(after the painting by Max Ernst)

He spoke early. Not the *goo goo goo* of infancy,
but *I am God.* Joseph kept away, carving himself
a silent Pinocchio out in the workshed. He said
he was a simple man and hadn't dreamed of this.

She grew anxious in that second year, would stare
at stars saying *Gabriel? Gabriel?* Your guess.
The village gossiped in the sun. The child was solitary,
his wide and solemn eyes could fill your head.

After he walked, our normal children crawled. Our wives
were first resentful, then superior. Mary's child
would bring her sorrow...better far to have a son
who gurgled nonsense at your breast. *Googoo. Googoo.*

But I am God. We heard him through the window,
heard the smacks which made us peep. What we saw
was commonplace enough. But afterwards, we wondered
why the infant did not cry. And why the Mother did.

Plainsong

Stop. Along this path, in phrases of light,
trees sing their leaves. No Midas touch
has turned the wood to gold, late in the year
when you pass by, suddenly sad, straining
to remember something you're sure you knew.

Listening. The words you have for things die
in your heart, but grasses are plainsong,
patiently chanting the circles you cannot repeat
or understand. This is your homeland,
Lost One, Stranger who speaks with tears.

It is almost impossible to be here and yet
you kneel, no one's child, absolved by late sun
through the branches of a wood, distantly
the evening bell reminding you, *Home, Home,
Home*, and the stone in your palm telling the time.

Warming Her Pearls
(for Judith Radstone)

Next to my own skin, her pearls. My mistress
bids me wear them, warm them, until evening
when I'll brush her hair. At six, I place them
round her cool, white throat. All day I think of her,

resting in the Yellow Room, contemplating silk
or taffeta, which gown tonight? She fans herself
whilst I work willingly, my slow heat entering
each pearl. Slack on my neck, her rope.

She's beautiful. I dream about her
in my attic bed; picture her dancing
with tall men, puzzled by my faint, persistent scent
beneath her French perfume, her milky stones.

I dust her shoulders with a rabbit's foot,
watch the soft blush seep through her skin
like an indolent sigh. In her looking-glass
my red lips part as though I want to speak.

Full moon. Her carriage brings her home. I see
her every movement in my head...Undressing,
taking off her jewels, her slim hand reaching
for the case, slipping naked into bed, the way

she always does...And I lie here awake,
knowing the pearls are cooling even now
in the room where my mistress sleeps. All night
I feel their absence and I burn.

In Your Mind

The other country, is it anticipated or half-remembered?
Its language is muffled by the rain which falls all afternoon
one autumn in England, and in your mind
you put aside your work and head for the airport
with a credit card and a warm coat you will leave
on the plane. The past fades like newsprint in the sun.

You know people there. Their faces are photographs
on the wrong side of your eyes. A beautiful boy
in the bar on the harbour serves you a drink – what? –
asks you if men could possibly land on the moon.
A moon like an orange drawn by a child. No.
Never. You watch it peel itself into the sea.

Sleep. The rasp of carpentry wakes you. On the wall,
a painting lost for thirty years renders the room yours.
Of course. You go to your job, right at the old hotel, left,
then left again. You love this job. Apt sounds
mark the passing of the hours. Seagulls. Bells. A flute
practising scales. You swap a coin for a fish on the way home.

Then suddenly you are lost but not lost, dawdling
on the blue bridge, watching six swans vanish
under your feet. The certainty of place turns on the lights
all over town, turns up the scent on the air. For a moment
you are there, in the other country, knowing its name.
And then a desk. A newspaper. A window. English rain.

Prayer

Some days, although we cannot pray, a prayer
utters itself. So, a woman will lift
her head from the sieve of her hands and stare
at the minims sung by a tree, a sudden gift.

Some nights, although we are faithless, the truth
enters our hearts, that small familiar pain;
then a man will stand stock-still, hearing his youth
in the distant Latin chanting of a train.

Pray for us now. Grade I piano scales
console the lodger looking out across
a Midlands town. Then dusk, and someone calls
a child's name as though they named their loss.

Darkness outside. Inside, the radio's prayer –
Rockall. Malin. Dogger. Finisterre.

KATHLEEN JAMIE

(*born* 1962)

Kathleen Jamie was born in Renfrewshire and educated at Edinburgh University. She lives in Fife. Her poetry uses Scots (dialect and phonetics) in ways that refresh its traditions. On the one hand, as in 'Arraheids', she employs Scots for critique. The 'hard tongues o grannies' suggest a female genealogy for Jamie's own sharpness in the poem; while that sharpness is simultaneously used against the repressive elements in Scottish culture which the grannies personify. On the other hand, Jamie also exploits Scots for her own positive purposes. In 'Ultrasound' she subtly harmonises tone, idiom, sound and natural image. The tender, all-embracing world of 'Bairnsang' is created by a melodic interplay between terms of endearment, words that signify or mimic natural phenomena, and the place-names that mysteriously clinch each stanza. While most of her work maintains a backbone of stanzaic shape, we primarily hear Jamie's poems as flexible, sinuous rhythms that carry intense images lightly. Like the child scanned in the womb, they are 'hauled silver-quick / in a net of sound'.

Arraheids

See thon raws o flint arraheids
in oor gret museums o antiquities
awful grand in Embro –
Dae'ye near'n daur wunner at wur histrie?
Weel then, Bewaur!
The museums of Scotland are wrang.
They urnae arraheids
but a show o grannies' tongues,
the hard tongues o grannies
aa deid an gaun
back to thur peat and burns,
but for thur sherp
chert tongues, that lee
fur generations in the land
like wicked cherms, that lee
aa douce in the glessy cases in the gloom
o oor museums, an
they arenae lettin oan. But if you daur

arraheids: arrowheads; *raws:* rows.

sorn aboot an fancy
the vanished hunter, the wise deer runnin on;
wheesht ... an you'll hear them,
fur they cannae keep fae muttering
ye arenae here tae wonder,
whae dae ye think ye ur?

from Ultrasound
(for Duncan)

I *Ultrasound*

Oh whistle and I'll come to ye,
my lad, my wee shilpit ghost
summonsed from tomorrow.

Second sight,
a seer's mothy flicker,
an inner sprite:

this is what I see
with eyes closed;
a keek-aboot among secrets.

If Pandora
could have scanned
her dark box,

and kept it locked –
this ghoul's skull, punched eyes
is tiny Hope's,

hauled silver-quick
in a net of sound,
then, for pity's sake, lowered.

sorn aboot: loaf about; *fae:* frae, from.

shilpit: pale; *keek-aboot:* peeping.

V *Bairnsang*

Wee toshie man,
          gean tree and rowan
gif ye could staun
yer feet wad lichtsome tread
granite an saun,
but ye cannae yet staun
sae maun courie tae ma airm
an greetna, girna, Gretna Green

Peedie wee lad
          saumon, siller haddie
gin ye could rin
ye'd rin richt easy-strang
ower causey an carse,
but ye cannae yet rin
sae maun jist courie in
and fashna, fashna, Macrahanish Sand

Bonny wee boy
          peeswheep an whaup
gin ye could sing, yer sang
wad be caller
as a lauchin mountain burn
but ye cannae yet sing
sae maun courie tae ma hert
an grieve nat at aa, Ainster an Crail

My ain tottie bairn
          sternie an lift
gin ye could daunce, yer daunce
wad be that o life itsel,
but ye cannae yet daunce
sae maun courie in my erms
and sleep, saftly sleep, Unst and Yell

toshie: tidy; *gean:* cherry; *courie tae:* nestle into; *greetna:* don't cry; *girna:* don't whimper; *peedie:* tiny; *siller haddie:* silver haddock; *causey:* causeway; *carse:* flat land near a river; *fashna:* don't vex yourself; *peeswheep:* peewit, lapwing; *whaup:* curlew; *caller:* fresh; *sternie:* star; *lift:* sky.

VII *Prayer*

Our baby's heart, on the sixteen-week scan
was a fluttering bird, held in cupped hands.

I thought of St Kevin, hands opened in prayer
and a bird of the hedgerow nesting there,

and how he'd borne it, until the young had flown
– and I prayed: this new heart must outlive my own.

Lochan
(for Jean Johnstone)

When all this is over I mean
to travel north, by the high

drove roads and cart tracks
probably in June,

with the gentle dog-roses
flourishing beside me. I mean

to find among the thousands
scattered in that land

a certain quiet lochan,
where water lilies rise

like small fat moons,
and tied among the reeds,

underneath a rowan,
a white boat waits.

SIMON ARMITAGE

(*born* 1963)

Simon Armitage was born in Huddersfield. A former probation officer, he lives in the same part of West Yorkshire where he grew up (which he mythologises as a border, 'a cultural fault-line'). He has published several books, including a collaboration with Glyn Maxwell, *Moon Country* (1996), an update of Auden's and MacNeice's *Letters from Iceland*. Armitage's poetic potential is suggested by 'Zoom!', a poem about the potential of poetry. 'Zoom!' represents poetry as the sum of everything from the Mechanics' Institute to the universe. Similarly, both in his career and in individual poems, he moves from reportage to cosmic parable. 'Millet: The Gleaners' and 'Drawing the Arctic Circle' show his interest in how the imagination works: its obsessions, its horizons. His sequence *The Whole of the Sky* makes the Zodiac an excuse for engaging in every kind of observation and fancy. Armitage's poles of reportage and parable, together with his homage to Auden and MacNeice, suggest an effort to restore a kind of 1930s scope to poetry. Armitage may also have been influenced by Paul Muldoon's inventiveness, and by various ways in which Irish poets, following Kavanagh, have made parish and universe a basis for poetic structure. His memoir *All Points North* (1998) is a part-satirical, part-serious return (in prose) to "roots". Armitage defines an imagined Yorkshire against the poetic parishes of Ted Hughes and Tony Harrison. He has said that his 'word pool' is coloured by the West Riding and by the language of 'my friends, family or heroes'. Two poems in Yorkshire dialect establish an extraordinary intimacy with their subjects.

Zoom!

It begins as a house, an end terrace
in this case
    but it will not stop there. Soon it is
an avenue
    which cambers arrogantly past the Mechanics' Institute,
turns left
    at the main road without even looking
and quickly it is
    a town with all four major clearing banks,
a daily paper
    and a football team pushing for promotion.

On it goes, oblivious of the Planning Acts,
the green belts,
    and before we know it it is out of our hands:
city, nation,
    hemisphere, universe, hammering out in all directions
until suddenly,
    mercifully, it is drawn aside through the eye
of a black hole
    and bulleted into a neighbouring galaxy, emerging
smaller and smoother
    than a billiard ball but weighing more than Saturn.

    People stop me in the street, badger me
in the check-out queue
    and ask 'What is this, this that is so small
and so very smooth
    but whose mass is greater than the ringed planet?'
It's just words
    I assure them. But they will not have it.

Poem

And if it snowed and snow covered the drive
he took a spade and tossed it to one side.
And always tucked his daughter up at night.
And slippered her the one time that she lied.

And every week he tipped up half his wage.
And what he didn't spend each week he saved.
And praised his wife for every meal she made.
And once, for laughing, punched her in the face.

And for his mum he hired a private nurse.
And every Sunday taxied her to church.
And he blubbed when she went from bad to worse.
And twice he lifted ten quid from her purse.

Here's how they rated him when they looked back:
sometimes he did this, sometimes he did that.

Millet: The Gleaners

No one's twisting her arm but there it is,
locked backwards in a half-nelson, broken
like a shotgun. In hand, a spray of corn
spills out like a tail of peahen feathers.

The nearest is standing but bends also.
Like a forced branch or a trained limb, something
which has given, she curves, disarmed, a bow
without string hemmed in under the skyline.

The third shadows the first, and if the sunset
is a spotlight then she steals the finale
with a bow, not a curtsy. Past caring
she forgets the task, if it was picking
or planting, whether it was corn or barley.

Let me say this: we trip across the fields
like tourists; take flowers, tell huge stories –
lies, and think only of the poppies.
It could be midnight when the evening fades;

the hammock, the hats, the picnic basket,
the day like an apple – not even bruised
but somehow bottled, the road in sight, the car
where we left it. It will right itself, that square
of flattened grass where we laid the blanket.

Drawing the Arctic Circle

The last blizzard softens into sleet.
A certain heat gets under the shingle.
Glaciers rupture with the echo of metal.
Pack-ice is putting out to sea.

Arctic poppies bend in the breeze.
Bones sweat in the Eskimo middens.
Kelp slackens back to the meltwater-streams.
Atoms glitter in the solar wind.

Helen, you are the sweetest sister.
It's kind of you and Tom to offer.
Greenland is much as we imagined.
We've brought enough Scotch to sink the *Titanic*.

The stars seem almost close enough to touch.
God help us both if this is summer.
The sun shines all day and all night
but it has no warmth, no light, no colour.

On an Owd Piktcha
(from tJerman)

Int swelterin eet, mongst birds n tbeez,
side cool watter n rushes n reeds,
tChrahst Chahld sithee, born baht taint,
laikin arahnd on tVirgin's knee.

N pooakin its nooas aht o tleaves n tmoss,
already green, tTree o tCross.

from The Whole of the Sky

The Mariner's Compass

Living alone, I'm sailing the world
single-handed in a rented house.
Last week I rounded the Cape of Good Hope,
came through in one piece;

this morning, flying fish
lying dead in the porch with the post.
I peg out duvet covers and sheets
to save fuel when the wind blows,

tune the engine so it purrs all night
like a fridge, run upstairs
with the old-fashioned thought
of plotting a course by the stars.

Friends wave from the cliffs,
talk nervously from the coast-guard station.
Under the rules, close contact
with another soul means disqualification.

Taurus

So we tracked it down to where it was finally stood,
remote, dumb as a cloud, the ring in its nose
held out like a child's hand, and we guided it home
through the sky's fields and the open gate of the sun.

The Phoenix

Tvillage cuckoo wer caught one spring
to trap tgood weather, an kept in a tower baht roof.
Tnext mornin tbird'd sprung; tMarsdeners reckoned
ttower wernt builded igh enuff. A ladder wer fetched

to bring tbird dahn, but nubdy'd clahm.
Trust, tha sees. Tladder maht walk. Chap maht be stuck
in clahdcuckooland till Kingdomcumsdy, Godknowswensdy.
Meanwahl, tbird wer nested in Crahther's chimney.

Ursa Minor

Arctic fox, arctic hare, arctic tern, polar bear;
region of the egg-race of the goose,
the snowy owl mistaken for a lynx,
the endless patience of the moose.

Region of the flight-path and the vapour-trail of swans,
the soup-spoon tennis racket of the beaver's tail,
the flagship of the elk, the royal trout,
the dog face and the wet-suit of the seal.

Region of the silver-plated sturgeon,
region of the loose electron of the ermine,
region of the walrus in its punctured zeppelin;
arctic skua, arctic hare, arctic fox, polar bear.

Apus

In 1596, de Houtman and Keyser were taking the piss
when they christened eight dull stars the Bird of Paradise.
Legless and sky-high the bird certainly was; nevertheless
its feathers were those of a head-dress or a lady's hat,

and its eggs were the seeds of the paradise plant
with its bird-bud heads that flower in the rain.
Apus, the Bird of Paradise, sixty-seventh in rank,
without a bright star or a meteor shower to its name.

The Flying Fish

Blue-backed, silver-bellied, half-imagined things;
six of them, blown off course by the solar wind.
They were coated with salt or snuff – interstellar dust –
and we picked the granules out of their tails and wings.

We carried them out to the beach in a budgie cage,
lowered them down and opened the door. They went deep,
then turned about, breaking the surface, launching themselves
wholeheartedly out of the sea at their own stars.

DON PATERSON
(*born* 1963)

Don Paterson was born in Dundee, where he grew up, leaving school at 16 to
work as a professional musician. A guitarist, he co-leads the jazz-folk ensemble
Lammas. He is also a freelance writer. Paterson has published two collections,
Nil Nil (1993) and *God's Gift to Women* (1997), and *The Eyes* (1999), versions
from the Spanish of Antonio Machado. He hones his poems into highly con-
centrated formal shapes. As a musician, Paterson feels 'no ideological conflict
between either form and expression...or sound and meaning'. One structural
model is the American pianist Ritchie Bierach because: 'There's never one single
note in his tunes that isn't advancing the argument in some way.' Paterson's
mainly psychological scenarios make an interesting contrast with the more
extraverted world of Simon Armitage. Yet his images 'decode the world' (to
quote 'Heliographer') in their own way. Some poems take up the problematic
question of selfhood where MacNeice and Larkin left off. 'Bedfellows' revisits
the disturbingly paired occupants of Mr Bleaney's room, while 'The Ferry-
man's Arms' seems in dark dialogue with MacNeice's 'Charon'.

The Ferryman's Arms

About to sit down with my half-pint of Guinness
I was magnetised by a remote phosphorescence
and drawn, like a moth, to the darkened back room
where a pool-table hummed to itself in the corner.
With ten minutes to kill and the whole place deserted
I took myself on for the hell of it. Slotting
a coin in the tongue, I looked round for a cue –
while I stood with my back turned, the balls were deposited
with an abrupt intestinal rumble; a striplight
batted awake in its dusty green cowl.
When I set down the cue-ball inside the parched D
it cracked on the slate; the nap was so threadbare
I could screw back the globe, given somewhere to stand –
as physics itself becomes something negotiable
a rash of small miracles covers the shortfall:
I went on to make an immaculate clearance.

A low punch with a wee dab of side, and the black
did the vanishing trick while the white stopped
before gently rolling back as if nothing had happened,
shouldering its way through the unpotted colours.

The boat chugged up to the little stone jetty
without breaking the skin of the water, stretching,
as black as my stout, from somewhere unspeakable
to here, where the foaming lip mussitates endlessly,
trying, with a nutter's persistence, to read
and re-read the shoreline. I got aboard early,
remembering the ferry would leave on the hour
even for only my losing opponent;
but I left him there, stuck in his tent of light, sullenly
knocking the balls in, for practice, for next time.

Heliographer

I thought we were sitting in the sky.
My father decoded the world beneath:
our tenement, the rival football grounds,
the long bridges, slung out across the river.
Then I gave myself a fright
with the lemonade bottle. Clunk –
the glass thread butting my teeth
as I bolted my mouth to the lip.

Naw...copy me. It's how the grown-ups drink.
Propped in my shaky,
single-handed grip,
I tilted the bottle towards the sun
until it detonated with light,
my lips pursed like a trumpeter's.

Wind-Tunnel

Sometimes, in autumn, the doors between the days
fall open; in any other season
this would be a dangerous mediumship
though now there is just the small exchange of air
as from one room to another. A street
becomes a faint biography: you walk
through a breath of sweetpea, pipesmoke, an old perfume.

But one morning, the voices carry from everywhere:
from the first door and the last, two whistling draughts
zero in with such unholy dispatch
you do not scorch the sheets, or wake your wife.

Bedfellows

An inch or so above the bed
    the yellow blindspot hovers
where the last incumbent's greasy head
    has worn away the flowers.

Every night I have to rest
    my head in his dead halo;
I feel his heart tick in my wrist;
    then, below the pillow,

his suffocated voice resumes
    its dreary innuendo:
there are other ways to leave the room
    than the door and the window

ACKNOWLEDGEMENTS

The poems in this anthology are reprinted from the following books, and thanks are due to the copyright holders cited below for their kind permission:

Fleur Adcock: *Poems 1960-2000* (Bloodaxe Books, 2000), by permission of Bloodaxe Books Ltd.

Simon Armitage: *Zoom!* (Bloodaxe Books, 1989), by permission of Bloodaxe Books Ltd; *Kid* (Faber, 1992), *CloudCuckooLand* (Faber, 1997), by permission of Faber & Faber Ltd.

W.H. Auden: *Collected Poems*, ed. Edward Mendelson (Faber, 1991) and *The English Auden: Poems, Essays and Dramatic Writings 1927-1939*, ed. Edward Mendelson (Faber, 1977) for 'September 1, 1939' and the version used here of 'In Memory of W.B. Yeats', by permission of Faber & Faber Ltd.

Basil Bunting: *Complete Poems* (Bloodaxe Books, 2000), by permission of Bloodaxe Books Ltd.

Norman Cameron: *Complete Poems and Selected Translations*, ed. Warren Hope & Jonathan Barker (Anvil Press, 1990), by permission of Anvil Press Poetry Ltd.

Ciaran Carson: *The Irish for No* (Gallery Press, 1987/Bloodaxe Books, 1988), *Belfast Confetti* (Gallery Press, 1989/Bloodaxe Books, 1990), by permission of the Gallery Press.

Austin Clarke: *Collected Poems* (Dolmen Press in association with Oxford University Press, 1974), by permission of R. Dardis Clarke, 21 Pleasants St, Dublin 8.

Keith Douglas: *Complete Poems*, ed. Desmond Graham (Faber, 2000), by permission of Faber & Faber Ltd.

Carol Ann Duffy: *Selling Manhattan* (Anvil Press, 1987), *The Other Country* (Anvil Press, 1990), *Mean Time* (Anvil Press, 1993), by permission of Anvil Press Poetry Ltd.

Ian Duhig: *The Bradford Count* (Bloodaxe Books, 1991), *Nominies* (Bloodaxe Books, 1998), by permission of Bloodaxe Books Ltd.

Douglas Dunn: *Terry Street* (Faber, 1969), *The Happier Life* (Faber, 1972), *Love or Nothing* (1974), *Elegies* (Faber, 1985), *Dante's Drum-kit* (Faber, 1993), by permission of Faber & Faber Ltd.

Paul Durcan: *A Snail in My Prime: New and Selected Poems* (Harvill, 1993), by permission of The Harvill Press; and *The Selected Paul Durcan*, ed. Edna Longley (Blackstaff Press, 1982), *The Berlin Wall Café* (Blackstaff Press, 1985), by permission of Blackstaff Press Ltd.

T.S. Eliot: *The Complete Poems and Plays* (Faber, 1969), by permission of Faber & Faber Ltd.

William Empson: *Collected Poems* (Hogarth Press, 1984), by permission of Lady Empson and the Hogarth Press.

James Fenton: *The Memory of War and Children in Exile: Poems 1968-1983* (Penguin, 1983), by permission of Peters, Fraser & Dunlop Group Ltd and the author.

Ian Hamilton Finlay: from various publications, with the kind permission of the author and of Polgon Books for 'Orkney Interior'.

Robert Garioch: *Complete Poetical Works*, ed. Robin Fulton (Macdonald, Edinburgh, 1983), by permission of the Saltire Society, Edinburgh.

W.S. Graham: *Collected Poems* (Faber, 1979), by permission of Michael and Margaret Snow.

Robert Graves: *Complete Poems*, ed. Beryl Graves and Dunstan Ward (Carcanet, 1995-1999), by permission of Carcanet Press Ltd.

Thom Gunn: *Collected Poems* (Faber, 1993) and *Boss Cupid* (Faber, 2000), by permission of Faber & Faber Ltd.

Ivor Gurney: *Collected Poems*, ed. P.J. Kavanagh (Oxford University Press, 1984), by permission of Penny Ely.

Thomas Hardy: *Complete Poems*, ed. James Gibson (Macmillan, 1981).

Tony Harrison: *Selected Poems* (Penguin, 1987), by permission of Gordon Dickerson and the author.

Seamus Heaney: *Opened Ground: Poems 1966-1996* (Faber, 1998), by permission of Faber & Faber Ltd.

John Hewitt: *Collected Poems*, ed. Frank Ormsby (Blackstaff Press, 1991), by permission of Blackstaff Press Ltd.

Geoffrey Hill: *Collected Poems* (Penguin, 1985), by permission of Penguin Books Ltd.

Selima Hill: *Trembling Hearts in the Bodies of Dogs: New & Selected Poems* (Bloodaxe Books, 1994), by permission of Bloodaxe Books Ltd; *Saying Hello at the Station* (Chatto, 1984), by permission of the author.

Ted Hughes: poems from *New Selected Poems* (Faber, 1995), reprinted from his Faber collections *The Hawk in the Rain* (1957), *Lupercal* (1960), *Wodwo* (1967) and *Moortown* (1979), by permission of Faber & Faber Ltd.

Kathleen Jamie: *The Queen of Sheba* (Bloodaxe Books, 1994), by permission of Bloodaxe Books Ltd; *Jizzen* (Picador, 1999), by permission of Macmillan Publishers Ltd.

Patrick Kavanagh: *Selected Poems*, ed. Antoinette Quinn (Penguin, 1996), reprinted here by permission of the Trustees of the Estate of the late Katherine B. Kavanagh, and through the Jonathan Williams Literary Agency.

Philip Larkin: *Collected Poems*, ed. Anthony Thwaite (Faber, 1990), by permission of Faber & Faber Ltd; 'Going', 'Wedding-Wind' and 'Deceptions' are reprinted from *The Less Deceived* (1955) by permission of The Marvell Press, England and Australia.

D.H. Lawrence: *Complete Poems*, ed. Vivian de Sola Pinto and Warren Roberts (Penguin, 1977), by permission of Laurence Pollinger Ltd.

Tom Leonard: *Intimate Voices: Selected Work 1965-1983* (Vintage, 1985), by permission of the author.

Alun Lewis: *Collected Poems*, ed. Ceri Archard (Seren, 1994), by permission of Seren Books.

Michael Longley: *Selected Poems* (Jonathan Cape, 1998), *The Weather in Japan* (Jonathan Cape, 2000), by permission of Lucas Alexander Whitley.

Norman MacCaig: *Collected Poems* (Chatto & Windus, 1990), by permission of the Hogarth Press.

Hugh MacDiarmid: *Complete Poems*, ed. Michael Grieve & W.R. Aitken (Penguin, 1985), by permission of Carcanet Press Ltd.

Medbh McGuckian: *The Flower Master* (Oxford University Press, 1982; Gallery Press, 1993) and *Selected Poems* (Gallery Press, 1998), by permission of the Gallery Press.

Louis MacNeice: *Collected Poems*, ed. E.R. Dodds (Faber, 1979), by permission of David Higham Associates Ltd.

Derek Mahon: *Collected Poems* (Gallery Press, 1999), by permission of the Gallery Press.

John Montague: *Collected Poems* (Gallery Press, 1995), by permission of the Gallery Press.

Edwin Morgan: *Collected Poems* (Carcanet, 1990), by permission of Carcanet Press Ltd.

Edwin Muir: *Collected Poems* (Faber, 1984), by permission of Faber & Faber Ltd.

Paul Muldoon: *New Selected Poems 1968-1994* (Faber, 1996), *Hay* (Faber, 1998), by permission of Faber & Faber Ltd.

Eiléan Ní Chuilleanáin: *The Second Voyage: Selected Poems* (Gallery Press/ Bloodaxe Books, 1986), *The Magdalene Sermon* (Gallery Press, 1990), *The Brazen Serpent* (Gallery Press, 1994), by permission of the Gallery Press.

Wilfred Owen: *The Complete Poems and Fragments*, ed. Jon Stallworthy (Chatto & Windus, the Hogarth Press and Oxford University Press, 1983), by permission of the Estate of Wilfred Owen, the editor and Chatto & Windus.

Don Paterson: *Nil Nil* (Faber, 1993), *God's Gift to Women* (Faber, 1997), by permission of Faber & Faber Ltd.

Sylvia Plath: *Collected Poems*, ed. Ted Hughes (Faber, 1981), by permission of Faber & Faber Ltd.

Henry Reed: *Collected Poems*, ed. Jon Stallworthy (Oxford University Press, 1991), by permission of Oxford University Press.

Isaac Rosenberg: *Collected Works* (Chatto and Windus/The Hogarth Press, 1979).

Carol Rumens: 'The Impenitent' and 'Stealing the Genre' from *Thinking of Skins: New & Selected Poems* (Bloodaxe Books, 1993), 'Prayer for Northern Ireland' from *Best China Sky* (Bloodaxe Books, 1995), by permission of Bloodaxe Books Ltd; 'Stanzas for a New Start' from *Holding Pattern* (Blackstaff Press, 1998), by permission of Blackstaff Press Ltd.

Siegfried Sassoon: *Collected Poems* (Faber, 1984), by permission of Barbara Levy Literary Agency.

Jo Shapcott: *Her Book: Poems 1988-1998* (Faber, 2000), by permission of Faber & Faber Ltd.

Stevie Smith: *Collected Poems*, ed. James MacGibbon (Penguin, 1985), by permission of the James MacGibbon Estate.

Charles Hamilton Sorley: *Collected Poems*, ed. Jean Moorcroft Wilson (Woolf, 1985).

Dylan Thomas: *Collected Poems* (J.M. Dent, 1988), by permission of David Higham Associates.

Edward Thomas: *Collected Poems*, ed. R. George Thomas (Oxford University Press, 1978).

R.S. Thomas: *Selected Poems 1946-1968* (Bloodaxe Books, 1986), by permission of Bloodaxe Books Ltd; *Collected Poems 1945-1990* (J.M. Dent, 1993), by permission of the Orion Publishing Group Ltd.

W.B. Yeats: *The Poems*, ed. Richard J. Finneran (Macmillan, 1991), by permission of A.P. Watt Ltd.